MARITIME HISTORY SERIES

Series Editor

John B. Hattendorf, *Naval War College*

Volumes Published in this Series

Pietro Martire d'Anghiera, et al.
The history of travayle in the West and East Indies (1577)
Introduction by Thomas R. Adams,
John Carter Brown Library

Willem Ysbrandsz. Bontekoe
Die vier und zwantzigste Schiffahrt (1648)
Introduction by Augustus J. Veenendaal, Jr.,
Instituut voor Nederlandse Geschiedenis, The Hague

Josiah Burchett
A complete history of the most remarkable transactions at sea (1720)
Introduction by John B. Hattendorf,
Naval War College

Alvise Cà da Mosto
Questa e una opera necessaria a tutti li naviga[n]ti (1490)
bound with:
Pietro Martire d'Anghiera
Libretto de tutta la navigatione de Re de Spagna (1504)
Introduction by Felipe Fernández-Armesto,
Oxford University

Martín Cortés
The arte of navigation (1561)
Introduction by D. W. Waters,
National Maritime Museum, Greenwich

John Davis
The seamans secrets (1633)
Introduction by A. N. Ryan,
University of Liverpool

Francisco Faleiro
Tratado del esphera y del arte del marear (1535)
Introduction by Onesimo Almeida,
Brown University

Gemma, Frisius
De principiis astronomiae & cosmographiae (1553)
Introduction by C. A. Davids,
University of Leiden

Tobias Gentleman
Englands way to win wealth, and to employ ships and marriners (1614)
bound with:
Robert Kayll
The trades increase (1615)
and
Dudley Digges
The defence of trade (1615)
and
Edward Sharpe
Britaines busse (1615)
Introduction by John B. Hattendorf,
Naval War College

William Hacke
A collection of original voyages (1699)
Introduction by Glyndwr Williams,
Queen Mary and Westfield College, University of London

Marine architecture:
or Directions for carrying on a ship from the first laying of the keel
to her actual going to sea (1739)
Introduction by Brian Lavery,
National Maritime Museum, Greenwich

Pedro de Medina
L'art de naviguer (1554)
Introduction by Carla Rahn Phillips,
University of Minnesota

Thomas Pownall
The administration of the colonies (4th ed., 1768)
Introduction by Daniel A. Baugh, Cornell University,
and Alison Gilbert Olson,
University of Maryland, College Park

St. Barthélemy and the Swedish West India Company:
A selection of printed documents, 1784-1821
Introduction by John B. Hattendorf,
Naval War College

John Seller
Practical navigation (1680)
Introduction by Michael Richey,
Royal Institute of Navigation

Shipbuilding Timber for the British Navy:
Parliamentary papers, 1729-1792
Introduction by R. J. B. Knight,
National Maritime Museum, Greenwich

Jean Taisnier
A very necessarie and profitable booke concerning navigation (1585?)
Introduction by Uwe Schnall,
Deutsches Schiffahrtsmuseum, Bremerhaven

Lodovico de Varthema
Die ritterlich un[d] lobwirdig Rayss (1515)
Introduction by George Winius,
University of Leiden

Gerrit de Veer
The true and perfect description of three voyages (1609)
Introduction by Stuart M. Frank,
Kendall Whaling Museum

Isaak Vossius
A treatise concerning the motion of the seas and winds (1677)
together with
De motu marium et ventorum (1663)
Introduction by Margaret Deacon,
University of Southampton

The Administration of the Colonies

(1768)

Thomas Pownall

A Facsimile Reproduction
With an Introduction by

DANIEL A. BAUGH
and
ALISON GILBERT OLSON

Published for the
JOHN CARTER BROWN LIBRARY
by
SCHOLARS' FACSIMILES & REPRINTS
DELMAR, NEW YORK
1993

SCHOLARS' FACSIMILES & REPRINTS
ISSN 0161-7729
SERIES ESTABLISHED 1936
VOLUME 487

New matter in this edition
© 1993 Academic Resources Corporation
All rights reserved

Printed and made in the United States of America

The publication of this work was assisted by a grant from the
National Endowment for the Humanities,
an agency of the Federal government

Reproduced from a copy in,
and with the permission of,
the John Carter Brown Library
at Brown University

Library of Congress Cataloging-in-Publication Data

Pownall, Thomas, 1722-1805.
  The administration of the colonies : 1768 /
a facsimile reproduction with an introduction by
Daniel A. Baugh and Alison Gilbert Olson.
        p.   cm. —
(Scholars' Facsimiles & Reprints, ISSN 0161-7729 ; v. 487)
  (Maritime history series)
  Originally published :
4th ed. : London : J. Walter, 1768.
  Includes bibliographical references.
  ISBN 0-8201-1487-1
  1. United States—Politics and government—To 1775.
2. Great Britain—Colonies—America—Administration.
I. Title. II. Series.
III. Series: Maritime history series (Delmar, N.Y.)
    E195.P895   1993
973.2´4—dc20   93-36377
              CIP

Introduction

The colonies of Governor Thomas Pownall's title are the British colonies in North America, and he wrote at a time when imperial reform was very much on the political agenda in London. In those days the word "administration" included policy, and the book deals mostly with policy issues and their background. The work stands out partly because it is a sympathetic, intelligent, and well informed discussion of the American question from the British side. There is of course a more famous writer in this category, Edmund Burke, and one immediately thinks of comparisons. Certainly Pownall's mind lacked the philosophical depth of Burke's, and his prose, though at times compelling, is on the whole not very good. But, unlike Burke, Pownall had lived among American colonists and had been directly involved in the workings of colonial politics, commerce, and defense. Possessing a trained mind and a strong inclination toward scientific curiosity and theoretical frameworks, he was a reflective observer. Anyone who has gained insight on the American colonial question from reading Burke will also gain much from reading Pownall.

The Administration of the Colonies was an evolving text. There were six editions, the first appearing anonymously in 1764, the fifth on the eve of the American Revolution, and the last in 1777. The first edition ran 131 pages; the fifth and sixth each occupied two volumes. The work grew by agglomeration, but Pownall had already stated in the first edition which topics he would treat at another time. Thus, in broad terms he foresaw the shape of the whole, but it is equally true that some features of the later editions were inspired by unfolding events.[1] The fourth edition has been selected for reprinting for three reasons. It is fuller and better integrated than earlier editions; it contains Pownall's mature thoughts on the whole range of subjects; and it appeared at a time (1768)

INTRODUCTION

when it could still have an influence on the ongoing debate over imperial policy in London.

It could play a role in that debate, but this does not mean that its proposals and general advice, if adopted by the British government in 1768, could have stopped the drift toward separation. Adoption of Pownall's ideas in 1764 might have made a big difference, but by 1768 the reservoir of imperial loyalty in America upon which Pownall's remedies were pitched was beginning to drain away. British ignorance and high-handedness had provoked violent protests in the colonies. Mistrust and self-righteousness now flourished on both sides of the Atlantic. Professor John Shy has observed that there is a tone of dismay, frustration, and despair in this edition which is not characteristic of earlier editions.[2] It does indeed appear that in 1768 Pownall was wondering whether, after so many blunders, British administrations would ever bother to learn; and he was doubly upset because the loyalty of the colonies—a point he had stressed repeatedly—no longer seemed assured.

So by 1768 *The Administration of the Colonies* did not provide many viable remedies. The book, however, should not be regarded as just a policy tract. Pownall wrote the first edition when the question of how to go about imperial reform had not yet been overtaken by the question of how to deal with the refractory colonists. His main purpose was to induce statesmen to think in a new and unfamiliar way about Britain's North American empire. His method was to provide a theory of empire and to show how each issue of imperial administration related to that theory. He offered lots of facts. Indeed, his leading administrative recommendation was designed to insure that policy decisions would be made by people who had up-to-date, accurate facts. The book retained this informational and theoretical character through all editions, and this is the main reason why it remains interesting.

How did it come about that Thomas Pownall knew so much, and thought so deeply and earnestly, about the problem of empire in North America? The short answer is that he had the benefit of a fine university education and spent most of the period between 1753 and 1760 in North America.[3] He was born in Lincoln in 1722. The family

INTRODUCTION

ranked as minor gentry; he was the eldest son. At Trinity College, Cambridge, he absorbed a bountiful and balanced education, Trinity having been recently rejuvenated academically by the distinguished Dr. Richard Bentley. After taking his degree in 1743 Pownall accepted a minor position at the Board of Trade, where his younger brother, John, had already made a good start on an administrative career. The Board of Trade's intimate connection with American affairs opened for him an opportunity to go to America as personal secretary to a newly appointed Governor of New York.

Upon their arrival in the autumn of 1753 the new governor, unable to throw off a bout of depression triggered by the death of his wife, promptly committed suicide, thus leaving Pownall's career in limbo. He did not pine away helplessly. Inquisitive and gregarious, he travelled energetically and made the acquaintance of numerous Americans in New York, Boston, Annapolis, and especially Philadelphia. Although it appears that he was brash and conceited, he was also a man who delighted in conversation and seems to have been free of Old World prejudice toward Americans. His natural disposition toward intellectual exchange and honest engagement with other people evidently gained him many friends, among them Benjamin Franklin and Lewis Evans. In a semi-official capacity he continued to report on American affairs to the Board of Trade; he attended, for instance, the Albany Congress of 1754.[4] In May 1755 Pownall was appointed Lieutenant Governor of New Jersey. During the years 1756 and 1757 he went back to England twice. On the first occasion, after a brief stay in England (the crossings took almost as long as the stay), he returned as administrative aide to Lord Loudoun, the Commander in Chief of British military forces in America. When he returned the second time, in August 1757, he came as the new Governor of Massachusetts; he was not quite 35 years of age.

Pownall not only loved conversation, he also loved to hike, and was much drawn to topography; it was his habit to carry a compass and a level. Even when he was Governor of Massachusetts he would venture into the countryside, effectively incognito, and talk with the locals. His interest in topography extended to geography, and his broad conception

INTRODUCTION

of North American geography formed the basis of his various memoranda on the subject of imperial defense.

The subject of defense was intensely important to the ministers at Whitehall in the 1750s. More than anything else, Pownall's memoranda on defense brought his name to the attention of the highest-placed statesmen. Although there was a lot about Pownall that Loudoun did not like, he did recognize his conceptual abilities. Pownall was directly in touch with William Pitt from about December 1756 to the end of the Seven Years War, either personally or by correspondence, and there is reason to believe that the plan to capture Quebec by land and sea, which was adopted by the Pitt government and successfully carried out in 1759-60, was influenced by Pownall's strategic analysis. (In the fourth edition his letter to Pitt of December 1758 is reprinted, with a commentary.)[5] Another matter on which Pownall eagerly sought information, especially for its bearing on the problem of colonial defense, was the Indian situation.[6]

The ordinary rough-and-tumble of Massachusetts politics was exacerbated by the demands of war. By 1757 the British had registered more failures than successes; the main strategic focus of the Anglo-French struggle was North America. The Governor of Massachusetts found himself in the thick of problems of military procurement—of soldiers, supplies, transport, and money to pay for them. Lord Loudoun's demands fell upon a legislature and colony that were already hard-pressed, and Pownall resisted his old chief, not in respect to substance really, but in respect to form. Loudoun insisted on his military authority to demand; Pownall insisted on the right of civil government to offer in response to requests. Pownall got his way, and thanks partly to the encouragement provided by Pitt's new burden-sharing program, the colony of Massachusetts wound up providing a great deal of substance to the war effort. When Pownall left in 1760 he was a successful and generally well-liked governor.[7] He was popular not just because the war had turned out successfully and Massachusetts could be proud of its contribution, but because he had upheld civil against military authority and respected the colony's political institutions.[8]

INTRODUCTION

Once back in England, Pownall kept up with American affairs through his brother at the Board of Trade, through correspondence with royal officials in Massachusetts such as Governor Bernard, merchants such as the Hancocks, and local political leaders such as Samuel Cooper. (Pownall had entered into business relations, first while in Pennsylvania, and later with Boston merchants, most notably the Hancock family with whom the association continued for many years. When Pownall was superseded and went home in 1760, John Hancock journeyed to England on the same vessel.) He also entertained a steady run of American visitors at his London home, including Benjamin Franklin. There are echoes of all these influences—the early experience at the Board of Trade, the associations formed in Philadelphia and Boston, and the frequent visitors in London—throughout *The Administration of the Colonies*.

Pownall had chosen to return to England in 1760; he did not have to leave America: he was appointed Governor of South Carolina and never took it up. After his return, he was offered Jamaica and turned it down. Both were more lucrative than Massachusetts in terms of salary, but Pownall was not ready at this time to cross the Atlantic again; in fact, he was searching for a wife. His initial efforts failed and he did not marry until 1765. (He married a widow and it was a happy match until broken by her death in 1777.) In 1761, he was offered, probably as a result of Pitt's influence, a position as First Commissary of Control for the Combined Army in Germany. He accepted, but just before leaving for Germany in June 1761 he wrote to Pitt asking to be kept in mind for employment in settling the situation of Canada; clearly he had not put the question of America behind him.[9]

His new employment was one for which his experience as Governor of Massachusetts in wartime had given him much preparation. His work was that of a top-level auditor, but not merely that: as the Treasury's top official on the spot he was also empowered to institute reforms. Anyone who knew Pownall could be sure that he would do so, and he did. The position terminated with the coming of peace and he returned to England in 1763. He appears to have worked hard and done a good job. A dismissed employee accused him of corrupt dealings, but the

INTRODUCTION

case fell apart and Pownall was easily exonerated. In May 1764 he became one of three Commissioners for Examining German Demands, appointed by the Treasury to sift through the myriad of claims for reimbursement from persons who had supplied food, fodder, and transportation to the Combined Army during the war. The three men saved the Treasury millions: £6,000,000 was applied for; they found justification for paying only £1,300,000. Toward the end, however, Pownall was accused of soliciting a bribe to speed the process; there was evidence that the Landgrave of Hesse-Kassel was prepared to offer a bribe, but no evidence to indicate that Pownall was a party to soliciting one or had ever received any bribe money. There will be reason to mention this episode again.[10]

It appears that Pownall wrote the first edition of *The Administration of the Colonies* in the winter of 1763-4. All editions began by laying the same majestic foundation. Britain's colonial possessions in America were to be viewed as parts of an Atlantic system, commercial and maritime, which held the key to wealth, power, and greatness. Although Pownall's "stage theory" of human society's development did not match that of the Scottish Enlightenment, it reached the same conclusion: the current stage was the age of commerce. Global commerce developed along its own "natural" paths: "While each [European] country supposes, that its own government actuates and governs the trade of its respective subjects and dependencies," the pattern of colonial commerce, Pownall declared, actually reflects "a general interest that is not concerned in, nor governed by the respective interests of Europe." All that European administrators could do was "to mark the nascent state of things, . . . [to] connect and combine our operations with it . . . and to build on its power"—in short, "to take the lead of it already formed." Because of the success of the Seven Years War, that lead was now clearly in Britain's hands. Therefore:

> It is now the duty of those who govern us, to carry forward this state of things, to the weaving this lead into our system, that our kingdom may be no more considered as the mere kingdom of this isle . . . [with

INTRODUCTION

> various appendages], . . . but as a grand marine dominion, consisting of our possessions in the Atlantic and in America united into one interest.

Britain's future greatness and security depended on recognizing this to be the only imperial course of action available. The task—"the precise duty" of the British government—was to take up the challenge and opportunity now presented, and see to the "forming . . . of some general system of administration, founded on this actual state of things." This concept of an ineluctably dynamic Atlantic commerce was the essential underpinning for all that followed. Without significant alteration Pownall placed it at the beginning of every edition. The quotations above are from the first edition; the reader will find almost identical words and ideas in the fourth.[11]

    The first step was to establish an administrative center. The challenge outlined above called for responsive administration, and that would be impossible unless there was a single office for colonial affairs to which all information flowed and in which the authority to make decisions was clearly located. In the four pages where Pownall discussed the urgent need for a central office he used the words "knowledge" and "information"—one or the other—no less than fourteen times.[12] It was not his object to strengthen British administration of the colonies in the sense of making it easier for the mother country to impose its will and exercise its power. That was the farthest thing from his mind. Success depended upon mutual interest and cooperation. Administrators had to have reliable facts as to how colonial trade was actually carried on, and statesmen had to learn to understand the subtle and circuitous ways in which the Atlantic empire provided its benefits to the mother country. Any attempt to bind the colonies and their trade to Great Britain by an ignorant exercise of power would bring ruin (pp. 38, 164-5).

    The point is important. The centralization of colonial administration was not a new idea; it had long been urged by the Board of Trade and was much in vogue in the early 1750s when Pownall was still an underling there. Pownall's own sense of its necessity was surely intensified by his experience as Governor of Massachusetts, where he could observe the manner in which orders and directions came across the

INTRODUCTION

Atlantic to their respective functionaries from the boards of Trade, Ordnance, Admiralty, and various branches of the Treasury as well as from a Secretary of State; lack of coordination was all too common. Others who were urging centralization (such as the Earl of Halifax, Pownall's superior and patron at the Board of Trade during most of the 1750s) also deplored the lack of coordination. But they were very greatly disturbed by another problem: the apparent weakness of the mother country's authority in North America.[13] Whereas they emphasized tighter control, Pownall emphasized need for a well informed responsiveness. He may have been aware of the fact that during the past decade (prior to 1764) the Board of Trade had become less responsive to North American concerns.[14]

The underlying assumptions about the nature of politics upon which Pownall based his proposals of the 1760s were essentially in keeping with those laid out in a youthful treatise he published in 1752 entitled *Principles of Polity*. Government was based on voluntary agreement among a variety of interest groups which recognized a natural interdependence. In the existing circumstances the American colonies, composed of different interests, could create such a voluntary interdependence either among themselves or with the mother country. Britain's imperial interest lay in preventing the Americans from doing the former.[15] They must interact governmentally with the mother country as they already did commercially, and the only way to make sure that they would do so, as Pownall saw it, was for the British government to shepherd the development of a cooperative empire, to establish a "dominion" whose strength would be derived from a harmonization of British Atlantic commercial interests.

There were serious political obstacles to this plan of a central office for the colonies. One involved a deep-seated constitutional issue that was by no means dead in the 1760s. If the office were located in Great Britain it would have to depend for its authority upon Parliament, not the monarchy, because Parliament had come to assume so extensive a supervisory role in colonial affairs that respect for the monarch alone was no longer sufficient to ensure colonial allegiance. Parliament must

INTRODUCTION

therefore create the administration and regulate the commerce and money supply which would enable his Grand Marine Dominion to work. Pownall recognized Parliament's position as an institutional fact of life. At the same time, however, he proposed that colonial administration be centered in a Secretary of State for the colonies, or else a Board of Trade of equal standing in government fashioned along lines proposed by the Earl of Halifax back in the 1750s.[16] He also urged that some great person under royal commission (he had the King's brother in mind) should be sent to gather "representations" from each colony about its situation.[17]

The Board of Trade had originally been established by William III in a successful effort to keep the colonies directly under royal authority after the Glorious Revolution. It was responsible to the Privy Council, not Parliament. In the mid-eighteenth century Parliament had gradually begun to address colonial issues but generally only those problems that the Board's resources were inadequate to handle. Halifax's recommendations had constituted an effort to shore up the Board's powers and, in effect, keep functional the old system in which colonial administration was considered primarily the job of the monarchy.[18] It is obvious that Pownall wished to depoliticize colonial administration as much as possible, but if his scheme amounted to reviving those recommendations, the effect would be to shift the center of imperial authority back to the monarchy.

The other and greater political obstacle concerned the relationship between the sovereign power in Great Britain and the "rights of Englishmen" that colonists believed they possessed, particularly in respect to their colonial legislatures. The question was not avoidable and Pownall had addressed it briefly, in an inconclusive manner, in the first edition. In the fourth edition he offered a full-scale treatment.

After five pages of transition, in which readers were again reminded that those who would undertake the reform of imperial government ought never to lose sight of the true object, a flourishing imperial commerce, he began the inquiry into the constitutional relationship (p. 43).

INTRODUCTION

Although he devised a logical plan of discussion the path is not easy to follow. It is not well marked (though he tried), the sub-sections are not plainly blocked out, and Pownall's sentences are often prolix and misleadingly punctuated even by eighteenth-century standards. Because the discussion involves close analysis of matters of law there is an added impediment to readability. (The first edition's brief treatment of the subject is inconclusive but much better written.) A tracing of the line of argument seems in order.

Pownall begins by pointing out that because no effort had been made, as he had urged in 1764, to settle these matters before introducing other measures, the question of sovereign rights had become the main focus of debate: "The question is now no longer of curiosity and theory; it is brought actually into issue" (p. 46)—by the uproar over the Stamp Act of course.

The first half deals with the rights and obligations which colonists derived solely from the authority of the King. All colonies, whether founded under royal charter or otherwise, stood outside the realm, and in the early decades Parliament had no role in their governance. Even during the Civil War and Interregnum, Pownall argues, Parliamentary or council rule of the colonies was executed in a manner which was not constitutionally different from the King's; the name and type of institution changed, but not the constitutional position. Even for colonies not under royal charter, he claims, royal methods of rule pervaded their relationships with the mother country. He concludes that under this form of authority the colonies possessed a constitutional right to reject, by action of their own legislatures, any laws published (merely) by royal authority.

He then turns to current matters of contention in respect to colonial administration under the Crown. There are, he asserts, "two great points which the Colonists labour to establish" (p. 67). The first concerns "their several rights and privileges, as founded in the rights of an Englishman." In the ten-page discussion which follows he makes the point that the King's power, vested in the governor, to veto acts of a colonial legislature solves few problems: in practice its use creates

INTRODUCTION

debilitating governmental confusion, and the colonists are also able to resort to devices which by-pass royal authority. One result is that the colonial legislatures have gained the whip hand. They have, in effect, acquired the executive as well as the legislative power (pp. 79-80). The second of the "great points" is colonial refusal to provide permanent salaries for royal officials, which he believes the colonies are legally obligated to do. He also suggests that a pension plan should be instituted for ex-governors (p. 83).

Holding that it is both a duty and a prudent course for the Crown as well as the colonists to uphold the political rights set forth in colonial charters, Pownall is certain that the establishing of a Commander in Chief of the army in North America during peacetime is a great mistake (pp. 86-101). Nothing, he avers, could be more dangerous, or better calculated to stir the various colonies into unifying against Great Britain; the mere hint of military threat to civil government would produce this result. The army in North America could be reduced in size and its command structure in the colonies subjected to civil authority.[19] He then discusses judicial reform (pp. 101-118) and the arrangement of material is not difficult to follow.

Pownall introduces the second part of his inquiry into the constitutional relationship by attempting to make clear the basic dichotomy that guides his analysis (pp. 118-25). Thus far he has examined "those points of colony administration which derive" from their original connections with the "King, as Sovereign." Now he moves to the question of how the colonies are related to King, Lords, and Commons, which in their collectivity had become the sovereign power of Great Britain and its empire. He asserts, in an important yet atrociously written sentence, that whereas the former relationship with the King alone will continue to "mark out the mode of administration by which they should be governed," the *settlement* of that relationship with regard to points "which have come into dispute" is determined by the sovereign power of King, Lords, and Commons (p. 119).[20] The next five pages review the former constitutional relationship. In them Pownall reiterates

INTRODUCTION

his interpretation of Parliament's rule during the Civil War and Interregnum.[21]

The "great alteration" came with the Restoration of 1660. At this juncture the King "participated" (*i.e.*, shared with) Parliament in the governance of the colonies. Acts of Parliament were passed which dealt not only with external trade but also internal affairs, even taxation (p. 125), and Parliament's power to make laws binding on the colonies "hath been constantly exerted by the government of England (afterwards Great Britain) and submitted to by the colonies." On this point Pownall in 1768 seems to be as unyielding as he had been in 1764 and 1766.[22]

But he immediately goes on to say that the issue is not simple. The doctrine—generally accepted in Great Britain and confirmed in the Declaratory Act (6 Geo. III c. 12)—that although the colonies were not part of the realm of Great Britain, the colonists were nevertheless subjects in every respect, raises, he believes, a profound question as to "the nature of this absoluteness" of King, Lords and Commons in this case. For if "the colonists, by birthright, by nature or by establishment, ever were entitled to all the rights, privileges, liberties and franchises of an Englishman, the absolute power must have some bounds," and he considers it doubtful whether they can be disfranchised just because "they are settled beyond the territorial limits to the realm" (pp. 127-33).

Whether Parliament has the right to levy taxes on the colonists (pp. 133-7) Pownall regards as a distinctly separate issue, which "depends upon quite other principles." He is here referring to the accepted doctrine that money bills must originate in the House of Commons, the rationale being that the members of that house do not vote, but rather grant, the various taxes upon the property of their constituents. Therefore, even if the principle "that the legislative power of parliament extends throughout America in all cases whatsoever" were not to be contested, there would remain the puzzling question of "how the commons do represent the property in America, when stated as being without the realm." If no good answer can be provided, the colonists will surely and understandably continue to protest against taxes levied by Parliament, using the very arguments on which the House of Commons

INTRODUCTION

in England has founded its constitutional power. All these constitutional "perplexities," he concludes, arise from stating the colonists to be "subjects of the realm, at the same time that the Colonies are stated as being no part of the realm."

How could this anomaly be resolved? One would start with the admission that by the very act of extending the power of King, Lords, and Commons over the colonies, as occurred at the Restoration, "the rights and liberties of the realm must be also extended to them." The "nature of the British constitution" required this, and if Parliament wishes to regard the colonies as "objects of taxation," they must have "knights and burgesses in parliament, *of their own election.*" This opened the almost untouchable question of whether Parliament's existing make-up was truly representative of wealth and property in Great Britain (in the later eighteenth century it certainly was not). Another question, the constitutional method by which the colonies could gain representation, was answered by recourse to ancient precedents—the annexing of Durham, Chester, and Wales—a point which was already familiar to many of Pownall's readers.

The colonists had in principle agreed to pay "customs and duties" on trade, as legislated by Parliament. The practice for granting other funds was "by requisition from the crown, to be laid before the assembly" by the governor. So long as the colonies continued to be regarded as separate from the realm, the British government should adhere to this practice, which was "wise, if not just also, from its having become, I had almost said, a constitutional mode of administration" by virtue of precedent (pp. 149-52). Pownall's conclusion is that the British government, if it cared about constitutional justice, confronted an alternative: either "to follow . . . this established mode" or to admit American representatives to Parliament.

The rest of his discussion of constitutional relations may be referred to summarily. The "requisition" method would require the kind of precise data indicated on pp. 155-62. The course he would prefer ("the measure") is to recognize the emergence of "*an actual system of dominion*" and to extend "the basis of its representative legislature,"

INTRODUCTION

thereby constituting politically "A GRAND MARINE DOMINION." He realizes that fellow Englishmen will generally look upon this idea as visionary and politically objectionable, and that Americans unfortunately appear to be no longer interested in obtaining Parliamentary representation: "To this measure, not only the Briton but the American also *now* objects" (p. 165). He thereupon attempts to answer the objections from each side (pp. 165-72). At the finish he predicts what may be expected if the "measure" he favors is not pursued. Under the existing "system of policy," Great Britain "must continue for a while, entangled in a series of hostile disputes with its Colonies, but must at length lose them," and thus "sink by the same pride, and same errors . . . as all other commercial states have done" (pp. 176-7).

It is obvious that by 1768 Pownall had come to the conclusion that Parliament's general right of taxation in the colonies rested on very dubious constitutional grounds. A degree of ambiguity remains, but the thrust of his ideas is clear. It also appears that his conception of a "grand marine dominion" had now come to depend upon American representation in Parliament. On the many aspects of the constitutional problem of British imperial relations in this epoch there is a large historical literature, and no attempt will be made here to delve into the subject. But it is necessary to explain why the Americans, by 1768, were not eager to resolve their complaint about "taxation without representation" by means of actually gaining representation in Parliament. In part, the Americans were mindful of the expense and inconvenience of sending representatives to England. But more importantly they were already realizing the difficulty of influencing a legislature with several hundred representatives from a multiplicity of constituencies. Lobbyists representing colonial interests had worked effectively over the years with the Board of Trade and the Privy Council but had found it hard to get anywhere with Parliament. There they not only came up against British domestic interests but against other imperial interests: wealthy absentee West India plantation owners, East India nabobs, or members of the Irish establishment, who were already stronger in Parliament than the American mainland interests could expect to become. Pownall toyed with

INTRODUCTION

the idea of offering the Americans a considerable number of representatives, proportional to their population. Not many Americans were ready to accept such a scheme, and no British politicians were.

Pownall, the ardent "futurist," eagerly foretold the unstoppable progress of expansive economic growth to the westward—in a passage fraught with Newtonian metaphor and prophetic grandeur.[23] Economic development would, in the course of time, cause the center of political power of the "grand marine dominion" to move across the Atlantic regardless of what the British government decided. All this may seem perspicacious from a twentieth-century vantage point, but it was not an idea that a British Parliament of the eighteenth century could possibly entertain.

Pownall turned next to the problem of colonial currency. Almost half of this rather long section (pp. 177-253) is devoted to printing a manuscript treatise on money by Tench Francis, Esq., a prominent Philadelphia lawyer.[24] We shall leave its particulars, and Pownall's own ideas on the subject, to historians of monetary theory. Politically and commercially, however, the question of an adequate colonial currency was of the first importance.

There is probably no clearer instance of the British government's incapacity, in the 1760s, to administer the Atlantic empire responsively than the matter of colonial currency. Every colony needed paper money despite the ever present danger of excessive issuance. Pownall's sensitivity to the plight of creditors paid off by inflated legal tender provoked him to vehemence, and he did not waver from the opinion that the Currency Act of 1764, which prevented the colonies from issuing paper that could be deemed legal tender, was a necessary measure. But he also knew that the American colonies could scarcely do without paper money. In 1764 he had stated that a certain amount of colonial paper money was always necessary. In 1768 he was more guarded about this in his introduction, giving strong emphasis to policies that would enable the colonies to trade for silver coin (p. 182), but later on (p. 227) the need for a paper currency is plainly stated.

INTRODUCTION

The colonists' complaints about the Currency Act during the first two years of its operation were mild, for three reasons: their sense of outrage was focused on the Sugar Act (1764) and Stamp Act (1765); wealthier colonial merchants, often creditors, generally welcomed a restraint on payment of debts by depreciated currency (pp. 230-1); and, perhaps most important, there was still a lot of paper money in circulation. By early 1766, however, a proportion of existing notes had attained their maturity dates in various colonies. The paper was thus retired and the resulting contraction affected economic activity, provoking a sense of urgency in colonial legislatures. Petitions for repeal of the act multiplied. When hopes for that faded, the different legislatures tried alternative proposals, all of which provided for notes that would not be legal tender. Nevertheless, with only one exception, their proposals were rejected in London. The Board of Trade simply fortified the position it had taken in 1764; in fact, it interpreted "legal tender" so broadly as to obstruct all subsequent proposals. Instead of responding to commercial and financial realities, the Board of Trade was locked into a doctrinaire posture of great severity. Royal governors pleaded for relief in vain until, in 1771, the new ministry under Lord North began to ease the policy.[25]

In the fourth edition Pownall offered two proposals. One was a scheme that he believed had been used to good advantage in Pennsylvania during the 1740s. The notes, to be issued by a "land office" established by each colony's legislature, were not to have the status of legal tender.[26] This scheme he now "proposed to . . . the colonies" to undertake on their own, but did so reluctantly. For he warned his British readers that if the colonies were to undertake it, whether because of "our bad policy, or their own prudence," they would thereby *take the lead*. They would in due course cooperate, and a system of intercolonial credit and currency regulation would gradually develop (pp. 232-4). This would bring on the very sort of commercial and political unification, centered in America, that British administration should seek to prevent. Therefore Pownall preferred a plan under which the British government would take the lead. He, together with Benjamin Franklin, had already

INTRODUCTION

shopped such a plan (a modified form of the Pennsylvania scheme) around Whitehall, to no avail. Still, he hoped that the British government would see the imperial advantage of taking the lead. One key modification in the proposed imperial plan was that the notes could serve as legal tender because they would be issued under Parliament's authority. An added feature of this plan, he pointed out, was that the profits could be used to pay permanent salaries to royal officials (pp. 242-3). By 1768, however, this feature rendered the plan unacceptable to the colonists because they saw it as a threat to the power of their legislatures.[27]

Of wider interest is Pownall's account of the circumstances which made a paper currency of some sort necessary in the North American colonies. Like Great Britain, North America had to trade for its precious metals, but unlike Great Britain its only considerable source of hard money was the foreign West Indies, and the influx from thence flowed out to pay for British manufactured goods as fast as it came in. Pownall addressed the problem in theoretical as well as situational terms, and it is obvious from his grasp of the role of "improvements" that he had a conception of what today is termed a developing country; if specie flowed out of such a country, that was not necessarily a sign of economic decline (pp. 177-8, 185-6). It is certain that Pownall picked up these ideas in America; some of the most interesting points were made in a Pennsylvania committee report of 1752 which he quoted at length (pp. 237-9).

Providing an adequate currency for commercial purposes, Pownall pointed out, harmonized with British imperial interests. A developing colonial economy could enlarge its consumption of British manufactures only insofar as it could pay for them, and if scarcity of money and poor terms of trade forced colonists to manufacture for themselves, not only their commercial but also their political ties to the mother country would weaken.

Pownall ended his section on the Indians of North America (pp. 254-81) by mentioning proposals for an imperial administration of Indian affairs and "proper regulations for the Indian trade," but spent no time on

INTRODUCTION

those proposals. He knew that questions about particular administrative remedies were secondary. His primary task—the task that completely dominates the discussion—was to convince statesmen that their policy with regard to the military security of the interior had to be based upon a policy of justice toward the natives.

According to his analysis the task and the policy were indeed inseparable. The inland frontier of the British colonies was, from any practical standpoint, incapable of defense; the concept of a military barrier was an illusion.[28] Yet since 1750 another idea had been gaining ascendancy: that of casting claims of British dominion into the interior. At first the idea was justified by a need to counter French expansion, but when French forces left North America in 1763 it was not given up. Pownall argued that the claim of dominion, and the postwar garrisons which were established to support it, did nothing to improve the situation of imperial defense. On the contrary, both the claim and the soldiers offended the Indians, serving to confirm suspicions they had held during the war (pp. 275-6). So long as this idea guided policy, the British empire would remain embroiled in bloody warfare against a people who might be extirpated perhaps, but never conquered (p. 262).[29] Moreover, even without active warfare, the military expense vastly outweighed any possible benefits. The paragraph in which Pownall lambasted this "idea of conquest, in support of this ambitious folly of dominion," is as succinct as it is incontrovertible (pp. 264-5). All this being so, the only sound policy for frontier security was that of getting and remaining on good terms with the Indians. In order to do this, Pownall concluded, the British colonial empire in North America must honor "the real spirit" of the alliances made with them, do "the Indians justice in their lands," and give up the "useless claim of dominion over them" (p. 280).

The whole discussion has the clarity, vigor, and coherence of a good essay, and readers will take their own measure of both Pownall's grasp of the situation and his moral assumptions. But there is one point that ought to be brought out. However much wisdom these pages contain—and they contain a good deal—the problem of "doing the Indians justice in their lands" could not be so felicitously handled as

INTRODUCTION

Pownall wished to think. He had beguiled himself with a hopeful assumption: "As hunters, their interest can never interfere with ours, as settlers." Indian men were hunters, to be sure, but in many regions Indian economies depended greatly upon agriculture, carried on largely by Indian women.[30] More obviously, "encroachments of the European settlers" on Indian lands, a prime complaint of theirs as he recognized (p. 261), were going to continue, and Pownall himself did not propose to slow the process down. On the contrary, he believed that the expansion of settlement, far from being detrimental to British imperial interests, was needed to prevent Americans from turning their labor toward manufacturing. The reader will not fail to notice that the Indian policy Pownall envisioned, though designed to avoid a violent and rapacious "destruction of these brave and free people," looked to a future in which their population would be "continually wearing away." Attrition would provide the solution: "as they diminish or retire, they cede their lands to us in peace" (p. 276). In sum, "hunters and wanderers" would naturally give way to "settlers and land-workers." One sees here an Enlightenment version of the march of civilization, the civilization in this case being the expanding empire of British America.

A long review of Pownall's first edition formed the lead-off article in *The Gentleman's Magazine* of March 1764. The reviewer devoted most of his attention to trade. The first edition (like the fourth) concluded with a discussion of imperial trade policy, and the reviewer did not miss or mistake Pownall's key points: Great Britain should look to expanding the scope of colonial trade, not confining it; there was "great danger that any severity of execution" of the existing laws of trade— enforcement at a level which would make them truly effective—would place the Americans in a position where they would be economically compelled to take up manufacturing rather than continue to depend upon British imports; and once that happened their governmental independence would not be "an event so remote as our leaders" might think. Pownall's specific proposals for enlarging the scope of colonial trade are also to be found in the first edition: the establishment of "*British*

INTRODUCTION

markets" by means of British merchant houses in those parts of Europe where a direct colonial trade would be profitable; a scheme whereby the East India Company's trade might be integrated; and, most strenuously argued of all, an insistence that trade between North America and the foreign West Indies must be allowed to flourish, it being indispensable to the whole British Atlantic system. The reviewer in *The Gentleman's Magazine* noted all this, and also remarked that Pownall's discussion of trade seemed to be "written with great knowledge of the subject, and upon the most enlarged and comprehensive principles."[31]

The fourth edition included all the points above, but was significantly improved. One defect of the first edition was that it lacked a coherent description of the existing Atlantic trading system. In the fourth edition Pownall included a long extract from the "New York Petition" for the purpose of illustrating the actual "circuit of North American commerce."[32] The picture thus became richer and clearer.

Another defect of the first edition was its failure to confront the issue posed by the old laws of trade and navigation, that is to say, the laws enacted a century earlier which were designed to restrict many aspects of colonial commerce. Pownall's whole purpose in this section was to argue for a more open American colonial trade, and he knew that statesmen in the 1760s were invoking those old laws to justify a policy of confining colonial trade. Yet he started off in 1768, just as in 1764, with a weak—really a self-contradictory—opening paragraph. Its first sentence reads:

> The principles on which the act of navigation is founded are just, and of sound policy; but the application of them, by the modes prescribed, as the laws now stand, to the present state of the Colony trade, is neither founded in justice nor prudence.[33]

It is very hard to see how he could have considered some of those century-old principles still to be "of sound policy." Merely to criticize their *application* was to dodge the issue. Presumably he did not dare challenge the almost sacred "act of navigation."[34] That may have been wise.

INTRODUCTION

But there is to be found in the fourth edition, unlike the first, a long and interesting second paragraph in which Pownall directly confronted the matter at issue. However sound the "laws of trade respecting America" were when they were originally "framed and enacted," he observed, they had been overtaken by commercial developments. Those laws of a century ago had been aimed at "regulating *mere plantations;*" now the colonies had grown into "a very complex and extensive commercial interest" which had the effect of "forming A GRAND MARINE EMPIRE." If those old laws were now carried "into strict and literal execution," he warned, "we must determine to reduce our Colonies again to such mere plantations." British statesmen must therefore "make a sincere, unprejudiced and candid review of these laws of trade."[35] There was no ambiguity in this.

One can certainly find a number of boldly revisionist pronouncements on trade policy in the first edition—perhaps none was bolder than the claim that the colonies in their current circumstances would hardly have any trade at all "without an absolute and entire infraction" of the universally held principle that their trade should be confined to the mother country.[36] But the first edition's section on trade had basically offered an ambiguous opening paragraph followed by a set of policy proposals sprinkled with warnings about injurious measures. The systemic reason why a strict enforcement of the old laws of trade would be disastrous was not made altogether clear. Now, by emphasizing the historical change that a century of colonial trading had wrought, and illustrating "the circuit of North American commerce" by reference to the New York petition, Pownall substantially repaired the defects. In so doing he brought the discussion more into line with the large theme laid out at the beginning of the book, where he portrayed a practically invincible "spirit of *commerce*" as the "predominant power" in the world (p. 4). Obviously, this section on trade should be read in conjunction with those opening pages.

Pownall's description and analysis of the British Atlantic trading system stands apart from the existing literature on colonial trade, which was preoccupied with pointing out foreign threats and promoting

INTRODUCTION

particular interests; such generalizations as the English writers invoked were borrowed from the accumulated maxims of an incoherent mercantilism. Pownall's discussion owes nothing to mercantilist doctrines. But the truly distinguishing qualities of his treatment are comprehensiveness, integration, and realism. His eyes were opened to the realities of the British Atlantic system through acquaintance with American merchants; his knowledge in this sphere was not based on books. His insight came from an appreciation of the dynamism of commerce.

The portrayal of oceanic commerce in this book stands in marked contrast to Adam Smith's. Pownall contemplated how Atlantic commerce actually worked. Smith found arguments to support his abhorrence of a system he imagined to be monopolistic. In September 1776 Pownall, after reading *The Wealth of Nations*, published an open letter to Smith. It was a long book review, for the most part sober and academic, and in fact Pownall's ideas about the circuit of oceanic trade assume their best theoretical form here. But when it came to Smith's handling of the subject of British imperial trade, Pownall delivered a rebuke that was as passionate as it was pointed:

> In consequence of this doctrine, you are not only for breaking up the monopoly, but for a dismemberment of the empire, by giving up the dominion over our colonies. This prompt and hasty conclusion is very unlike the author of 'the Treatise on the wealth of nations,' it savours more of the puzzled inexperience of an unpracticed surgeon, who is more ready with his amputation knife, than prepared in the skill of healing medicines. If we lose our colonies, we must submit to our fate; but the idea of parting with them on the ground of system, is much like the system which an ironical proverb recommends, '*of dying to save charges*'.[37]

Clearly, Pownall never abandoned the belief that, if properly managed, a British Atlantic empire based on commercial growth could have worked. As noted earlier, however, he did not believe that the center of this empire would always remain in Britain.[38]

INTRODUCTION

It is obvious that Pownall's experience in America influenced *The Administration of the Colonies* in almost every way. Did the publication of the book influence his later career? His career after 1760 was certainly a disappointment to him. Although it should be borne in mind that few ex-governors fared well in this respect, Pownall had unusually good credentials. He was clearly intelligent, still rather young, ambitious, energetic, and an acknowledged expert on military administration as well as American colonial affairs. But the appointments that he hoped for never came.

Anyone who had served the crown abroad suffered the political disadvantage of being out of personal contact at Westminster, but Pownall's problem may have been closer to the opposite. It is possible that British politicians who knew him personally found him to be insufferable. Lord Loudoun told the Duke of Cumberland in 1757: "He has no knowledge of Men. All merit consists in joining implicitly in his Opinions and in Adulation of his Perfections."[39] Loudoun was a far from perfect creature, and his was a soldier's view of an uppity young aide whose ideas on civil-versus-military power were the opposite of his own. But Loudoun's comment is reinforced by a piece of gossip relating to an early effort at courtship of Pownall's which failed: the lady "frankly told him that he had a *positiveness* in his temper she could not bear with and would certainly make her unhappy."[40] From other evidence as well, one forms the impression that for a career in politics or administration Pownall was too fond of ideas, especially his own.

Pownall had been angling to "be of some service in England" ever since his return to London in 1760. He sought on the one hand to be employed by the colony of Massachusetts as their London agent or better yet as the vaguely defined English "Patron" of the colony (or colonies), a position he himself suggested in the *Administration*.[41] On the other hand, he was also after a second-tier job with the ministry. He had written to Pitt, hoping for a London position concerned with North American affairs, but to no avail.[42] Before long Pitt was out of office. In 1764 the publication of a treatise demonstrating his expertise on imperial

INTRODUCTION

questions was therefore a means of attracting notice in a wider circle. Although in a memoir twenty years later Pownall said that "the publication of this treatise ruined me with those who had the real power of Government in their hands," it is certain that he had not anticipated such a consequence at the time.[43] He dedicated the second edition to George Grenville, who was still head of the government when it appeared in early 1765.

The dedication of that second edition to Grenville is in many ways understandable, but Pownall's persistence in dedicating the third and fourth editions to Grenville is puzzling. Grenville was out of office before the end of 1765 and remained in opposition for the rest of his life; everyone knew that George III detested him. In regard to American policy, Grenville was author of the Sugar Act (1764) and Stamp Act (1765), which had stirred the colonies to a furor. Although Pownall had not ruled out measures of their genre, he must have noticed by 1766, if not earlier, that the methods and spirit of Grenvillite colonial administration were plainly contrary to what he recommended. Information had not been carefully gathered and weighed; the initiatives had not been "wisely and firmly bottomed . . . as to be a *practical*" approach to administration. And as all knew, in the aftermath Grenville remained convinced that his measures had been sound. In spite of all this, Pownall prefaced the fourth edition with a fourteen-page letter to Grenville which has the character of a dedication. This letter has been interpreted as an attempt "to weasel out of having dedicated the second and third editions" to him.[44] But the letter is in fact more adulatory than Pownall would have needed to make it, if his aim had been simply and courteously to disengage himself.

Was Pownall as politically obtuse as these facts imply? It is interesting to consider his options for ministerial alliances. Pitt, in the 1760s, was erratic, unhealthy, and notoriously unhelpful to his followers. Pownall had no known connection with the Bedford group. Lord Rockingham and his party would appear to have been a logical choice in terms of commercial policy. During their brief moment in office (1765-6) the Rockinghams had made a determined legislative assault on Grenville's

INTRODUCTION

American program and eliminated some its worst blunders; they had shown a disposition to learn about American trade from merchants actually affected by it. Pownall was surely aware of these facts. The Rockinghams, however, managed to make sure that Pownall would remain an enemy. In consequence of the unconfirmed accusations that Pownall had solicited and received a bribe from the Landgrave of Hesse-Kassel (mentioned above), Lord Rockingham's Treasury denied him a bonus of £3000 which it allowed to the two other commissioners who served with him.[45] He cannot have entertained any notions of affiliating with the Rockinghams. Still, how can one explain the fact that as late as 1768 Thomas Pownall did not stand clear of George Grenville?

Strange as it may seem, Grenville, in the summer of 1768, was the best choice available. He was one of very few ministers or former ones who shared Pownall's advocacy of a comprehensive plan for the reform of empire. Pitt had shown no interest. The Rockinghams were inclined to leave things as they had been—the policy of "salutary neglect" as Burke later called it. Grenville was unusual among politicians of that epoch in that he was genuinely interested in administrative matters. Like Pownall, Grenville believed that the Atlantic commercial empire was of immense importance to the wealth and power of Great Britain. The problem, of course, was that Grenville's initial approach to reform had produced an imperial crisis. Presumably Pownall hoped that Grenville could learn, could be persuaded to try another tack. After all, Grenville had not opposed the idea of American representation in Parliament and was known to dislike a policy of military coercion. Finally, a point historians have too easily forgotten: after Pitt took a peerage Grenville was "the most effective debater in the House of Commons."[46]

Recent events had brought American affairs to a boil once again. The summer before the fourth edition came out, Parliament had passed a Revenue Act levying duties (the Townshend duties) on items the Americans imported from Britain—glass, tea, silk, lead, paper, and paints—and allocated the returns to the support of imperial civil government in America. In the same session, Parliament legislated the reorganization of the American customs service. By late spring of 1768

INTRODUCTION

word was filtering to Whitehall that the Americans were resisting both acts. The customs commissioners in Boston were finding it "totally impracticable to enforce the execution of the revenue laws." In February, the Massachusetts legislature approved a circular letter to be sent to other colonial legislatures. Drafted by Samuel Adams, the letter urged united action against the Revenue Act; it attacked the plan to pay colonial officials out of revenues raised by the new taxes and also rejected the idea of colonial representation in Parliament. The following month colonial non-importation associations, first created to resist the Stamp Act, began to be revived.

Meanwhile, politics in Great Britain were in disarray. There was no power of unified action in either the ministry or the opposition. The nominal prime minister, Pitt, now Earl of Chatham, was almost totally incapacitated by physical and mental illness, and the rest of the ministry, under the hesitant deputyship of the Duke of Grafton, was adrift. In opposition, rival parliamentary factions jockeyed for dominance, unable to coalesce because of their sharp divisions over American policy.[47] The newly appointed Secretary of State for the colonies, acting on his own, had ordered troops to be sent to back up the Massachusetts customs commissioners and had instructed the governor of that colony to require the assembly to disavow the circular letter and to dissolve them if they refused. The governor was rebuffed, the assembly dissolved, the populace inflamed, and riots broke out when the troops arrived. In embarrassed confusion the rest of the cabinet repudiated the Secretary's acts, but did not come up with alternatives.

Thus, Pownall's fourth edition appeared as George III's cabinet, without a leader and without a policy, was doing little but responding *ad hoc* to American encounters. The book was timely, and apparently circulated widely; it was commented on at length in contemporary reviews and seems to have been read and discussed among men of political influence, certainly by Rockingham, Burke, and Grenville.[48]

In the second half of 1768 George Grenville's attitude toward the American problem seems to have undergone a transformation. He now believed in moderation. Until the colonies knew where they stood on

INTRODUCTION

questions of taxation and sovereignty, imperial relations could not improve. Parliament must make up its mind about taxation. It would be better to give up the right to tax the colonies than to allow the issue to go on festering. If necessary, the government should revert to "requisitions" presented to colonial legislatures. Nothing should be done to invade chartered rights without a careful preliminary inquiry. He abhorred the use of British troops to enforce colonial policy. Stability in British America must be founded on civil government. Some of these ideas Grenville had held before. He had been already aware, for instance, of Chester and Durham as possible precedents for the colonies to follow in making application to be represented in Parliament. But his general attitude was new. As Philip Lawson has remarked, the contrast between Grenville's position in early 1766 and the years 1768-9 "could not have been more marked."[49] Grenville seems to have sensed that the imperial policy of Great Britain was headed toward a precipice.

Many of Grenville's newer ideas, and certainly the new attitude, were in accord with the contents of the fourth edition of *The Administration of the Colonies*. Pownall sent Grenville a prepublication copy in mid-July when asking permission to renew the dedication.[50] It is impossible to prove that the book stimulated Grenville's new line of thought, but the coincidence both in respect to timing and ideas is remarkable. On the matter of trade policy, though Grenville called for a full reappraisal, his schemes for giving the Atlantic trade a better balance[51] were the sort that Pownall would have considered "artificial," and thus ineffective or harmful. But on most issues the two men were now not far apart; in Parliamentary debates on American affairs during 1769-70 Pownall and Grenville were usually on the same side.

In 1767 Pownall had entered the House of Commons as member for Tregony, a Cornish borough. There is neither the need nor the space to trace here his subsequent conduct and role in Parliament, and its reception in the colonies.[52] His surviving Parliamentary speeches, much edited by himself, read well, but Pownall evidently lacked the gift of oratory, and probably a sense of proportion too. In any case, he seems to have been as effective as Edmund Burke at emptying the House when he

INTRODUCTION

stood up to speak. Yet he was clearly recognized as an expert on American affairs, and there were occasions when he managed to put before the House—those members still listening—some of the grand themes of *The Administration of the Colonies*.[53] Perhaps if Grenville had lived (he died in 1770), the temper of the House on this great imperial issue might have altered, and Pownall's sense of futility might have been somewhat alleviated. Perhaps he would have been less tempted to wander into the arms of Lord North in hopes of office, as he did in the early 1770s—a deviation which has not helped his historical reputation. In any case, he remained consistent in the hope that a reconciliation with the colonists might be worked out. And when the news of the battle of Saratoga arrived, he was among the first to declare that the only course was to grant independence.

In retrospect, it is impossible to put out of one's mind the futility of *The Administration of the Colonies* as a guide to policy. Its constitutional proposals may be dismissed as simply impracticable, or as coming too late to change the direction of politics on either side of the Atlantic. Its general conception of an enlarging empire with an eventually migrating center may be dismissed as politically unthinkable at the time, especially unthinkable to Englishmen. The idea that commerce could be allowed its course yet remain under the hand of a wise and responsive mode of imperial administration, which would manage to insure a due proportion of profit to the mother country, seems unduly hopeful. Pownall's notion that this imperial branch of administration could be insulated from British politics was naive. Indeed, an Enlightenment optimism pervades the whole book: political harmony would naturally follow commercial convenience; if various colonies had chosen to adopt the Pennsylvania currency plan they would soon have learned to coordinate their currencies harmoniously; good treatment of the Indians could solve the problem of frontier defense. The list could easily be extended.

Pownall acknowledged that his ideas would be generally regarded as visionary. But his reviling of "those declarations of power, with which we mock ourselves" (p. 164) certainly reads well in retrospect: those who

INTRODUCTION

believed they could force a set of ill-conceived policies on the Americans were beset by the worst delusion of all. Whatever career hopes he harbored, Pownall wrote his book in order to educate British statesmen and the British public as to the true conditions of transatlantic politics and commerce, and the limits thereby imposed on imperial governance. Of the assortment of works devoted to that task his was the best informed and, from an elongated perspective, perhaps the most realistic.

DANIEL A. BAUGH ALISON GILBERT OLSON
Cornell University *University of Maryland, College Park*

NOTES

1. The dates are as follows: First, 1764; second, 1765; third, 1766; fourth, 1768; fifth, 1774; sixth, 1777, all published in London. The last two bear the title, *The Administration of the British Colonies*. Their evolution is traced in G. H. Guttridge, "Thomas Pownall's *The Administration of the Colonies*: the Six Editions," *William and Mary Quarterly* 3rd ser. [hereafter *WMQ*], 26 (Oct. 1969), pp. 31-46. An important survey of the editions may also be found in John Shy, "Thomas Pownall, Henry Ellis, and the Spectrum of Possibilities, 1763-1775," in Alison Gilbert Olson and Richard Maxwell Brown, eds., *Anglo-American Political Relations, 1675-1775* (New Brunswick, 1970), pp. 155-86.

2. Ibid., p. 173.

3. For Pownall's early career see Charles A. W. Pownall, *Thomas Pownall, M.P., F.R.S., Governor of Massachusetts Bay, Author of the Letters of Junius* (London, 1908) Chs. I to VII; and John A. Schutz, *Thomas Pownall, British Defender of American Liberty* (Glendale, CA, 1951), pp. 15-180.

4. For the Albany Plan see Oliver Morton Dickerson, *American Colonial Government, 1696-1765* (New York, 1962), pp. 216-23; Alison Gilbert Olson, "The British Government and Colonial Union, 1754," *WMQ* 17 (Jan. 1960), pp. 22-34.

5. See below, Appendix, pp. 51-61 (Section II). By "Idea of the Service" (p. 52) he meant "strategy," a word that did not come into general English usage until the Napoleonic wars.

INTRODUCTION

6. Pownall's early reports on the situation of the Indians and his intercommunication with Pitt are noted in Francis Jennings, *Empire of Fortune: Crown, Colonies, and Tribes in the Seven Years War in America* (New York, 1988), pp. 96-100, 354-5. Pownall had formed a close partnership with Colonel William Johnson (later General Sir William Johnson), from whom he learned much of what he knew about this subject. For a succinct discussion of Johnson's views and activities see Michael Kammen, *Colonial New York: A History* (New York, 1975), pp. 308-14.

7. The opinion of Thomas Hutchinson ran entirely counter to this view; see William Pencak, *War, Politics, and Revolution in Provincial Massachusetts* (Boston, 1981), p. 151. Hutchinson and Pownall usually treated each other very badly: the animosity may have been personal; but it is certain that their political differences were marked; see generally Bernard Bailyn, *The Ordeal of Thomas Hutchinson* (Cambridge, MA, 1974), especially pp. 42-5.

8. He was praised by the prime minister, William Pitt, for his accomplishments, but reproved by the Board of Trade for allowing the Massachusetts legislature too much executive power; see Charles Pownall, *Thomas Pownall*, pp. 130-2.

9. Guttridge, "Six Editions," p. 32.

10. This paragraph is based on H. M. Little, "Thomas Pownall and Army Supply, 1761-1766," *Journal of the Society for Army Historical Research* 65 (1987), 92-104.

11. First edition (1764), pp. 3-9; fourth edition, pp. 1-12.

12. Pp. 12-16.

13. Halifax's early proposals are discussed in A. H. Basye, *The Lord's Commissioners of Trade and Plantations, Commonly Known as the Board of Trade, 1748-1782* (New Haven, 1925), pp. 84, 93-4, 102-4, 111.

14. Alison Gilbert Olson, *Making the Empire Work: London and American Interest Groups, 1690-1790* (Cambridge, MA, 1992), pp. 134-43.

15. P. 35: " . . . they must be guarded by this union against having or forming any principle of coherence with each other."

16. His recommendations on pp. 13, 17, and 19 may be compared with Halifax's earlier proposals.

17. P. 28. H.R.H. the Duke of York was proposed by Pownall; the ministry, however, rejected the idea. See the fifth edition (1774), I, 29-30.

18. Olson, *Making the Empire Work*, pp. 118, 138.

INTRODUCTION

19. On this subject he had been emphatic and consistent since at least 1755.

20. It is possible to ascertain the intended meaning of this sentence by reference to the fifth ed., I, 120-1, where the bad writing was cleaned up.

21. See also pp. 65-6, 122, 129. In this respect Pownall's interpretation is completely at variance with that which was set forth in Charles Howard McIlwain, *The American Revolution: A Constitutional Interpretation* (New York, 1923, repr. Ithaca, NY, 1958). McIlwain's argument rested heavily on what happened in 1649.

22. In an appendix to the third edition (1766), also published separately under the title *Considerations on the Points lately brought into Question as to Parliament's Right of Taxing the Colonies*, he had employed the most lurid language when describing the claims heard from the colonists that they were exempt from being taxed (pp. 9-11).

23. P. 37. A similar passage appears in the first edition.

24. Tench Francis: born in Ireland; studied law in London ca. 1720; Attorney General of Pennsylvania, 1741-55; Recorder of Philadelphia, 1750-55; died 1758. This treatise also appeared in the first edition.

25. See especially Jack P. Greene and Richard M. Jellison, "The Currency Act of 1764 in Imperial-Colonial Relations, 1764-1776," *WMQ* 18 (Oct. 1961), pp. 485-518. New England was exempt from the Currency Act, its system of paper money being judged benign. The exception south of New England was Maryland, where the paper was backed by British sterling funds.

26. Pownall's ready-to-hand distinction between "natural" and "artificial" played a role in his thoughts on money: any notes issued by authority of colonial legislatures through their "land offices" should not be legal tender, because the discipline of "natural" forces (*i.e.*, market forces) was needed to prevent them from becoming instruments of public mischief.

27. On Pownall's earlier cooperation with Franklin on behalf of this plan, as well as the colonists' fear that its profits would threaten the power of their legislatures, see Verner W. Crane, ed., *Benjamin Franklin's Letters to the Press, 1758-1775* (Chapel Hill, NC, 1950), pp. 25-30, 99-100.

28. Pownall's strongest statement of this point is to be found in a Memorial he wrote in 1756, printed below in the Appendix (Section I) pp. 31-3.

29. Almost certainly Pownall could have written something for the first edition very like what he published on this subject in the fourth. It was not an

INTRODUCTION

appropriate moment, he remarked in the 1764 edition, because the interior was then actually in a state of military embroilment with the Indians (*i.e.*, "Pontiac's rebellion"). In the second edition (1765) he did take up the subject to some extent.

30. For this point and other assistance relating to this subject the editors are much indebted to Prof. Daniel Usner of Cornell University.

31. *The Gentleman's Magazine*, XXXIV (March 1764), pp. 103-8. First edition (1764), pp. 113-31. Regarding trade with the foreign West Indies he asserted that, instead of curtailing North American trade with the foreign West Indies, "the duty of government [was] to permit, nay even to encourage" it, though under proper regulation (*ibid.*, p. 124).

32. Pp. 284-97. Internal evidence indicates that the date of this "New York Petition" was 1766 or afterwards, but we have been unable to trace it.

33. Pp. 281-2; first edition (1764), pp. 113-14.

34. In the discourse of the time, "act of navigation" rather than "acts" was often employed. The plural is correct, and the use of the singular had the effect of causing confusion even then.

35. Pp. 282-4. As he put it a few pages later, the colonies had become, in the course of time, "commercial states" (p. 299).

36. First edition (1764), p. 7.

37. *A Letter from Governor Pownall to Adam Smith* (London, 1776) is printed in Appendix A of *The Correspondence of Adam Smith*, ed. Ernest Campbell Mossner and Ian Simpson Ross (Oxford, 1977, repr. Indianapolis, 1987), pp. 337-76; this book is vol. 6 of The Glasgow Edition of the Works and Correspondence of Adam Smith. Smith's criticism of "a round-about trade" as being inherently inefficient provoked Pownall into analyzing the patterns and benefits of what he chose to call a "circuitous trade" (pp. 355-58). The quotation is from p. 366. See also Richard F. Teichgraeber, III, "'Less Abused than I had Reason to Expect': The Reception of *The Wealth of Nations* in Britain, 1776-90," *The Historical Journal*, 30 (1987), pp. 346-50. Smith and Pownall were almost exact contemporaries.

38. In *The Administration of the Colonies* Pownall's notion of the way in which the empire generated wealth and power was wholly commercial. While it is true that commerce was the wellspring, under the navigation acts the British empire was also designed to yield maritime resources for supporting naval needs. Pownall recognized the naval aspect in the *Letter* to Adam Smith (*op. cit.*, p. 357). This aspect is explored in Daniel A. Baugh, "Maritime Strength and

INTRODUCTION

Atlantic Commerce: The Uses of 'A Grand Marine Empire,'" in *An Imperial State at War*, ed. Lawrence Stone (London, 1993, forthcoming).

39. Loudoun to Cumberland, 17 Oct. 1757, Stanley Pargellis, ed., *Military Affairs in North America, 1748-1765: Selected Documents* (New York, 1936), p. 404.

40. William Coney to Sir William Johnson, undated but perhaps autumn 1760, quoted by Charles Pownall, *Thomas Pownall*, p. 161. Italics in the original.

41. Michael Kammen, *A Rope of Sand; the Colonial Agents, British Politics, and the American Revolution* (Ithaca, NY, 1968), p. 247.

42. Schutz, *Thomas Pownall*, pp. 195-6; Guttridge, "Six Editions," p. 32. The fact that his brother, John, was secretary to the Board of Trade and occupied a key position in the conduct of American affairs undoubtedly afforded some advantages to the ex-governor, but it may have complicated the problem of finding Thomas suitable employment in this sphere in England. It is hard to know because, to our knowledge, the political relations between the two brothers have not been investigated by historians. For John Pownall's career see Franklin B. Wickwire, "John Pownall and British Colonial Policy," *WMQ* 20 (Oct. 1963), pp. 543-54.

43. Charles Pownall, *Thomas Pownall*, p. 175.

44. Shy, "Thomas Pownall, Henry Ellis, and the Spectrum," p. 173.

45. Little, "Thomas Pownall and Army Supply," pp. 102-3.

46. John Brooke, *The Chatham Administration, 1766-1768* (London, 1956), p. 45.

47. For a brief survey see Ian R. Christie, *Crisis of Empire: Great Britain and the American Colonies, 1754-1783* (New York, 1966), chap. 4.

48. Burke's copy survives in the British Library; it contains numerous marginal jottings. Guttridge briefly discussed some of Burke's constitutional disagreements with Pownall in "Six Editions," pp. 42-3. See also Charles Pownall, *Thomas Pownall*, pp. 205-6.

49. Philip Lawson, "George Grenville and America: The Years of Opposition, 1765 to 1770," *WMQ*, 37 (Oct. 1980), pp. 561-76; the source for everything in this paragraph.

50. Pownall to Grenville, 14 July 1768, *The Grenville Papers*, ed. William J. Smith, 4 vols. (London, 1852-3), pp. 312-14; see also Grenville to Pownall, 17 July 1768, pp. 316-19.

51. Lawson, "George Grenville and America," p. 571.

INTRODUCTION

52. The best guide is Charles Pownall, *Thomas Pownall*, pp. 192-307. For Pownall's speeches see R. C. Simmons and P. G. D. Thomas, eds., *Proceedings and Debates of the British Parliaments Respecting North America, 1754-1783* 6 vols. (Millwood, NY, 1982-in progress).

53. See *ibid.*, especially vol. 3, pp. 103-10, 153-60, 229-38.

INTRODUCTION

SUGGESTIONS FOR FURTHER READING

Governor Pownall's life, writings, and speeches:

Guttridge, G. H. "Thomas Pownall's *The Administration of the Colonies*: the Six Editions." *William and Mary Quarterly*, 3rd ser. 26 (Oct. 1969), pp. 31-46.

Little, H. M. "Thomas Pownall and Army Supply, 1761-1766." *Journal of the Society for Army Historical Research*, 65 (1987), 92-104.

Pownall, Charles A. W. *Thomas Pownall, M.P., F.R.S., Governor of Massachusetts Bay, Author of the Letters of Junius*. London, 1908.

Schutz, John A. *Thomas Pownall, British Defender of American Liberty*. Glendale, CA, 1951.

Shy, John. "Thomas Pownall, Henry Ellis, and the Spectrum of Possibilities, 1763-1775." In *Anglo-American Political Relations, 1675-1775*, edited by Alison Gilbert Olson and Richard Maxwell Brown. New Brunswick, 1970, pp. 155-86.

Simmons, R. C. and Peter G. D. Thomas, eds. *Proceedings and Debates of the British Parliaments Respecting North America, 1754-1783*. 6 vols. Millwood, NY, 1982-in progress.

Note: An extensive list of Thomas Pownall's writings and publications is attached to the entry under his name in the *Dictionary of National Biography*. A list of his speeches in Parliament may be found in Charles Pownall's biography (above), Appendix, p. 6.

INTRODUCTION

General background:

Andrews, Charles M. *The Colonial Period of American History*. 4 vols. New Haven, 1934-8.

Christie, Ian R. *Crisis of Empire: Great Britain and the American Colonies, 1754-1783*. New York, 1966.

Christie, Ian R. and Benjamin W. Labaree. *Empire or Independence, 1760-1776: A British-American Dialogue on the Coming of the American Revolution*. New York, 1976.

Jack P. Greene, "'A Posture of Hostility': A Reconsideration of Some Aspects of the Origins of the American Revolution," *Proceedings of the American Antiquarian Society*, 87 (1977-8), pp. 27-68.

Tucker, Robert W. and David C. Hendrickson. *The Fall of the First British Empire: Origins of the War of American Independence*. Baltimore and London, 1982.

Political background:

Bailyn, Bernard. *The Ordeal of Thomas Hutchinson*. Cambridge, MA, 1974.

Bullion, John L. *A Great and Necessary Measure: George Grenville and the Genesis of the Stamp Act, 1763-1765*. Columbia, MO, 1982.

Kammen, Michael. *A Rope of Sand; the Colonial Agents, British Politics, and the American Revolution*. Ithaca, NY, 1968.

Lawson, Philip. "George Grenville and America: The Years of Opposition, 1765 to 1770." *William and Mary Quarterly*, 37 (Oct. 1980), pp. 561-76.

INTRODUCTION

Maier, Pauline. *From Resistance to Revolution: Colonial Radicals and the Development of American Opposition to Britain, 1765-1776.* New York, 1972.

Thomas, Peter D. G. *British Politics and the Stamp Act Crisis: The First Phase of the American Revolution.* Oxford, 1975.

Thomas, Peter D. G. *The Townshend Duties Crisis: The Second Phase of the American Revolution, 1767-1773.* Oxford, 1987.

Constitutional and administrative:

Keith, Arthur Berriedale. *Constitutional History of the First British Empire.* Oxford, 1930.

Olson, Alison Gilbert. *Making the Empire Work: London and American Interest Groups, 1690-1790.* Cambridge, MA, 1992.

North American Indians and the use of military forces:

Dowd, Gregory Evans. *A Spirited Resistance: The North American Indian Struggle for Unity, 1745-1815.* Baltimore and London, 1992.

Jennings, Francis. *Empire of Fortune: Crown, Colonies, and Tribes in the Seven Years War in America.* New York, 1988.

Shy, John. *Toward Lexington: The Role of the British Army in the Coming of the American Revolution.* Princeton, 1965.

INTRODUCTION

Currency and the balance of payments:

Ernst, Joseph Albert. *Money and Politics in America, 1755-1775: A Study in the Currency Act of 1764 and the Political Economy of Revolution.* Chapel Hill, NC, 1973.

Greene, Jack P. and Richard M. Jellison. "The Currency Act of 1764 in Imperial-Colonial Relations, 1764-1776." *William and Mary Quarterly*, 18 (October 1961), pp. 485-518.

Trade:

McCusker, John J. and Russell R. Menard. *The Economy of British America, 1607-1789.* 2d ed., with supplementary bibliography, Chapel Hill, NC, 1991.

Baugh, Daniel A. "Maritime Strength and Atlantic Commerce: The Uses of 'A Grand Marine Empire'." In *An Imperial State at War*, edited by Lawrence Stone. London, 1993, forthcoming.

INTRODUCTION

Editors' Table of Contents
of *The Administration of the Colonies*
(4th ed., 1768)

Dedicatory letter to George Grenville	v
Copy of the petition of the county Palatine of Chester, 1450, with the King's answer, as printed by Daniel King in 1656	xxi

The Administration of the Colonies

Commerce and marine dominion	1
A central office of authority for the American colonies	12
Proposal for inquiring into colonial affairs and achieving a comprehensive settlement	27
Beneficial results of the above proposals	34
Constitutional and administrative relations between the colonies and the mother country as established by law	43
—rights and powers which derive from the King, as sovereign (dangers of military power, 86-101) (the judiciary, 101-18)	46
—the sovereign power of King, Lords and Commons (taxation and representation, 133-72)	118

INTRODUCTION

Currency and the balance of payments	177
(treatise on paper currency by Tench Francis, 190-226)	
(paper currency proposal based on a method formerly used	
in Pennsylvania, 230-7)	
(that proposal modified for Parliamentary sponsorship, 240-53)	
North American Indians and the use of military forces	254
The British Atlantic system of trade	281

Appendix

Section I. Pownall's memorandum on the conditions that shape military strategy in North America, 1756	1
Section II. Pownall's strategy proposal for the campaign of 1759; a letter to William Pitt, 5 Dec. 1758	51
Sections III, IV, V. Miscellaneous documents	62

THE ADMINISTRATION OF THE COLONIES.

(THE FOURTH EDITION.)

WHEREIN THEIR

RIGHTS AND CONSTITUTION

Are discussed and stated,

By THOMAS POWNALL,

Late Governor and Commander in Chief of his his Majesty's Provinces, Massachusetts-Bay and South-Carolina, and Lieutenant-Governor of New-Jersey.

Pulchrum est benefacere Reipublicæ, etiam benedicere haud absurdum est. SALLUSTIUS.

LONDON:
Printed for J. WALTER, at Homer's Head, Charing-Cross. MDCCLXVIII.

TO THE RIGHT HONOURABLE

GEORGE GRENVILLE, Esq;

SIR,

WHEN I first published my opinions upon the administration of the Colonies, I addressed the book to you. You was then minister in this country, and had taken an active and leading part in the administration of those affairs. I did not by that address dedicate, as is the usual phrase, my opinions to the minister, for our opinions differed on several points: But as disputes upon a question, pregnant with the most dangerous consequences, began to be agitated between the minister of this country and the Colonists, which I saw must soon extend themselves in contentions with

with parliament itself: As I saw a spirit of suspicion and alarm arising, a temper of ill blood infusing itself into the minds of men; I endeavoured to obviate these mischiefs, by marking in that address, that, as there were neither arbitrary intentions on one hand against the liberties of the Colonies, nor rebellious designs on the other against the just imperium of government; so there was a certain good temper and right spirit, which, if observed on all sides, might bring these matters of dispute to such a settlement as political truth and liberty are best established upon.

You had conceived, that government hath a right to avail itself in its finances, of the revenues of all its dominions, and that the imposing taxes, by parliament, for the said purpose, was the constitutional mode of doing this. The Colonists who were not represented in parliament by knights and burgesses of their own election, " did appre-
" hend, they had reason to fear some dan-
" ger of arbitrary rule over them, when
" the supreme power of the nation had
" thought

"thought proper to impose taxes on his Majesty's American subjects, with the sole and express purpose of raising a revenue, and without their consent."

Parliament had, by a solemn act, declared that it hath a right to make laws, which shall be binding upon the people of the Colonies, subjects of Great Britain, in *all cases whatsoever*,—while the Colonists say, in *all cases which can consist with the fundamental rules of the constitution*; by which limitation, they except the case of taxation, where there is not representation. Hence the Colonists have, by many, been deemed factious, undutiful and disloyal, and even chargeable with treason itself.——

I had been sufficiently conversant in these affairs, although neither employed nor consulted in them, since I left America, to know that these alternate charges were false and groundless; that there were neither arbitrary intentions on one hand, nor seditious views on the other. As therefore, by my address, I meant to do justice to your principles, which I knew to be those of peace and government established on political liberty,—so I took that occasion, as I will ever esteem it a duty to do, to bear my testimony to the affection which the Colonists ever bore to the mother country, to their zeal for its welfare, to their sense of government and their loyalty to their sovereign, as also how much they have merited from this country, and how much they deserve to be considered by it, in order to put these matters of dispute on a footing of reconciliation, fair discussion and equitable settlement,——

It is great pity that questions of this nature were ever raised, * " for, it is a very " unsafe thing in settled governments, to " argue the reason of the fundamental con- " stitutions."—But when contrary propositions are alternately brought forward by the representatives of two people, as the avowed principles of their respective constituents; when an inferior government, which invariably acknowledges its dependence on a supe-

* Comm. Journal 1672.

rior and fupream government, thinks it hath a right to call into queftion fome particular exertions of power in that government, by rules which limit the extent of that power, it is abfolutely neceffary to decide fuch queftion, or to give fuch explanations of the matter, that it may ceafe to be a queftion;— for fo long as it continues in doubt, the parties will alternately charge each other with arbitrary principles, and a fpirit of fedition, with tyranny and rebellion;——and frequent injurious acts of violence, which numberlefs events will ever give occafion to, muft neceffarily be animated with a fpirit too nearly allied to the one and to the other. —The matter is in that ftate that it ought to come before parliament, it muft, it will,— it is neceffary to the fupport of government that it fhould;—it is neceffary to the fecurity of the nation and its intereft;—it is neceffary to the peace, liberties, and conftitution of the Colonies; it is neceffary to the fafety of minifters.

Many matters therefore, the publication of which I had fufpended, while I thought that

that this question might be waved, or some way compromised, I now publish in this edition. I continue my address, Sir, to you, now you are no longer minister, nor perhaps ever likely to be. I address myself to the private country gentleman, who will alway have a great share in the business of his country;—to Mr. George Grenville, as to one who hath, and alway will have great interest, lead and authority in parliament, from an opinion really and deeply grounded in the minds of the most serious of his countrymen, that, while for the sake of the peace and liberties of the whole, he means to support the constitutional powers of government in the crown; so is he equally, by principle, determined, as by abilities able, to guard the civil rights of the subjects with a peculiar regard to, and management of, their interests in their property.

This American question, in which liberty and the rights of property are so deeply engaged, must now come forward. From the part which you have already taken, you must still bear a considerable part in the debates

bates and confultations which will be held upon it. I therefore addrefs, to your moſt ſerious confideration, that ſtate of this buſineſs which the following book contains; nor will I defpair of your affent to what fo firmly eftabliſhes the rights of property, on the foundations of liberty, by an equal extenſion and communication of government, to wherefoever the people and dominions, having theſe rights, do extend. In the matters which I propoſe, I ſpeak my own ſentiments, not yours. I addrefs them to your ſerious confideration, as I do to every man of bufinefs in the nation, with an hope that from conviction of the juſtice, policy and neceffity of the meaſure, they may become the general ſentiments of the government, and of the people of Great Britain. From the ſame ſentiments, and with the ſame view of general peace and liberty, I could wiſh to recommend the ſame propoſitions to the Americans. Nor would I defpair of their affent to things, were there no jealouſies of, no prejudices againſt men. I am convinced that theſe maxims are true in theory, and do fincerely believe, that they are the only

prin-

principles, by which the peace, the civil liberty, and commercial prosperity of the British dominions can be maintained and supported. I am no Partizan. I do not palliate the errors of Great Britain. I do not flatter the passions of America. My zeal and many services towards the one, have appeared in the effect of those services; and my affection to the other, if it be not already known, will be seen, as, under the accident of a certain event, I mean to end my days there in a private character.

I have, in this present edition, gone into the discussion of this matter, *as it lies in fact*, and as it hath, at the first settlement of the Colonies, and in the different periods of their progress, *existed in right*, established on such fact. I have stated the fact, and the right, in hopes to point out what is the true and constitutional relation between Great Britain and the American Colonies, what is the precise ground on which this dangerous question ought to be settled: How far they are to be governed by the vigour of external principles, by the supreme superintending power of the mother country: How far,

by

by the vigour of the internal principles of their own peculiar body politic: And what ought to be the mode of administration, by which they are to be governed in their legislative, executive, judicial and commercial departments, in the conduct of their money and revenues in their power of making peace or war.—

Analysing by the experience of fact, this inquiry,———I mark the false policy which derives by necessary consequence from stating the Colonies, as subject only to the King in his seignoral capacity.———I show also that no precedents can be drawn from that period, when the two houses of parliament assumed the exercise of the sovereignty, and considered the Colonies *as their subjects*.—I show how the Colonies ought to be considered as parts of the realm, and by showing the perplexities in reasoning, and the dangerous consequences in practice, which attend the stating of the Colonies as without, and no part of the realm, at the same time that they are stated as subjects of the King, Lords and Commons collectively taken as sovereign. I mark the false ground and superstructure of that position.

In

In the course of this reasoning, while I state the rights of the Colonists, as those of Englishmen, to all intents and purposes; while I state *how* the Colonies have been administered, as distinct, free communities, and *how* they ought still to be administered, if they are not united to the realm.——I show that the Colonies, although without the limits of the realm, are yet in fact, of the realm; are *annexed*, if not yet *united* parts of the realm; are precisely in the predicament of the counties Palatine of Durham and Chester; and therefore ought, in the same manner, to be *united* to the realm, in a full and absolute communication and communion of all rights, franchises and liberties, which any other part of the realm hath, or doth enjoy, or ought to have and to enjoy: in communication of the same burthens, offices, and emoluments, in communion of the same foedoral and commercial rights, in the same exercise of judicial and executive powers,—in the same participation of council.—And that therefore, in the course and procedure of our government with the Colonies, there must arise a

duty

duty in government to give, a right in the Colonies to claim, a share in the legislature of Great-Britain, by having Knights and Burgesses of their own election, representing them in parliament.

It makes no difference in the matter of the truth, whether the government of England should be averse to the extending of this privilege to the Colonies, or whether the Colonies should be averse to the receiving of it:—Whether we, from pride and jealousy, or they, from fears and doubts, should be repugnant to this union. For, whether we reason from *experience* and the authority of *example*: Or whether we consider the policy, justice, and necessity of the measure, the conclusion is unavoidably the same; the proposition invariably *true*. *That the British isles, with our possessions in the Atlantic and in America, are in* FACT, UNITED INTO A ONE GRAND MARINE DOMINION: *And ought therefore, by policy, to be united into a one Imperium, in a one center, where the seat of government is. And ought to be governed from thence, by*

an

an administration founded on the basis of the whole, and adequate and efficient to the whole.

I have not stated the necessity of this measure, for reasons which cannot but be obvious to any prudent man; but I have ventured to affirm, that such is the actual state of the system of the British dominions, that neither the power of government, over these various parts, can long continue under the present mode of administration; nor the great interest of commerce, extended throughout the whole, long subsist under the present system of the laws of trade.

As I do, from my best judgment, sincerely believe, that a general and intire union of the British dominions, is the only measure by which Great Britain can be continued in its political liberty, and commercial prosperity, perhaps in its existence: So I make no scruple to averr, that if this measure be not adopted in *policy*, as it really exists in *fact*, it will soon become the duty of the several disunited parts, to look narrowly

rowly to, and stand firm in, the maintenance of their undoubted rights in that state and relation, in which the administration of government shall hold them. As I have pointed out the mode, how government may pursue its duty, consistent with the fundamentals of the constitution; so have I suggested, through every step, how the American may fortify himself in these rights, consistent with his alliance.

When I had first an opportunity of conversing with, and knowing the sentiments of, the * commissioners of the several provinces in North America, convened at Albany; of learning from their experience and judgment, the actual state of the American business and interest; of hearing amongst them, the grounds and reasons of that *American union* which they then had under deliberation, and transmitted the plan of to England: I then first conceived the idea, and saw the necessity of a general

* Appointed by their respective provinces, to attend a congress at Albany, in 1754, to which they were called by the crown.

British

British union. I then first mentioned my sentiments on this subject to several of those commissioners,—and at that time, first proposed my considerations on a general plan of union,———I had the satisfaction to find many of the measures, which I did then propose, adopted; and the much greater satisfaction of seeing the good effect of them: But this particular measure was at that time, I dare say, considered as theory and vision, and perhaps may, at this time, be thought so still: but every event that hath since arisen, every measure which hath since been taken, through every period of business in which I have been concerned, or of which I have been cognisant, hath confirmed me in my idea of the state of things, and of the truth of the measure: At this period, every man of business in Britain, as well as in America, sees the effect of this state of things, and may, in future, see the necessity of this measure. The whole train of events, the whole course of business, must perpetually bring forward into practice, and necessarily in the end, into establishment—*either an American or a British union.*—There is no other alternative, the

the only confideration which remains to every good man, who loves the peace and liberties of mankind, is whether the one or the other fhall be forced into exiftence, by the violence of parties, and at the hazard of events; or whether by the deliberate legiflative advice of the reprefentative of all who are concerned.——

May both the Briton and the American take this confideration to heart: and, whatever be the fate of parties and factions, of patriots or minifters, may the true government of laws prevail, and the rights of men be eftablifhed in political liberty.

With the higheft efteem and regard, I have the honour to be,

Sir,

Your moft obedient humble fervant,

T. POWNALL.

ADVERTISEMENT.

THAT I may obviate thofe prejudices by which many people might be led to think, that the doctrines and reafonings contained in the following book are novel, and theories of imagination: That I may at leaſt crave a fufpenfion of thofe opinions, from whence many people pronounce, that the application made by the Colonies, to deprecate the levying of taxes, when impofed by parliament, is unconftitutional and unprecedented: I have here inferted, as publifhed by Daniel King in 1656, the record of a like application from the county palatine of Chefter in the like cafe. With the King's anfwer, and ordinance made out in form. Wherein not only fimilar reafonings are exhibited, but a precedent alfo is holden forth. By which, government, on one hand,

hand, may fee, that this county Palatine was exempted from taxes laien by parliament, while the said county had not Knights and Burgesses of their own election, to represent them in parliament: and wherein the Colonies may see on the other hand, by pursuing the precedents relative to this county, that when it was thought proper and adviseable to subject it to taxes imposed by parliament, the privilege of sending Knights and Burgesses to parliament was the proper and constitutional remedy sought and obtained.

Copy

Copy of a Supplication, exhibited to King Henry VI. by the inhabitants of the County Palatine of Chester.

To the KING, our Sovereign Lord.
Anno D. 1450.

MOST Chriſtian Benigne, and Gracious King; We your humble ſubjects, and true obaiſant liege people, the Abbots, Priors, and all the clergy; your Barons, Knights, and Eſquires; and all the Commonalty of your County Palatine of Cheſter, meekly prayen and beſeechen your Highneſs: Where the ſaid county is, and hath been a county palatine, as well before the conqueſt of England, as continually ſince, diſtinct and ſeparate from the crown of England: within which county, you, and all

all your noble progenitors sithen it came into your hands, and all rulers of the same, before that time, have had your high courts of parliment to hold at your wills, your chancery, your exchequer, your justice to hold pleas, as well of the crown, as of common pleas. And by authority of which parliament, to make or to admit laws within the same, such as be thought expedient and behovefull for the weal of you, of the inheritors, and inheritance of the said county. And no inheritors or possessioners within the said county, be not chargeable, lyable, nor have not been bounden, charged nor hurt, of their bodies, liberties, franchises, land, goods, nor possessions, within the same county, [* *but by such laws as they*] have agreed unto. And for the more proof and plain evidence of the said franchises, immunities,

---

* The above is a literal transcript of the Record as published by Daniel King. I have not the means of consulting the original, there is certainly some omission or default in the copy. I have inserted the words, *but by such laws as they*, printed between hooks. I see no other way of making sense of it. I have also in the same manner between hooks inserted the words *be wrong*.

and freedoms; The moſt victorious King William the conqueror your moſt noble progenitor, gave the ſame county to Hugh Loup his nephew, to hold as freely to him and to his heirs *by the ſword*; as the ſame King ſhould hold all England *by the crown*. Experience of which grant, to be ſo in all appeals and records, out of the ſame; where, at your common-law it is written, contra coronam et dignitatem veſtram: It is written in your time, and your noble progenitors, ſinth the ſaid Earldome came into your hands, and in all Earls times afore. Contra dignitatem gladii ceſtriæ. And alſo they have no Knights, Citizens, ne Burgeſſes ne ever had, of the ſaid county, to any parliament holden *out of the ſaid* county; whereby they might, in any way of reaſon be bounden, And alſo ye and your noble progenitors, and all Earles, whoſe eſtate ye have in the ſaid Earledome; as Earles of Cheſter, ſith the conqueſt of England have had within the ſame; regalem, poteſtatum, jura regalia, præ-rogativa regia. Which franchiſes notwith-ſtanding, there be your commiſſions directed out to ſeveral commiſſioners of the ſame county, for the levy of ſubſidy, granted by

† the

the commons of your land, in your parliament, late begun at Westminster, and ended at Leicester, to make levy thereof within the said county, after the form of their grant thereof, contrary to the liberties, freedoms, and franchises, of the said county, and inheritance of the same, at all times, before this time used, that please your noble grace, of your blessed favour, the premises graciously to consider: and also, how that we your beseechers, have been as ready of our true hearts, with our goods, at times of need, as other parts of your lands; and also ready to obey your laws and ordinances, made, ordained, and admitted within the said county, and if any thing amongst us [*be wrong*,] ready to be reformed by your Highness, by the advice of your councel, within the said county; and hereupon to discharge all such commissioners of levy of the said subsidy within the said county, and of your special meer grace, ever, to see that there be never act in this parliment, nor in any parliment hereafter, holden out of the said county, made to the hurt of any of the inheritors, or inheritance of the said county, of their bodies, liberties, franchises, goods, lands, tenements, or possessions, being within the said county. For if any such act should be made, it were clean contrary to the liberties, freedoms, immunities, and franchises of the said county. And as to the resigning of such possessions, as it hath liked your Highness, to grant unto any of your subjects: all such as have ought of grant within the said county, will be ready to surrender their letters pattents, which they have of your grant, for the more honourable keeping of your estate; as any other person or persons within any other part of your land; or else they shall be avoided by us, under your authority committed unto us, within your said county. And furthermore, considering that your beseechers are, and ever have been true, dreading, obaisant, and loving unto you, and of you, as unto you; and of our most dowted Sovereign Lord, our Earle and natural Lord: We the said Barons, Knights, Esquires, and Commons, are ready to live and die with you, against all earthly creatures; and by your licence, to shew unto your Highness, for the gracious expedition of this our most behoveful

peti-

petition. And we the said Abbots, Priors, and clergy, continually to pray to God for your most hounerable estate, prosperity, and felicity, which we all beseek God to continue, with as long life to reign, as ever did prince upon people; with issue coming of your most gracious body, perpetually to raign upon us for all our most singular joy and comfort.

The Kings will is, to the subsidy in this bill contained: Forasmuch as he is learned, that the beseechers in the same, their predecessors, nor ancestors, have not been charged afore this time, by authority of any parliament holden out of the saide county, of any quindisme, or subsidy, granted unto him or any of his progenitors, in any such parliament; That the beseechers, and each of them be discharged of the paying and levy of the said subsidy. And furthermore, the King willeth, that the said beseechers, their successors and heirs, have and enjoy all their liberties, freedoms, and franchises, as freely and entirely as ever they, their predecessors or ancestors in his time, or in time of his progenitors, had and enjoyed it.—

Pro-

Profecuta fuit ifta Billa ad Dominum Regem per Johannem Manwaring Militem, Radulphum Egerton, Robertum Foulfhurſt, Robertum Leigh de Adlington, et Johannem Needham Anno. R. R. H. 6. poſt conqueſtum Anglie viceſſimo nono.

By the King.

TRUSTY and wellbeloved in God, and truſty and well beloved we greet you well. And foraſmuch as we have underſtanding, by a ſupplication preſented unto us, on the behalf of all our liege people within our county palatine of Cheſter: How

their

their predeceffors nor anceftors, have not been charged before this time, with any fifteenth or fubfidy granted unto us, or any of our progenitors, by authority of any parliament, holden out of our faid county, for which caufe, we have charged our chamberlain of our faid county, to make our writs, directed to all our commiffioners, ordained for the affeffing and levy of the fubfidy laft granted unto us: Charging them to furceafe of any execution of our letters of commiffion, made unto them, in that parties. Wherefore, according to our commandment late given by us, unto our faid Chamberlain: We will that ye in our behalf, open and declare unto all our faid liege-people: How it is our full will and intent, that they be not charged with any fuch grant, otherwife than they, their predeceffors and anceftors have been charged afore time. And that they have and hold, poffide, and enjoy, all their liberties, freedoms, and franchifes, in as ample and large form, as ever they had in our, or any of our faid progenitors days. And that ye

fail

fail not thereof, as we truſt you, and as you deem to pleaſe us.

Given under our ſignet of the Eagle, at our pallace of Weſtminſter the eighth day of March, Anno. R. R. H. 6. Viceſſimo Nono.

To our truſty and wellbeloved in God, the Abbot of our monaſtry of Cheſter; and to our truſty and wellbeloved Knights Sir Thomas Stanley, our Juſtices of Cheſter, Sir John Manwaring, and to every of them.

THE ADMINISTRATION OF THE COLONIES.

THE several changes of territories, which at the last Peace took place in the Colonies of the European world, have given rise to a new system of interests, have opened a new channel of business, and brought into operation a new concatenation of powers, both commercial and political.—This system of things ought, at this crisis, to be actuated by a system of politics, adequate and proportionate to its powers and operations: But while we find not any one comprehensive or precise idea of the crisis now arising; we see that all which is proposed as measures, is by parts, without connection to any whole, by temporary expedients,

pedients, and shiftings off of present dangers, without any reference to that eventual state of things, which must be the consequence of such measures, and such expedients; much less by reference to that eventual state of things, by which the true system ought to be framed, and actuated.

This state of the business has tempted me to hazard my sentiments on the subject. My particular situation in time past gave me early opportunity of seeing and observing the state of things, which have been long leading to this crisis. I have seen and mark'd, where it was my duty, this nascent crisis at the beginning of the late war, and may affirm, have foreseen and foretold the events that now form it. My present situation by which I stand unconnected with the politics of ministry, or of the colonies, opens the fairest occasion to me of giving to the public, whom it concerns, such an impartial uninfluenced opinion of what I think to be the right of things, as I am convinced the following sheets contain. I know what effect this conduct will have, what it has had, on this work and on myself. I may be thought neither by the ministry nor the Colonists to understand this subject, the one may call this work the vision of a theorist, the other will represent the doctrine which it contains, as

the

the prejudices of power and ambition. The one may think me an advocate for the politicks of the colonies, the other will imagine me to be an evil counsellor against the colonies to the ministry: But as I know that my aim is, without any prudential view of pleasing others, or of my own interest, to point out and to endeavour to establish an idea of the true interest of the colonies, and of the mother country as related to the colonies, I shall equally disregard what varies from this on the one hand, and equally reject what deviates from it on the other.

In the first uncultur'd ages of Europe, when men sought nothing but to possess, and to secure possession, the power of the *sword* was the predominant spirit of the world; it was that, which formed the Roman empire; and it was the same, which, in the declension of that empire, divided again the nations into the several governments formed upon the ruins of it.

When men afterward, from leisure, began to exercise the powers of their minds in (what is called) learning; religion, the only learning at that time, led them to a concern for their spiritual interests, and consequently led them under their spiritual guides. The power of *religion* would hence as naturally predominate and rule, and did actually become the ruling spirit of the policy of Europe. It was this spirit, which, for many ages formed, and gave away kingdoms; this which created the anointed Lords over them, or again excommunicated and execrated these sovereigns; this that united and allied the various nations, or plung'd them into war and bloodshed; this, that formed the ballance of the power of the whole, and actuated the second grand scene of Europe's history.

But since the people of Europe have formed their communication with the commerce of Asia; have been, for some ages past, settling on all sides of the Atlantic Ocean, and in America, have been possessing every seat and channel of commerce, and have planted and raised that to an interest which has taken root;---since they now feel the powers which derive from this, and are extending it to, and combining it with others; the spirit of *commerce* will become that predominant power, which will form the general policy, and rule the powers of Europe: and hence a grand commercial interest, the basis of a great commercial dominion, under the present scite and circumstances of the world, will be formed and arise. The rise and forming of this commercial interest is what precisely constitutes the present crisis.

The

The European poſſeſſions and intereſts in the Atlantic and in America lye under various forms, in plantations of ſugar, tobacco, rice, and indigo, in farms of tillage and paſture, in fiſheries, Indian hunts, foreſts, naval ſtores, and mines; each different ſcite produces ſome ſpecial matter of ſupply neceſſary to one part of that food and raiment become requiſite to the preſent ſtate of the world; but is, as to it's own local power of produce, totally deſtitute of ſome other equally neceſſary branch of ſupply. The various nature of the lands and ſeas lying in every degree and aſpect of climate, and the ſpecial produce and vegetation that is peculiar to each, forms this local limited capacity of produce. At the ſame time that nature has thus confined and limited the produce of each individual ſcite to one, or at moſt to few branches of ſupply, at the ſame time hath ſhe extended the neceſſities of each to many branches beyond what its own produce can ſupply. The Weſt India iſlands produce ſugar, meloſſes, cotton, &c. they want the materials for building and mechanics, and many the neceſſaries of food and raiment: The lumber, hides, the fiſh, flour, proviſions, live-ſtock, and horſes, produced in the northern colonies on the continent, muſt ſupply the iſlands with theſe requiſites. On the other hand, the ſugar and meloſſes of the sugar islands is become a necessary intermediate branch of the North American trade and fisheries. The produce of the British sugar islands cannot supply both Great Britain and North America with the necessary quantity; this makes the mellosses of the foreign sugar islands also necessary to the present state of the North American trade. Without Spanish silver, become necessary to the circulation of the British American trade, and even to their internal course of sale and purchase, not only great part of that circulation must cease to flow, but the means of purchasing the manufactures of Great Britain would be equally circumscribed: Without the British supplies, the Spanish settlements would be scarce able to carry on their culture, and would be in great distress. The ordinary course of the labour and generation of the negroes in the West India islands makes a constant external supply of these subjects necessary, and this connects the trade of Africa with the West Indies; the furr and Indian trade, and the European goods necessary to the Indian, are what form the Indian connection.----I do not enter into a particular detail of all the reciprocations of those wants and supplies, nor into a proof of the necessary interconnections arising from thence; I only mark out the general *traites* of these, in order to explain what I mean when I say, that by the limitation

of

of the capacities and extent of the necessities of each, all are interwoven into a necessary intercourse of supplies, and all indissolubly bound in an union and communion of *one general composite interest* of the whole of the Spanish, French, Dutch, Danish, and British settlements. This is the *natural state* of the European possessions in the Atlantic and in America; this general communion is that natural interest under which, and by which, they must subsist. On the contrary, the spirit of policy, by which the mother countries send out and on which they establish colonies, being to confine the trade of their respective colonies solely to their own special intercourse, and to hold them incommunicable of all other intercourse or commerce, the *artificial or political state* of these colonies becomes distinct from that which is above described as their natural state.---The political state is that which policy labours to establish by a principle of repulsion; the natural one is that state under which they actually exist and move by a general, common, and mutual principle of attraction. This one general interest thus distinct must have some one general tendency or direction distinct also, and peculiar to its own system. There must be some center of these composite movements, some lead that will predominate and govern in this general interest---

That particular branch of busineſs and its connections in this general commercial intereſt, which is moſt extenſive, neceſſary, and permanent, ſettles and commands the market; and thoſe merchants who actuate this branch muſt acquire an aſcendency, and will take the lead of this intereſt. This lead will predominate throughout the general intercourſe, will diſſolve the effect of all artificial connections which government would create, and form the natural connections under which theſe intereſts actually exiſt,—will ſuperſede all particular laws and cuſtoms, and operate by thoſe which the nature and actual circumſtances of the ſeveral intereſts require. This lead is the foundation of a commercial dominion, which, whether we attend to it or not, will be formed: whether this idea may be thought real or viſionary is of no conſequence as to the exiſtence and proceſſion of this power, for the intereſt, which is the baſis of it, is already formed;—yet it would become the wiſdom, and is the duty of thoſe who govern us, to profit of, to poſſeſs, and to take the lead of it already formed and ariſing faſt into dominion; it is our duty ſo to interweave thoſe naſcent powers into, and to combine their influence with, the ſame intereſts which actuate our own government; ſo to connect and combine the operations of our trade with this intereſt, as to partake of

its

its influence and to build on its power. Although this interest may be, as above described, different and even distinct from the peculiar interests of the mother countries, yet it cannot become independent, it must, and will fall under the dominion of *some* of the potentates of Europe. The great question at this crisis is, and the great struggle will be, which of the states of Europe shall be in those circumstances, and will have the vigour and wisdom so to profit of those circumstances, as to take this interest under its dominion, and to unite it to its government. This lead seemed at the beginning of the late war to oscillate between the English and French, and it was in this war that the dominion also hath been disputed. The lead is now in our hands, we have such connection in its influence, that, whenever it becomes the foundation of a dominion, that dominion must be ours.

It is therefore the duty of those who govern us, to carry forward this state of things to the weaving of this lead into our system, that Great Britain may be no more considered *as the kingdom of this Isle only, with many appendages of provinces, colonies, settlements, and other extraneous parts*, but as A GRAND MARINE DOMINION CONSISTING OF OUR POSSESSIONS IN THE ATLANTIC AND

IN

in America united into a one empire, in a one center, where the seat of government is.

As the rising of this crisis above described, forms precisely the *object* on which government should be employed; so the taking leading measures towards the forming all those Atlantic and American possessions into one Empire of which Great Britain should be the commercial and political center, is the *precise duty* of government at this crisis.

The great minister, whose good fortune shall have placed him at this crisis, in the administration of these great and important interests—will certainly adopt the system which thus lies in nature, and which by natural means alone, if not perverted, must lead to a general dominion, founded in the general interest and prosperity of the commercial world, must build up this country to an extent of power, to a degree of glory and prosperity, beyond the example of any age that has yet passed;—* *id est viri et ducis non deesse fortunæ præbenti se, et oblata casu flectere ad concilium.*

The forming some general system of administration, some plan which should be

* Liv. l. 28. § 44.

(whatever

(whatever may be the changes of the ministry at home, or in the governors and officers employed abroad) uniformly and permanently purfued by meafures founded on the actual ftate of things as they arife, leading to this great end, *is, at this crifis, the precife duty of government.* This is an object which ought not to be overlooked or miftaken. It ought not to be a ftate myftery, nor can be a fecret. If the Spanifh, French, and Dutch governments can oppofe it, they will; but if it be founded in nature, fuch oppofition will only haften its completion, becaufe any meafures of policy which they can take to obftruct it, muft either deftroy the trade of their own colonies, or break off their connection. If they attempt to do this by force, they muft firft form an alliance, and fettle the union of their mutual interefts, and the eventual partition of the effect of it; but this will prove a matter of more difficulty, than can eafily be compaffed, and under the difadvantages created thereby, there will be much hazard of the utmoft effort of their united forces.

To enable the Britifh nation to profit of thefe prefent circumftances, or of the future events, as they fhall fucceffively arife in the natural proceffion of effects, it is neceffary, that the adminiftration form itfelf into fuch eftablifhments establishments for the direction of these interests and powers, as may keep them in their natural channel, as may maintain their due connections with the government, and lead them to the utmost effect they are capable of producing towards this grand point.

The first spring of this direction, the basis of this government, is the administration at home. If that department of administration, which should have the direction of these matters, be not wisely and firmly bottomed, be not so built, as to be a *practical*— be not so really supported by the powers of government, as to be an *efficient administration*, all measures for the administration of these interests, all plans for the government of these powers are vain and self-delusive; even those measures that would regulate the movements and unite the interests under a practical and efficient administration, become mischievous meddling impertinencies where that is not, and must either ruin the interests of these powers, or render a breach of duty necessary to the colonies that they may avoid that ruin.

That part of government, which should administer this great and important branch of business, ought, in the first place, to be the center of all information and application from

from all the interests and powers which form it; and ought from this center, to be able, fully, uniformly, and efficiently, to distribute its directions and orders. Wherever the wisdom of state shall determine that this center of information shall be fixed; from whatever department all appointments, orders, and executive administration shall issue, it ought somewhere to be fixed, known, of record, and undivided; that it may not be partial, it ought to extend to all times, and all cases. All application, all communication, all information should center immediately and solely in this department: this should be the spring of all nominations, instructions, and orders.———It is of little consequence where this power of administration is placed, so that the department be such, as hath the means of the knowledge of its business—is specially appropriated to the attention necessary to it—and officially so formed as to be in a capacity of executing it. Whether this be a Secretary of State, or the Board of Trade and Plantations, is of no consequence; but it ought to be entirely in either the one or the other. Where the power for the direction is lodged, there ought all the knowledge of the department to center; therefore all officers, civil or military, all servants of the government, and all other bodies or private persons ought to correspond immediately ly with this department, whether it be the Secretary of State or the Board of Trade. While the military correspond with the Secretary of State, the civil in one part of their office with the Secretary of State, in another with the Board of Trade; while the navy correspond in matters not merely naval with the Admiralty, while the engineers correspond with the Board of Ordnance, officers of the revenue with the several boards of that branch, and have no communication with the department which has, or ought to have, the general direction and administration of this great Atlantic and American, this great commercial interest, who is to collect? who does, or ever did collect, into a one view, all these matters of information and knowledge? What department ever had, or could have, such general direction of it, as to discuss, compare, rectify and regulate it to an official real use? In the first place, there never was yet any one department form'd for this purpose; and in the next, if there was, let any one acquainted with business dare to say, how any attempt of such department would operate on the jealousies of the others. Whenever, therefore, it is thought proper (as most certainly it will, some time or other, tho' perhaps too late) to form such department, it must (if I may so express myself)

be

be sovereign and supreme, as to every thing relating to it; or to speak plainly out, *must be a secretary of state's office in itself.* When such is form'd, although the military, naval, ordnance, and revenue officers, should correspond, in the matters of their respective duties, with the departments of government to which they are more immediately subordinate and responsible, yet, in general matters of information, or points which are matters of government, and the department of this state office, they should be instructed to correspond and communicate with this minister. Suppose that some such minister or office now existed, is it not of consequence that he should be acquainted with the Geography of our new acquisitions? If, therefore, there have been any actual surveys made of them, should not such, or copies of such, be sent to this minister or office? If a due and official information of any particular conduct in our colonies, as to their trade, might lead to proper regulations therein, or might point out the necessity of a revision of the old laws, or the making further provision by new ones, would it not be proper that the custom-house officers settled there should be directed to correspond and communicate with this minister, or office, on these points? Would it interfere with their due subordination, as officers of

the

the revenue, to the commissioners of the customs?—If there were any events arising, or any circumstances existing, that might affect the state of war or peace, wherein the immediate application of military operations were not necessary or proper, should not the military and naval officers be directed to communicate on these matters with this minister, or office? Should not, I say, all these matters of information come officially before this minister, if any such state minister, or office, was established?

As of information and knowledge centering in a one office, so also of power of executing, it should spring from one undivided department. Where the power of nominating and dismissing, together with other powers, is separated from the power of directing, the first must be a mere privilege or perquisite of office, useless as to the king's business or the interest of his colonies, and the latter must be inefficient. That office, which neither has the means of information, nor can have leisure to attend to the official knowledge produced thereby, nor will be at the trouble to give any official directions, as to the ordinary course of the administration of the American matters, must certainly be always, as it is, embarrassed with the power of nomination, and fetter'd with the

chain

chain of applications, which that power drags after it. On the other hand, what effect will any instructions, orders or directions, have from that board, which has not interest to make or dismiss one of the meanest of its own officers: this, which is at present the only official channel, will be despised; the governors, nay, every the meanest of the officers in the plantations, looking up solely to the *giving power*, will scarce correspond with the *directing*—nay, may perhaps contrive to make their court to the one, by passing by the other. And in any case of improper conduct of these officers, of any neglect of duty, or even of misdemeanour; what can this directing power do, but complain to the minister who nominates, against the officers appointed by him? If there be no jealousies, no interfering of interests, no competitions of interfering friends, to divide and oppose these two offices to each other: if the minister is not influenced to continue, upon the same motives upon which he first appointed; if he does not see these complaints in a light of opposition to his nomination and interest; some redress may, after a due hearing between the party and the office, be had;—the authority of the board may be supported, and a sort of remedy applied to the special business, but a remedy worse than the disease—a remedy that

C dishonours

dishonours that board, and holds it forth to the contempt of those whom it ought to govern.

It is not only from the natural impracticability of conducting this administration under a divided State of power and direction, that the necessity of forming a some one state office, or minister of state, for the executing it arises: but the very nature of the business of this department, makes the officer who is to administer it a state officer, a minister for that department, and who ought to have immediate access to the closet. I must here repeat, that I am no partizan of the Secretary of State's office, or for the Board of Trade: I have ceased to have any connection of business with either, and have not the least degree of communication with the one or the other. Without reference, therefore, to either, but with all deference to both, I aim to point out, that the department of the administration of Trade and plantations, be it lodged where it may, should be a State office, and have a minister of state. That office, or officer, in a commercial nation like this, who has the cognizance and direction (so far as government can interfere) of the general trade of the kingdom—whose duty it is to be the depository and reporter of the state and condition of it; of every thing which

which may advance or obstruct it, of the state of manufactures, of the fisheries, of the employment of the poor, of the promoting the labour and riches of the country, by studying and advising every advantage, that can be made of every event which arises in commercial politics, every remedy, which can remove any defect or obstruction;—who is officially to prepare every provision or revision necessary in the laws of trade, for the consideration of parliament; and to be the conductor of such thro' the necessary measures—is certainly an officer of state, if the Secretary of State, so call'd, is. That office, or officer, who has cognizance and direction of the plantations in every point of government, in every matter judicial or commercial; who is to direct the settlements of colonies, and to superintend those already settled; who is to watch the plantations in all these points, so far as they stand related to the government, laws, courts and trade of the mother country———is certainly an officer of state, if the Secretary of State, so called, is. That office or officer, who is to report to his Majesty in council on all these points; whose official *fiat*, or negative, will be his Majesty's information in council, as to the legislature in the colonies—is certainly an officer of state. That office, or officer, who is to hear and determine on all matters of complaint, and mal-administration, of the crown officers and others, in the plantations; and can examine witnesses on oath ---is surely an officer of state. That office, or officer, who is to correspond with all the servants of the crown on these points, and to be the issuer of his Majesty's orders and instructions to his servants, on these many, great, and important points of state—is certainly his Majesty's secretary, and certainly a secretary of state.

But if it be considered further, who the persons are, that are of this very great and extensive commission of the Board of Trade and Plantations; namely, all the great officers of state for the time being, with the bishop of London, the secretaries of state for the time being, and those more especially called the commissioners of trade, it will be seen, that it is no longer a doubt or a question, as to its being an office of state: it is actually so; and has, as an office, as a board, immediate access to his Majesty in council, even to the reporting and recommending of officers. This was the plan whereon it was originally founded, at its first institution, by Lord Sommers.

That great statesman and patriot saw that all the powers of government, and several departments

departments of administration *disunited*, were interfering with, and obstructing each other on this subject, and not they only here in England, but that the respective officers of these several departments carried all this distraction into the detail of their business in the colonies, which I am afraid is too much the case even at this day: he saw that this administration could not be conducted but by an intire union of all the powers of government, and on that idea formed the board of trade and plantations, where, and where alone, these powers were *united in a one office*. In which office, and in which alone, all the business of the colonies ought therefore to be administred; for if such union be necessary, here alone is that *official union*. Unhappily for the true interest of government, partly from an intire neglect of this administration in time past, and partly from the defective partial exercise of it, since some idea of these matters began again to revive, this great and wise plan hath been long disused; but it is fortunate for the public in this important crisis, that such is the temper of particulars, such the zeal of all for his Majesty's service, such the union of his servants, that the spirit of service predominates over these natural defects: so that all who wish well to the interest of this country, in its trade and colonies, may hope to see that

that union, at prefent only minifterial, become *official* in this bufinefs, and revive again that great, wife and conftitutional plan of office, actuated under the real fpirit of it.

The only queftion at prefent is, who fhall be the executive officer of this department of ftate; whether the fecretary of ftate, properly fo called; or the firft lord, and other commiffioners, properly called *the board of trade*; or whether it fhall remain divided, as it is, between the feveral great departments of adminiftration; *or whether fome more official and practical divifion of this adminiftration may not be made.*

Suppofe now, it fhould be thought proper, that this adminiftration be placed in the fecretary of ftate's office, all the adminiftration of the plantations may be given to the fouthern department: yet the great object of the general trade of Great Britain muft be divided between the fouthern and the northern, as the matters of confideration happen to lie in the one or in the other department; and how will the fouthern department act, when any matter of commerce arifes in the plantations, that has fpecial connections or interferings with the Dutch, Hamborough, Danifh or Ruffian trade?

It

It cannot lie in the board of trade, properly so called, until it be found proper, and becomes a measure of government to erect that board into a secretary of state's office for this department, which, first or last, it most certainly will do. That, therefore, the great business of trade and plantations may not run into confusion, or be at a stand;—that it may be carried to the effect proposed, held forth, and desired by government, and necessary to it; all that can be done at present is, to put the whole executive administration, the nomination, correspondence, issuing of instructions, orders, &c. under the secretary of state, if he has leisure to attend to it, and can undertake it; and to make the board of trade a mere committee of reference and report; instead of reporting to the king in council, to report to the secretary of state, who shall lay the matters before his Majesty, and receive and issue his orders;—who shall refer all matters to this committee, for their consideration, and shall conduct through the legislature all measures necessary to be determined thereby. If this be not practicable, there is no other alternative, than to do directly what ought to be done, and what, some time or other, must be done; the making the officer who conducts this department a minister for that department, with all the powers necessary thereto. For until

until a practical and efficient administration be formed, whatever the people of this country may think, the people of the colonies, who know their business much better than we do, will never believe government is in earnest about them, or their interest, or even about governing them; and will, not merely from that reasoning, but from necessity of their circumstances, act accordingly.

Until an effective administration for Colony affairs be established by government, all plans for the governing of those countries under any regular system of policy, will be only matter of speculation, and become mere useless opprobrious theory. All official information given and transmitted by those whose duty it is to give it, will, as accident shall decide, or as the connexions of parties shall run, be received or not; nay, it may so happen, that those officers who should duly report to government the state of these matters, will, as they find themselves conscientiously or politically disposed, direct that information to those who are in, or to those who are out of administration. Every leader of every little flying squadron will have his runner, his own proper channel of information; and will hold forth his own importance in public, by bringing *his plan*

plan for American affairs before it. All true and regular knowledge of these affairs being dispersed, will be evaporated; every administration, even Parliament itself, will be distracted in its councils by a thousand odds and ends of proposals, by a thousand pieces and parcels of plans, while those surely, who are so deeply concerned as the Americans themselves are, will not be excluded from having their plan also; they will have their plan also, for however peaceably they may submit to the direction of the powers of government, derived through a regular established permanent mode of administration, they will by any means that they can justify, refuse to have their interests directed and disposed of by every whim that every temporary empiric can force into execution. If therefore we mean to govern the Colonies, we must previously form at home some practical and efficient administration for Colony affairs.

Before the erection of the Board of Trade as a particular office, the business of the Colonies was administered with efficiency; the king himself in council administered the government of his Colonies; the state officer, each in his proper department was no otherwise Minister than as ministerially executing the orders which he received, or officially

officially reporting from his refpective department, the information which he had to lay before the king in council. Since the eftablifhment of that office called the Board of Trade, the adminiftration of the Colonies has either laid dormant, or been overlaid; or, if taken up, become an occafion of jealoufy and ftruggle for power between that Board and every ftate officer who hath been deemed the Minifter for the time being. From this jealoufy and this ftruggle, this Board hath been fuppofed to interfere at different times with every other office, while at one time it hath had the powers and held the port of a minifter's office, and at another hath become a mere committee, inefficient as to execution, unattended to as reporting. The Colonies, and the officers of the Colonies, have one while been taught to look up to this Board as the Minifter for their affairs, and at another, have learned to hold it in that contempt which inefficiency gives; which contempt, however, hath not always ftopped there.

To prevent, on this critical occafion, all fuch appearances on one hand, from mifleading thofe who are to be governed, and to put an end on the other, to all interfering amongft thofe who are to govern in this line of bufinefs---The Board of Trade fhould either

either be made what it never was intended to be, a Secretary of State's office for the Plantations, or be confined to what it really is, a committee of reference for examination and report, for stating and preparing business, while the affairs of the Colonies are administred solely by the King in council, really acting as an efficient board for that purpose. Somewhere there ought to be an efficiency, and in this supreme board is the proper residence of it. To place it here would be really and in fact the establishing of an administration for colony affairs.

The first step that such administration would take to fix the basis of an established, permanent and effective system of government for the mother country and the Colonies, must be made by some *leading measure*, which shall, on real fact, and by actual representation of the parties concerned, examine into the various interests which have arisen, the various claims which are derived from those interests, and the various rights that may, or may not, be admitted, as founded on these, and as consistent with the general government and interest of the whole.

To obtain this with truth and certainty, and to engage the colonists to co-operate in this view with that confidence which a free
people

people muſt have, if they co-operate at all---. government would ſend out to America, *ſome very conſiderable perſon*, under commiſſion and inſtructions, to hear and examine on the ſpot, the ſtate of things there, and by ſuch proper repreſentations and aſſiſtance as can no where be had but upon the ſpot, and from the people themſelves, to form ſuch authentic matter of information for the king in council, as may become the ſolid baſis of real government, eſtabliſhed by the principles of real liberty.

To ſuch conſiderable perſon, and to ſuch commiſſion, only, would the coloniſts give their confidence; they would know that *there* there was no ſpirit of party or faction, that there could be no jobb---They would be convinced that government was in earneſt, and meant to act fairly and honourably with them. They would meet ſuch perſon in the abundance of their loyalty, with diſpoſitions of real buſineſs in their temper, and with the ſpirit of real union in their hearts.

What commiſſion could be more honourable and glorious, even to the higheſt character, than that of acting for the rights and liberties of a whole people, ſo as to be the means of eſtabliſhing thoſe rights and liberties

liberties, by an adequate system of freedom and government, extended to the whole? What can be more suited to the most elevated character, than to be the *great reconciler* between the mother country and her colonies, mis-represented to, and mis-informed of each other?

I am almost certain that this measure will not be adopted, that it will be, as it has been already, rejected---that there never will be any systematical union of government between the mother country and the colonies---that the opportunity when such might be established on true principles will be neglected---and that the course of business will, on this occasion, be, as the history of mankind informs us it always has been, that those errors which might be rectified by the spirit of policy, will be permitted to go on piling up one mischief over another, until nothing but power can interpose, which will then interpose when the spirit of policy is no more.

The mother country and her colonies will continue to live on in perpetual jealousies, jarrings and disputes. The colonies will for some time *belong to some faction here,* and be the tool of it, until they become powerful enough to hold a party for themselves, and
make

make *some faction their tool.* The latter stage of this miserable connection will be one continued struggle, whether Great Britain shall administer the rights and interests of the colonies, or whether the interest and power of the colonies shall take a lead in that administration which shall govern Great Britain. This convulsion may agitate for a while, until some event shall happen that will totally break all union between us, and will end in the ruin of the one or the other, just as the accident of the die shall turn.

Although I am convinced that this will be the state of things, yet, as I know that what I have here recommended, is founded on precedents of better and wiser times than the present, is not founded barely on my own experience, but in that of men who have long had the lead of business in those countries, is what every true friend of the colonies, who lives and has his property there, would recommend---what every man of business here, who wishes well to the government of Great Britain, must approve. I now propose it to the public as a measure, of which if administration should neglect or refuse to take the lead, the colonies may profit by those means of communication with one another, and by those powers which their constitutions and establishments give them

them for the preservation of their civil and commercial interests; yet, taking it up, as a measure, which, for the sake of Great Britain, I wish administration to adopt, I say, government should send out some considerable person, with a council to assist him, under a commission and instructions, to call a congress of commissioners from the several colonies.---He should have power and be instructed to call to his aid and assistance, the governors, or any other his Majesty's servants, as occasion should require.

By the representations and assistance of this congress and these persons, he should inquire into the *actual* state of the crown's authority, as capable of being executed by the King, and by his governor, and other the immediate executors of the power of the crown.

He should inquire into the extent of the exercise and claim of the legislative powers, and examine dispassionately and without prejudice, on what grounds of necessity or expediency any precedents which stretch beyond perhaps the strict line of the commissions or charters, are founded.

He should inquire into the state of their laws, as to their conformity to the laws of Great Britain, and examine the real state of the

the facts or business which may have made any deviation necessary or not.

He should examine into the powers and practice of their courts of judicature, whether, on one hand, they have not extended their authority beyond their due powers; or whether, on the other hand, they have not been restrained by instructions, or by the acts of the colony legislatures, within bounds too narrowly circumscribed to answer the ends for which such courts are erected.

He should, which can only be known upon the spot, inquire into and examine the actual state of their commerce, that where it deviates unnecessarily from the laws of trade, it may be restrained by proper regulations---or where the laws of trade are found to be inconsistent with the interest of a commercial country having colonies which have arisen from, and depend upon trade, a revision may be made of those laws, so as that the system of our laws may be made conform to the system of our commerce, and not destructive of it.

Under all these various heads, he may hear all the grievances which the officers of the crown, or the people, complain of, in order

order to form a just and actual representation for the King in council.

He should inquire into the state of the King's revenues, his lands, his naval stores; and he should review the state of the military service, the forts, garrisons and forces.--- With the assistance of proper commissioners from the provinces and colonies concerned, he should settle the several disputes of the colonies amongst themselves, particularly as to their boundary lines. He should also inquire into all fraudulent grants.

All these matters duly examined and inquired into, a report of the whole business, should be drawn up, and being authenticated by the original documents, should be laid before the King in council: Those points which were of the special department of any of the boards or offices under government, would be refered from thence to those respective offices, for them to report their opinion upon the matter. ---And when the whole, both of matter and of opinion, was by the most authentic representations, and by the best advice, thus drawn together, the King in council would be enabled to form, and by and with the advice and authority of Parliament to establish, the only system of government and
commercial

commercial laws, which would form Great Britain and her colonies into a one united commercial dominion.

If this measure be adopted, a general bill of rights, and an act for the establishment of government and commerce on a great plan of union, will be brought forward; the colonies will be considered as so many corporations, not without, but united to, the realm; they will be left in all the free and full possession of their several rights and liberties, as by grant, charter, or commissions given; yet, for every power which they exercise or possess, they will depend upon the government of the whole, and upon Great Britain as the center. Great Britain, as the center of this system, of which the colonies by actual union shall become organized, not annexed parts, must be the center of attraction to which these colonies, in the administration of every power of their government, in the exercise of their judicial powers, in the execution of their laws, and in every operation of their trade, must tend. They will remain under the constant influence of the attraction of this center; and cannot move, but that every direction of such movement will converge to the same. And as it is not more necessary to preserve the several governments subordinate

subordinate in their respective orbs, than it is essential to the preservation of the whole empire to keep them disconnected and independent of each other, *they must be guarded by this union against having or forming any principle of coherence with each other, above that whereby they cohere to this center, this first mover.* They should alway remain incapable of any coherence, or of so conspiring amongst themselves, as to create any other equal force which might recoil back on this first mover. Policy acting upon a system of civil union, may easily and constitutionally provide against all this. The colonies and provinces, as they stand at present, are under the best form as to this point, which they can be under. They are under the best frame and disposition for the government of the general and supreme power (duly applied) to take place, having at present no other principle of civil union between each other, than that by which they naturally are, and in policy should be, in communion with Great Britain, as the common center of all. The different manner in which they are settled; the different modes under which they live; the different forms of charters, grants, and frames of government they possess; the various principles of repulsion that these create; the different interests which they actuate; the different religious interests by which they are actuated; the rivalship and jealousies which arise from hence; and the impracticability of reconciling and accommodating these incompatable ideas and claims, will keep them for ever so, so long as the spirit of civil policy remains, and is exerted to the forming and maintaining of this system of union.

However visionary this may seem to those who judge by parts, and act by temporary expedients, those truly great ministers who shall ever take up the administration of the colonies as a system, and shall have a general practical and adequate knowledge of that system, as interwoven in that of the mother country, will, on the contrary, find this measure prudential if not a necessary one, as leading to that great and absolutely necessary measure of uniting the Colonies to Great Britain as parts of the realm, in every degree and mode of communication of its rights and powers. And until some steps are taken which may lead and approach to this system of union, as the interest and power of the Colonies approach to the bearing of a proportion with that of Great Britain, the real interest of Great Britain and her Colonies will continue to be very inadequately and very unhappily administred, while the business of the Colonies shall
in

in the mean time become a faction instead of a constitutional part of the administration.

The center of power, instead of remaining fixed as it now is in Great Britain, will, as the magnitude of the power and interest of the Colonies increases, be drawn out from the island, by the same laws of nature analogous in all cases, by which the center of gravity in the solar system, now near the surface of the sun, would, by an encrease of the quantity of matter in the planets, be drawn out beyond that surface. Knowing therefore the laws of nature, shall we like true philosophers follow, where that system leads, to form one general system of dominion by an union of Great Britain and her Colonies, fixing, while it may be so fixed, the common center in Great Britain, or shall we without ever seeing that such center must be formed by an inter-communion of the powers of all the territories as parts of the dominions of Great Britain, like true modern politicians, and from our own narrow temporary ideas of a local center, labour to keep that center in Great Britain by force against encreasing powers, which will, finally, by an overbalance heave that center itself out of its place? Such measures would be almost as wise as his who standing in a scale should thrust his stick up against the beam to prevent it from descending, while his own weight brought it the faster down. That policy which shall ever attempt to connect the Colonies to Great Britain *by power*, will in that very instant connect them *to one another in policy.*

Before we enter into these matters, I do not think it would be impertinent just to mark the idea of colonies, and their special circumstances, which makes it a measure in commercial governments, to establish, cultivate, and maintain them.

The view of trade in general, as well as of manufactures in particular, terminates in securing an extensive and permanent vent; or to speak more precisely, (in the same manner as shop-keeping does) in having many and good customers: the wisdom, therefore, of a trading nation, is to gain, and to create, as many as possible. Those whom we gain in foreign trade, we possess under restrictions and difficulties, and may lose in the rivalship of commerce: those that a trading nation can create within itself, it deals with under its own regulations, and makes its own, and cannot lose. In the establishing colonies, a nation creates people whose labour, being applied to new objects of produce and manufacture, opens new

new channels of commerce, by which they not only live in ease and affluence within themselves, but, while they are labouring under and for the mother country, (for there all their external profits center) become an increasing nation, of appropriated and good customers to the mother country. These not only increase our manufactures, increase our exports, but extend our commerce; and if duly administered, extend the nation, its powers, and its dominions, to wherever these people extend their settlements. This is, therefore, an interest which is, and ought to be dear to the mother country: this is an object that deserves the best care and attention of government: and the people, who through various hardships, disasters and disappointments; through various difficulties and almost ruinous expences, have wrought up this interest to such an important object, merit every protection, grace, encouragement, and privilege, that are in the power of the mother country to grant.---It is on this *valuable consideration*, (as Mr. Dummer, in his spirited defence of the colonies, says) that they have a right to the grants, charters, privileges and protection which they receive; and also on the other hand, it is from these grants, charters, privileges and protection given to them, that the mother country has an exclusive right

right to the external profits of their labour, and to their custom. As it is the right, so it becomes the duty of the mother country to cultivate, to protect and govern the colonies: which nurture and government should precisely direct its care to two essential points. 1st, That all the profits of the produce and manufactures of these colonies center finally in the mother country: and 2dly, That the colonies continue to be the sole and proper customers of the mother country.---To these two points, collateral with the interests, rights and welfare of the colonies, every measure of administration, every law of trade should tend: I say collateral, because, rightly understood, these two points are mutually coincident with the interests, rights and welfare of the colonies.

It has been often suggested, that care should be taken in the administration of the plantations; lest, in some future time, these colonies should become independent of the mother country. But perhaps it may be proper on this occasion, nay, it is justice to say it, that if, by becoming independent, is meant a revolt, nothing is further from their nature, their interest, their thoughts. If a defection from the alliance of the mother country be suggested, it ought to be, and can be truly said, that their spirit

rit abhors the sense of such; their attachment to the protestant succession in the house of Hanover will ever stand unshaken; and nothing can eradicate from their hearts their natural, almost mechanical, affection to Great Britain, which they conceive under no other sense, nor call by any other name, than that of *home*. Besides, the merchants are, and must ever be, in great measure allied with those of Great Britain; their very support consists in this alliance, and nothing but false policy *here* can break it. If the trade of the colonies be protected and directed from hence, with the true spirit of the act of navigation, that spirit under which it has risen, no circumstances of trade could tempt the Colonists to certain ruin under any other connections. The liberty and religion of the British colonies are incompatible with either French or Spanish government; and they know full well, that they could hope for neither liberty nor protection under a Dutch one. Any such suggestion, therefore, is a false and unjust aspersion on their principles and affections, and can arise from nothing but an intire ignorance of their circumstances. Yet again, on the other hand, while they remain under the support and protection of the government of the mother country; while they profit of the beneficial part of its trade; while their attachment to the

the prefent royal family ftands firm, and their alliance with the mother country is inviolate, it may be worth while to inquire, whether they may not become and act in fome cafes independent of the *government and laws* of the mother country:—and if any fuch fymptoms fhould be found, either in their government, courts, or trade, perhaps it may be thought high time, even now, to inquire how far thefe colonies are or are not arrived, at this time, in thefe cafes, at an independency of the government of the mother country:—and if any meafure of fuch independency, formed upon precedents unknown to the government of the mother country at the time they were formed, fhould be infifted on, when the government of the mother country was found to be fo weak or diftracted at home, or fo deeply engaged abroad in Europe, as not to be able to attend to, and affert its right in America, with its own people,—perhaps it may be thought, that no time fhould be loft to remedy or redrefs thefe deviations—if any fuch be found; or to remove all jealoufies arifing from the idea of them, if none fuch really exift.

But the true and effectual way to remove all jealoufies and interfering between the feveral powers of the government of the mother

ther country, and the several powers of the governments of the colonies, in the due and constitutional order of their subordination, is to inquire and examine what the colonies and provinces really are; what their constitution of government is; what the relation between them and the mother country; and in consequence of the truth and principles established on such examination—to maintain firmly, both in claim and exercise, the rights and power of the supreme government of the mother country, with all acknowledgement of the rights, liberties, privileges, immunities and franchises of the Colonists, both personal and political, treating them really as what they are.—Until this be done, there can be no government properly so called; the various opinions, connections and interests of Britains, both in this island, and in America, will divide them into parties—the spirit of mutual animosity and opposition, will take advantage of the total want of established and fixed principles on this subject, to work these parties into faction; and then the predominancy of the one faction, or the other, acting under the mask of the forms of government, will alternately be called government.

In the former editions of this book, I had marked out what points of colony government

ment had fallen, in the courſe of adminiſtration, into diſpute; what the different apprehenſions were, which had given riſe to the different meaſures purſued on thoſe points—I had ſtated the nature of each queſtion—what was the true iſſue to which the diſpute ought to be brought; and at the ſame time that I ſtated the effect of theſe diſputes in matters of adminiſtration, I ſhewed how neceſſary it was that they ſhould be ſome way or other decided. I did not proceed to give any opinion or deciſion—I thought the firſt ſufficient, and thought it was all that was neceſſary. But yet as that was neceſſary, and as I ſaw an attention to American affairs ariſing in the minds of moſt men of buſineſs, I was in hopes that theſe points might have been diſpaſſionately conſidered, and prudently ſettled; that they might be fixed on ſuch legal and conſtitutional grounds: that that true ſyſtem of efficient government founded in political liberty (which all ſeemed to profeſs here) might be eſtabliſhed in the colonies: I was ſure, from the ſpirit and genius of the people, it would be nouriſhed and maintained there, ſo as to become in ſome future, and perhaps not very diſtant age, an aſylum to that liberty of mankind, which, as it hath been driven by the corruption and the conſequent tyranny of government, *hath been conſtantly retiring*

retiring westward—but from the moment that American affairs became an object of politics, they became the tools and instruments of faction. Such hath been their fate, that as on one hand they have given real occasion to those who mean well to the peace and liberty of mankind; so on the other have they supplied specious pretences to those who mean only to profit of the force of parties—to dispute the state and application of every case in politics relative to the colonies, by recurring back to the principles on which they appear to have been settled, established, and afterwards governed; and these principles, from the variableness and fluctuation of the opinion and spirit of government, have been so often changed, that propositions the very reverse of each other, may strictly be deduced from the conduct of the crown and state towards the colonies. Hence it is, that at this day the constitution and rights of the colonies, in the actual exercise of them, are unsettled; the relation in which they stand connected with the realm and with the King, are disputed; and Parliament, as well as ministers, are balancing in opinion what is the true, legal, and constitutional mode of administration by which those colonies are to be governed. Whether the colonies be demesnes of the crown, without the realm, or parts and parcels of the realm;

realm; whether these foreign dominions of the King be as yet annexed to the realm of England; whether the colonists be subjects of the King in his foreign dominions, or whether they be subjects of, and owe allegiance to the realm; has been at various times, and is at this day called into dispute. This question is now no longer of curiosity and theory; it is brought actually into issue. It is now by deeds and overt acts discussed, and must be decided. To do this truly and justly, it must be thoroughly considered, what were the circumstances of their migration; under what political constitutions they were established and chartered; and by what mode of administration their affairs have been conducted and governed by the King, and by the government of England.

When the lands of America were first discovered, the sovereign of that subject, in each particular case, who discovered them, either from a power given by the Pope, or from some self-derived claim, assumed the right of possession in them. If these lands were really derelict, preoccupancy might have created a right of possession: yet even in this case, some further circumstances of interconnection with that land, such as the mixing labour with it, must attend that occupancy, or the right would have been very defective.

defective. Where the lands were already occupied by the human species, and in the actual possession of inhabitants, it will be very difficult to show on what true principle or grounds of justice, the Pope, or any other christian prince, assumed the right to seize on, dispose, and grant away, the lands of the Indians in America. Surely, the divine author of our holy religion, who declared that his kingdom was *not of this world*, hath not bequeathed to christians an *exclusive charter*, giving right of possession in the lands of this world, even where the supreme Providence hath already planted inhabitants in the possession of it: and yet, absurd, unjust, and groundless as this claim is, it is the only claim we Europeans can make, the only right we can plead. However, the English title is as good as any other European title, and indisputable against any other European claim.

Let us see the first assumption and exercise of this right in our government, contained in the grant which Henry the Seventh made to Cabot.———Copy of the grant, as it is a curious act, is printed in the appendix. —It contains a grant to Cabot, and his sons, of power, to set up the King's standard in any lands, islands, towns, villages, camps, &c. which he shall discover not in the occupancy of any christian power: and that this Cabot, his sons, and their heirs, may seize, conquer, and occupy any such lands, islands, towns, camps, or villages: and as his liege vassals, governors, locumtenentes, or deputies, may hold dominion over and have exclusive property in the same.

As the sovereigns of Europe did thus on one hand assume, without right, a predominant claim of possession, against the Indians in these lands; so our sovereigns also thus at first assumed against law an exclusive property in these lands, to the preclusion of the jurisdiction of the state. They called them their foreign dominions; their demesne lands in partibus exteris, and held them as their own, the King's possessions, not parts or parcels of the realm, † " as not yet annexed " to the crown." So that when the House of Commons, in those reiterated attempts which they made by passing a bill to get a law enacted for establishing a free right of fishery on the coasts of Virginia, New-England, and Newfoundland, put in the claim of the state to this property, and of the parliament to jurisdiction over it; they were told in the House by the servants of the crown, † " That it was not fit to make

† Journal of the House of Commons, April 25, 1621.

laws

"laws here for those countries which are not yet annexed to the crown." ‡ "That this bill was not proper for this house, as it concerneth America." Nay, it was doubted by others, "whether the house had jurisdiction to meddle with these matters." And when the house, in 1624, was about to proceed upon a petition from the settlers of Virginia, to take cognizance of the affairs of the plantations, "upon § the Speaker's producing and reading to the house a letter from the king concerning the Virginia petition, the petition, by general resolution, was withdrawn." And although the bill for a free fishery, to the disannulling some clauses in the King's charters, passed the house; as also the house came to some very strong resolutions upon the nullity of the clauses in the charters; yet the house from this time took no further cognizance of the plantations till the commencement of the civil wars. Upon this ground it was the King considered the lands as his demesnes, and the colonists as his subjects in these his foreign dominions, not his subjects of the realm or state.

The plantations were settled on these lands by his licence and grant; the constitutions

‡ Ditto, April 29, 1621.
§ Ditto, April 29.

and powers of government were framed by the King's charters and commissions; and the colonists understanding themselves as removed out of the realm, considered themselves in their executive and legislative capacity of government, in immediate connection and subordination to the King, their only sovereign lord.

In the same manner as this state and circumstances of a people migrating from, and settling in vacate countries, without, or out of the territories of the realm, operated to the establishment of the King's sovereignty there, he having assumed an exclusive right to the property. In the same manner it must and did necessarily operate to the establishment of the people's liberty, both personal and political—they had either tacit or express permission to migrate from the realm, and to settle in places out of the realm: those who settled under charters, had, in those charters, licence, by an express clause, to *quit* the realm, and to *settle* on lands *out of the realm*; as also acknowledgement that they and their posterity were entitled to enjoy all the liberties, franchises, and immunities, of free denizons and natural subjects, to all intents and purposes, as if they had been abiding and born within the realm.

So

So long as they were considered as natural born English subjects *of the realm,* they must retain and possess in the full enjoyment and exercise thereof, all the same rights and liberties in their persons, all the same franchises and privileges in their property, that any other English subject did possess.—If their freehold was part of any manor in any county of the realm, and that freehold was worth forty shillings by the year, such freehold undoubtedly gave the possessor a vote for the representative of such county; and these rights must give this subject, this freeholder, claim to the same participation of council in the legislative part of government, to the same communication of power in the executive part, the same right to act and trade, as every other English freeholder had.

If by migrating from out the realm the colonists ceased to have participation, such legislative participation in the councils as the English freeholder hath; if they ceased to have communication in the offices, burthens, and exercise of government; if being without the realm they ceased to be bound by laws made only for the internal regulation and government of the realm; if they ceased in future to be bound by laws wherein they were not expressly named; if they

ceased

ceased to be under the protection of those laws which were made, and those powers and magistracies which were created for the preservation of the peace within the realm; if they were (no matter how) separated from participation of the benefits of our holy religion, according to the established church; and if the colonies at the same time were not parts or parcels of the realm, they undoubtedly ceased to be subjects of the realm. But being by law, both established and natural, possessed of all the rights, privileges, franchises and immunities of a free-born people—no government less free than that which they had left, could, by any justifiable power, be established over or amongst them; and therefore the colonists were established in a government conformable to the government of England. They had power of making laws and ordinances, and of laying impositions, by a general assembly, or representative legislature—the power of erecting courts and creating magistrates, of the same power and operations, by the same modes and proceedings, *mutatis mutandis*, as were used in the government of England; nay, in some cases, by a mode adapted to a democratic, and even elective, government. The administrative and executive part had all the same checks, and the legislative all the same powers and privileges, only restrained from

from not acting contrary to the laws of England. And upon the same ground those colonies, of whose first settlement the crown took no care or cognizance, the colony of Plymouth, || that of Massachusetts, Providence Plantation, and the colony of Connecticut, established among themselves the like powers of free government.

And here we may venture to affirm, that if the colonies were to be deemed without the realm, not parts or parcels of it, not annexed to the crown of England, though the demesnes of the King; if the colonists by these means ceased to be subjects of the realm, and the Parliament had no right or jurisdiction to make laws about them; if the government of them resided in the King, only as *their* sovereign, *dum Rex ei præfit, ut caput istius populi, non ut caput alterius populi,* they were certainly a people *sui juris ---nam imperium quod in rege est ut in capite, in populo manet ut in toto, cujus pars est caput,* * and having an undoubted claim, by the nature of their liberties, to a participation in legislature, had an undoubted right, when

---

|| Vide Mr. Prince's New-England Chronology; and Lt. Gov. Hutchinson's Hist. of Massachusetts.
* *Grotius de B. & P. lib.* 2. *c.* 9. § 8.

formed

formed into a state of government, to have a representative legislature established, as part of their government; and therefore when so formed, being a body politic in fact and name, they had within themselves, the King, or his deputy, being part, full power and authority, to all intents and purposes, both legislative and executive, for the government of all the people, whether strangers or inhabitants, within their jurisdiction, independent of all external direction or government, except what might constitutionally be exercised by their sovereign lord the King, or his deputy, and except their subordination, not allegiance, to the government of the realm of England *(ut alterius populi)*. They acknowledged themselves to be a government subordinate to the government of England, so that they might justly be restrained from doing or becoming any thing repugnant to the power, rights and interest of England---but held their allegiance as due only to their sovereign; therefore, these premises admitted, as they did on one hand truly measure the duties of this allegiance, by the same rights and claims as the King's English subjects of the realm did; so on the other did they justly maintain that in every exercise of their own rights, privileges and powers,---they were free and independent of all controul, except what was

interwoven

interwoven into their conftitution, fo as to operate in the internal movements of thefe powers, or to be externally exercifed by the legal powers and negative refiding in the King their fovereign, or in his deputy.

They certainly were not provinces in the fimple idea of Roman provinces governed by laws and power, not deriving from their own rights, and arifing within their own government, but impofed on them by the *imperium alterius populi*, and adminiftered under provincial officers commiffioned from this *imperium*, abfolute as to them. Our colonies and provinces being each a body politic, and having a right to, and enjoying in fact, a certain legiflature, indented rather with the cafe of the Grecian colonies, as ftated by Grotius, — *Huc referenda & difceffio quæ ex confenfu fit in colonias, nam fic quoque novus populus fui juris nafcitur.* οὐ γαρ ἐπὶ τῷ Δῦλοι, ἀλλ' ἐπὶ τῷ ὁμοιοι ἔιναι ἐκπέμπονται. *Non enim ut fervi fint fed ut pari jure fint dimituntur.**—Many inftances may be collected from Thucydides, which would fhew that the dependence of the colonies of Greece on their mother cities, was only the

---

* It fhould be remarked here, though Grotius has omitted to do it, That this is a Pofition of the Locreans, a Colony of Corinth, obviating the Charge of Revolt. *Thucyd. Lib.* 1. *c.* 37.

connection of *Fœderates* acknowledging precedence, not the subordination of subjects acknowledging allegiance. But having, as above, stated the circumstances of the migration and first settlement of the English colonists, I shall confine myself to the instances and facts of the English colonies.

They were bodies corporate, but certainly not corporations in the sense of such communities *within the realm*. They were erected into provinces, had the *jura regalia*, the patentee as the King's deputy, or the King's governor, as part of their constitution, whether by commission or by charter, was vested with all the same royal powers which the King hath in his palace, both executive and legislative.

These provinces were all, in the true spirit, intent, and meaning of the thing, COUNTIES PALATINE; and some of them were actually and expressly created such.

The Caribbee Islands, granted by Charles the first, in the third year of his reign, to the Earl of Carlisle, were erected into a province or county, by the name of The Province of Carlisle, " with all and every such " like and so large privileges, jurisdictions, " prerogatives, royalties, liberties, freedoms,
" regal

" regal rights and franchises whatsoever, as
" well by sea as land, within the limits of
" the said islands, to have, use, exercise,
" and enjoy, as any Bishop (according to
" the custom of Duresme) within the said
" bishoprick or county palatine of Duresme,
" in our kingdom of England, ever before
" hath, had, keepeth, useth, or enjoyeth,
" or of right could or ought to have, keep,
" use, or enjoy."

The grant in 1630, to Sir Robert Heath, and his heirs, of the lands now called Louisiana, ran in the same manner.——" We
" erect the same into a province, and in-
" corporate it by the name of Carolanea,
" or the province Carolanea, with all and
" singular such like, and as ample rights,
" jurisdictions, privileges, prerogatives, roy-
" alties, liberties, immunities, and franchi-
" ses, as well by sea as land, within the
" regions, territories, islands, and limits
" aforesaid, to have, exercise, use, and en-
" joy the same, as any Bishop of Duresme,
" in the bishoprick or county palatine of
" Duresme, &c. &c."

In the charter of Maryland is granted as follows, " We have thought fit to erect the
" same into a province, with all and singu-
" lar the like, and as ample rights, juris-
" dictions,

"dictions, privileges, prerogatives, royal-
"ties, liberties, immunities, royal rights
"and franchises, of what kind soever, tem-
"poral, as well by sea as by land, within
"the country, isles, islets, and limits afore-
"said, to have, exercise, use, and enjoy the
"same, as amply as any Bishop of Durham
"within the bishoprick or county palatine
"of Durham, in our kingdom of England,
"hath any time heretofore had, held, used,
"or enjoyed, or of right ought, or might
"have had, held, used or enjoyed."

The charter of the 15th of Charles the first, to Sir Ferdinando Gorges, erects, creates, and incorporates, all the premises granted into a province or county, called the province or county of Main, granting him all and singular, and as large and ample rights, jurisdictions, privileges, prerogatives, royalties, liberties, and immunities, franchises and preheminencies, as well by sea as land, within the premises, as the Bishop of Durham hath within the county palatine of Durham.

The charter of Pensylvania *erects the said country into a province or seignory*, in the recital of the powers of which all the *regalia* are granted; and especially the power and privilege

privilege of not being taxed but by the consent of the freemen, or in parliament.

By the charter of William and Mary, the provinces of the Massachusets-bay was " *erected and incorporated into a real province,*" in the powers of which the Jura Regalia are described and fully granted.

All these provinces have the power of peace and war, of exercising law martial, of life and death, of creating towns, counties, and other corporations within themselves; and the powers of their general assemblies are very different from, and go beyond the powers of our common councils within the realm.

The fact is, that the constitution of the government of England, as it stood at that time, founded upon, or built up with the feudal system, could not extend beyond the realm. There was nothing in the nature of the constitution providing for such things as colonies, or provinces. Lands without or beyond the limits of the realm, could not be the property of the realm, unless by being united to the realm. But the people who settled upon these lands in *partibus exteris*, being the King's liege subjects, the King, as sovereign Lord, assumed the right of of property, and of government. Yet the people being intitled to the rights, privileges, &c. of freemen, the King eſtabliſhed by his commiſſion of government, or charters, theſe colonies as free ſtates, ſubordinate according to ſuch precedents or examples as his miniſtry thought ſuitable to the preſent caſe; and the county palatine of Durham became this precedent, and the model of this conſtitution as to the *regalia*. This was the actual ſtate of the circumſtances of our coloniſts at their firſt migration, and of the colonies at their firſt ſettlement; and had nothing further intervened, would have been their conſtitution at this day. Let us examine what has intervened, and mark as preciſely as we can, where power has attempted, and where right has effected any change in theſe circumſtances.

Notwithſtanding this mode of conſtitution, acknowleged *de jure*, as well as eſtabliſhed *de facto*, we find, that from the moment that theſe our Kings, and their council, took up the idea of comparing theſe plantations to the duchies of Gaſcoigne or Normandy, as we find in the journals of the Houſe of Commons, before referred to. From that moment the conſtitution of the colonies were treated as being the ſame with that of Jerſey, part of the duchy of Normandy;

and the same mode of administration was adopted for the colonies as had been used and accustomed for the government of that island.

Appeals from the provincial law courts were established; not to the courts of equity here in England, not to the House of Lords, according to the constitution and custom of England, but as appeals from the courts in Normandy were brought before the King, as Duke in council; so here in the plantations, appeals were made to the King in council, according to the ancient custom of Normandy. And the same rules for these appeals were adopted—" Appeals (says Mr. Falle in his account of Jersey) " may be " brought before the council board, in mat- " ters of civil property, * above the value of " 300 livres Tournois, but no appeal is ad- " mitted in matters of less value; nor in " interlocutories, nor in criminal causes, " which are judged here to be without " appeal."

As the laws of Jersey may be reduced under these three heads: 1. The ancient custom of Normandy, as it stood before the alienation of that duchy, called in the rolls of the itinerant judges *La Somme de Mançel*. This makes what the statute law is in England.

* In the same manner appeals may be brought from the colonies, in matters where the value is £ 300.

2. Muni-

2. Municipal or local usages, which are the unwritten and traditionary law, like the common law in England. 3. Constitutions and ordinances made by the King, or his commissioners royal; with such regulations and orders, as are from time to time transmitted to Jersey, from the council board.—So Charles the First took up the idea, that the colonies in like manner, his demesnes in his foreign dominions, might be governed by laws, ordinances, and constitutions, made and published with his consent,* by his royal commissioners, established for governing the plantations, together with such further instructions as should be transmitted from the council board; and that these commissioners, being his council for plantation affairs, might be the dernier court of appeal from the colonies. He left indeed the colonies in some degree in possession of the statute law of England, as it stood before their migration, and allowed them, as far as was consistent with the legislation of this his council, the making and using their municipal and local laws.

Under these Norman ideas of the constitution of our colonies, it was a most fortunate circumstance for them, That the island

* Vide Appendix, for the Commission at length.

of Jersey had, by its constitution, a right to hold a "convention or meeting of the three "orders or estates of the islands, in imitation "of those august assemblies, known by "that or some other name, in great king- "doms and monarchies, a shadow, and "resemblance of an English parliament." In which, "the King's governor, or lieute- "nant, had a negative voice. The great "business of which meetings, was the raising "money to supply public occasions. For, "(Mr. Falle says) as in England, money "cannot be raised upon the subject, but by "authority of parliament, so here it is a re- "ceived maxim, that no levies can be made "upon the inhabitants, but by their own "consent, declared by their representatives "assembled in common-council." It was fortunate, I say, for our colonies, that this was the case of Jersey; for there can be no other reasonable account given, how our co- lonies preserved this essential right of English- men, but that it happened to be also a con- stitutional right of his Majesty's foreign French-Norman subjects. This commission indeed was annulled, and a board of planta- tions (at the head of which, as a marine department, the Earl of Warwick was placed, being admiral) was appointed by an ordi- nance of parliament; and after the restora- tion, a council of trade and plantations was established,

established, and upon that being dissolved in December, 1674, these matters were conducted by a committee of council, until after the revolution, when the present board of trade and plantations was appointed. But although, as political liberty became better understood, and more effectually established, in our own constitution, the very idea of a privy council making laws for English subjects, though in America, began to be more warily touched upon, and was at last finally dropped: Yet the idea of directing, restraining, and suspending, in some cases, the exercise of their constitutional powers of government, by the King's further powers and instructions, and authorities under his signet, or sign manual, or by his order in privy council, or even by letters from secretaries of state, doth continue too deeply rooted to this day; as also this fragment of the Norman custom of appeal to the King, as Duke in council, continues to be the corner-stone in the edifice of their judicatories. From the state of matters as above, it is clear, that so far as refers to the relation between the King and them, while the King by himself, or by his royal commissioners, his council, or his committee, assumed a right to make and publish laws, constitutions, and ordinances, as binding upon, and penal against, the people of the colonies, without the intervention

vention of their legislature. They undoubtedly had a right, and it was their duty to reject them, and to refuse obedience to them; as also to consider all his royal commands and instructions, whether by orders in council, by sign manual, or by letters from secretaries of state, when they assumed the port of laws or ordinances, to be no otherwise binding on the colonies and provinces, than as royal proclamations, which have in many cases, a certain authority, *quoad terrorem*, though not that of law. If the colonists had at their migration, as natural liberties as above described, and were, by the commissions of government or charters (for I see no difference, both equally providing for an uninterrupted and continual succession of civil government) established in the same; no orders or instructions, which might derive thus from the King alone, to the suspending, restraining, or obstructing the enjoyment of these rights and liberties, or the exercise of these powers, could take effect, or have the force of law.

And as thus of the King's power in the government of the colonies, so we may with the stronger reason venture to pronounce that parliament without the King, as by that committee, or board of plantations, instituted by order of parliament in the year 1643,

F could

could have none of those powers which might supercede the rights and liberties of the colonies.

How far the power of King and parliament, the whole imperium of Great Britain, may go in conjunction with right, is matter of more difficulty to ascertain; and of more danger to decide. If the provinces have any rights, however much subordinate, even this imperium must be bounded by them. However, I have formed my opinion on this subject, and I will speak it out;—if I am in an error, even error may give occasion to the rise of truth.---But this is not the place.

Having said so much on the liberties of the people in the colonies, it is right, perhaps necessary, to say, I am sure it may be said with the utmost precision and conviction, That the King must retain in himself, and in his deputy set over them in his government of them, all those same preheminences, royal rights, powers and prerogatives, which are vested in the crown, as part of the government of England. And that whenever the people, or their representatives in the colonies, act towards his royal person, or towards his representative, in derogation of these rights and powers, they can neither be justified by right, or the constitution, or even

good

good policy towards themselves, whatever specious temporary reasons they may assign for it; for this mode of conduct will be permitted to a certain degree only, and for a certain time; but will alway in the end, as it alway hath in fact done, call forth some remedy, so far as relates to the colonists ideas, worse than the disease. I will instance in one case only---The constant refusal of the Assemblies to fix permanent salaries for the civil establishment of government.

The above is the actual and rightful relation between the King and the American colonies; and by the rule of this relation, we ought to review and decide those several points wherein the crown, or its Governors acting under its commission and instructions, differ with the people.

Upon such review it will appear, under this first general head, in various instances, that the two great points which the Colonists labour to establish, is the exercise of their several rights and privileges, as founded in the rights of an Englishman; and secondly, as what they suppose to be a necessary measure in a subordinate government, the keeping in their own hands the command of the revenue, and the pay of the officers of government, as a security for the conduct of those officers towards them.

Under the first head come all the disputes about the King's instructions, and the governor's power, as founded on them.

The King's commission to his governor, which grants the power of government, and directs the calling of a legislature, and the establishing courts, at the same time that it fixes the governor's power, according to the several powers and directions granted and appointed by the commission and instructions, adds " and by such *further powers, instruc-*" tions, and authorities, as shall, at any " time hereafter, be granted or appointed " you, under our signet or sign manual, or " by our order in our privy council." It should here seem, that the same power which framed the commission, with this clause in it, could also issue its *future orders and instructions* in consequence thereof: but the people of the colonies say, that the inhabitants of the colonies are entitled to all the privileges of Englishmen; that they have a right to participate in the legislative power; and that no commands of the crown, by orders in council, instructions, or letters from Secretaries of State, are binding upon them, further than they please to acquiesce under

such,

such, and conform *their own actions* thereto; that they hold this right of legislature, not derived from the grace and will of the crown, and depending on the commission which continues at the will of the crown; that this right is inherent and essential to the community, as a community of Englishmen: and that therefore they must have all the rights, privileges, and full and free exercise of their own will and liberty in making laws, which are necessary to that act of legislation,—uncontrouled by any power of the crown, or of the governor, preventing or suspending that act; and, that the clause in the commission, directing the governor to call together a legislature by his writs, is declarative and not creative; and therefore he is directed to act conformably to a right actually already existing in the people, &c. and therefore that such clause ought not to be in the commission, or to be understood as being of no effect, so far as concerns the colonists.

When I speak of full uncontrouled independent powers of debate and result, so far as relates to the framing bills and passing them into laws, uncontrouled by any power of the crown or of the governor, as an essential property of a free legislature; I find some persons in the colonies imagine, that I represent

present the colonies as claiming a power of legislature independent of the King's or governor's negative.---These gentlemen knowing that it is not my intention to do injustice to the colonies, wish me so to explain this matter, that it may not bear even the interpretation of such a charge---I do therefore here desire, that the reader will give his attention to distinguish a full, free, uncontrouled, independent power, in the act of legislation,—from a full, free, uncontrouled, independent power, of carrying the results of that legislation into effect, independent either of the Governor's or King's negative. The first right is that which I represent the colonists claiming, as a right essential to the very existence of the legislature: The second is what is also essential to the nature of a subordinate legislature, and what the colonists never call in question. That therefore the point here meant to be stated as in debate, is, Whether a subordinate legislature can be instructed, restricted, and controuled, in the very act of legislation? whether the King's instructions or letters from secretaries of state, and such like significations of his Majesty's will and pleasure, is a due and constitutional application of the governors, or of the royal negative?---The colonists constantly deny it,—and ministry, otherwise such instructions would not be given, constantly maintain it.

After

After experience of the confusion and obstruction which this dubitable point hath occasioned to business, it is time surely that it were some way or other determined. Or whether in fact or deed, the people of the colonies, having every right to the full powers of government, and *to a whole legislative power*, are not under this claim entitled in the powers of legislature and the administration of government, to use and exercise in conformity to the laws of Great Britain, the same, full, free, independent, unrestrained power and legislative will in their several corporations, and under the King's commission and their respective charters, as the government and legislature of Great Britain holds by its constitution, and under the great charter.

Every subject, born within the realm, under the freedom of the Government of Great Britain, or by adoption admitted to the same, has an essential indefeasible right to be governed, under such a mode of government as has the unrestrained exercise of all those powers which form the freedom and rights of the constitution; and therefore " the " crown cannot establish any colony upon— " or contract it within *a narrower scale* than " the subject is entitled to, by the great " charter

"charter of England[*]." The government of each colony muſt have the ſame powers, and the ſame extent of powers that the government of Great Britain has,---and muſt have, while it does not act contrary to the laws of Great Britain, the ſame freedom and independence of legiſlature, as the parliament of Great Britain has. This right (ſay they) is founded, not only in the general principles of the rights of a Britiſh ſubject, but is actually declared, confirmed, or granted to them in the commiſſions and charters which gave the particular frame of their reſpective conſtitutions. If therefore, in the firſt original eſtabliſhment, like the original contract, they could not be eſtabliſhed, upon any ſcale ſhort of the full and compleat ſcale of the powers of the Britiſh government,---nor the legiſlature be eſtabliſhed on any thing leſs than the whole legiſlative power; much leſs can this power of government and legiſlature, thus eſtabliſhed, be governed, directed, reſtrained or reſtricted, by any poſterior inſtructions or commands by the letters of Secretaries of State. But upon the ſuppoſition, that a kind of general indetermined power in the crown, to ſuperadd inſtructions to the commiſſions and charter be admitted, where the coloniſts do

[*] Hiſtorical Review of the Conſtitution and Government of Penſylvania, p. 11.

not

not make a queſtion of the caſe wherein it is exerted, yet there are particular caſes wherein both directive and reſtrictive inſtructions are given, and avowedly not admitted by the coloniſts. It is a ſtanding inſtruction, as a ſecurity of the dependence of the government of the colonies, on the mother country, that no acts wherein the King's rights, or the rights of the mother country or of private perſons can be affected, ſhall be enacted into a law without a clauſe ſuſpending the effect thereof, till his Majeſty's pleaſure ſhall be known. This ſuſpending clauſe is univerſally * rejected on the principles above, becauſe ſuch ſuſpenſion disfranchiſes the inherent full power of legiſlature, which they claim by their rights to the Britiſh liberties, and by the ſpecial declarations of ſuch in their charters. It does not remove this difficulty by ſaying, that the crown has already in its hands the power of fixing this point, by the effect of its negative given to its governor. It is ſaid, that if the crown ſhould withdraw that inſtruction, which allows certain bills to be paſſed into laws with a ſuſpending clauſe, which inſtruction is not meant as a reſtriction upon, but an indulgence to the legiſlatures; that if the crown

* In ſome caſes of emergency, and in the caſes of the concerns of individuals, the inſtruction has been ſubmitted to, but the principle never.

ſhould

should withdraw this instruction, and peremptorily restrain its governor from enacting laws, under such circumstances as the wisdom of government cannot admit of, that then these points are actually fixed by the true constitutional power; but wherever it is so said, I must repeat my idea, that this does not remove the difficulty. For waving the doubt which the colonists might raise, especially in the charter colonies, how far the governor ought, or ought not, to be restricted from giving his assent in cases contrary only to instructions, and not to the laws of Great Britain; waving this point, let administration consider the effects of this measure. In cases where the bills, offered by the two branches, are for providing laws, absolutely necessary to the continuance, support, and exercise of government, and where yet the orders of the crown, and the sense of the people, are so widely different as to the mode, that no agreement can ever be come to in these points---Is the government and administration of the government of the colonies to be suspended? The interest, perhaps the being of the plantations, to be hazarded by this obstinate variance, and can the exercise of the crown's negative, in such emergencies, and with such effect, ever be taken up as a measure of administration? And when every thing is thrown into confusion,

fusion, and abandoned even to ruin by such measure, will administration justify itself by saying, that it is the fault of the Colonists? On the contrary, this very state of the case shows the necessity of some other remedy.

In the course of examining these matters, will arise to consideration the following very material point. As a principal tie of the subordination of the legislatures of the colonies on the government of the mother country, they are bound by their constitutions and charters, to send all *their acts* of legislature to England, to be confirmed or abrogated by the crown; but if any of the legislatures should be found to do almost every act of legislature, by votes or orders, even to the repealing the effects of acts, suspending establishments of pay, paying services, doing chancery and other judicatory business: if matters of this sort, done by these votes and orders, never reduced into the form of an act, have their effect without ever being sent home as acts of legislature, or submitted to the allowance or disallowance of the crown: If it should be found that many, or any of the legislatures of the colonies carry the powers of legislature into execution, independent of the crown by this device,—it will be a point to be determined how far, in such cases, the subordination of the legislatures of the colonies to the government of the mother country

country is maintained or suspended;—or if, from emergencies arising in these governments, this device is to be admitted, the point, how far such is to be admitted, ought to be determined; and the validity of these votes and orders, these Senatus-Consulta so far declared. For a point of such great importance in the subordination of the colony legislatures, and of so questionable a cast in the valid exercise of this legislative power, ought no longer to remain in question.

The next general point yet undetermined, the determination of which very essentially imports the subordination and dependance of the colony governments on the government of the mother country, is, the manner of providing for the support of government, and for all the executive officers of the crown. The freedom and right efficiency of the constitution require, that the executive and judicial officers of government should be independent of the legislative; and more especially in popular governments, where the legislature itself is so much influenced by the humours and passions of the people; for if they do not, there will be neither justice nor equity in any of the courts of law, nor any efficient execution of the laws and orders of government in the magistracy: according, therefore, to the constitution

tution of Great Britain, the crown has the appointment and payment of the several executive and judicial officers, and the legiflature settles a permanent and fixed appointment for the support of government and the civil list in general: The crown therefore has, *à fortiori*, a right to require of the colonies, to whom, by its commission or charter, it gives the power of government, such permanent support, appropriated to the offices, not the officers of government, that they may not depend upon the temporary and arbitrary will of the legiflature.

The crown does, by its instructions to its governors, order them to require of the legiflature a permanent support. This order of the crown is generally, if not universally rejected, by the legiflatures of the colonies. The assemblies quote the precedents of the British constitution, and found all the rights and privileges which they claim on the principles thereof. They allow the truth and fitness of this principle in the British constitution, where the executive power of the crown is immediately administered by the King's Majesty; yet say, under the circumstances in which they find themselves, that there is no other measure left to them to prevent the misapplications of public money, than by an annual voting and appropriation of the salaries

ries of the governor and other civil officers, issuing from monies lodged in the hands of a provincial treasurer appointed by the assemblies: For in these subordinate governments, remote from his Majesty's immediate influence, administered often times by necessitous and rapacious governors who have no natural, altho' they have a political connection with the country, experience has shewn that such governors have misapplied the monies raised for the support of government, so that the civil officers have been left unpaid, even after having been provided for by the assembly. The point then of this very important question comes to this issue, Whether the inconveniencies arising, and experienced by some instances of misapplications of appropriations (for which however there are in the King's courts of law, due and sufficient remedies against the offender) are a sufficient reason and ground for establishing a measure so directly contrary to the British constitution: and whether the inconveniencies to be traced in the history of the colonies, through the votes and journals of their legislatures, in which the support of governors, judges, and officers of the crown will be found to have been withheld or reduced on occasions, where the assemblies have supposed that they have had reason to disapprove the nomination,—or the person, or his conduct;—
whether,

whether, I say, these inconveniencies have not been more detrimental, and injurious to government; and whether, instead of these colonies being dependent on, and governed under, the officers of the crown, the scepter is not reversed, and the officers of the crown dependant on and governed by the assemblies, as the Colonists themselves allow, that this measure * " renders the governor, " and all the other servants of the crown, " dependant on the assembly."---But the operation of this measure does not end here; it extends to the assuming by the assemblies the actual executive part of the government in the case of the revenue, than which nothing is more clearly and unquestionably settled in the crown. In the colonies the treasurer is solely and entirely a servant of the assembly or general court; and although the monies granted and appropriated be, or ought to be, granted to the crown on such appropriations, the treasurer is neither named by the crown, nor its governor, nor gives security to the crown or to the Lord High Treasurer, (which seems the most proper) nor in many of the colonies, is to obey the governor's warrant in the issue, nor accounts in the auditor's office, nor in any one colony is it admitted, that he is liable to such account. In consequence of this supposed ne-

* Smith's History of New York, p. 118.

cessity,

cessity, for the assembly's taking upon them the administration of the treasury and revenue, the governor and servants of the crown, in the ordinary revenue of government, are not only held dependant on the assembly, but all services where special appropriations are made for the extraordinaries which such services require, are actually executed and done by commissioners appointed by the assembly, to whose disposition such appropriations are made liable. It would be perhaps inviduous, and might tend to prejudging on points which ought very seriously and dispassionately to be examined, if I were here to point out in the several instances of the actual execution of this assumed power, how almost every executive power of the crown lodged in its governor, is, where money is necessary, thus exercised by the assembly and its commissioners. I therefore rest the matter here.

In the first edition of this book I pointed out the measure of the government's settling fixed salaries on the officers of the crown in America, independant of the people. I afterwards withdrew this proposition, from an apprehension of the evils which might arise to the service by these fixed and permanent salaries, having a tendency to render the chief offices sinecures, procured by the

the corruptors for the corrupted, in reverſions, from generation to generation. This meaſure, hath been ſince eſtabliſhed by parliament. But why, thoſe who had the conduct of it would not admit a clauſe, providing that ſuch ſalaries, hereafter to be eſtabliſh'd, ſhould be given to no perſon but to ſuch as actually executed the office, is not very eaſy to conceive, unleſs from ſuggeſtions that one would not willingly take up againſt the integrity of their intentions.---If that act ſhould ever be explained, or amended by any ſubſequent law, it is to be hoped, that this clauſe would not again be omitted.

The ſame motive, and reaſon which weigh'd with government, to adopt this meaſure of fixing ſalaries for the civil officers of the crown in America during the time of their ſerving, ſhould operate, to induce government to take one ſtep further, in order to render the meaſure quite effectual, that is, to ſettling ſome half-pay or other penſion, on ſuch officers as are from age or ill health removed; or after long ſervices in that country, are permitted to return home. The appointments of the governors &c. are ſuch, wherein no fortunes can either be made, or ſaved with honor.---If they have no fortunes of their own,

own, they muſt, after their ſervices, return home to ſtarve. " There is no man" (ſays an American, the intelligent author of the Hiſtorical Review of Penſylvania) " long, or much converſant in this over-
" grown city [London] who hath not often
" found himſelf in company with the ſhades
" of departed governors, doomed to wan-
" der out the reſidue of their lives, full of
" the agonizing remembrance of their paſt
" eminence, and the ſevere ſenſation of
" preſent neglect. *Sir William Keith*, upon
" his return, was added to this unfortunate
" liſt, concerning whom, the leaſt that can
" be ſaid is, that either none but men of
" fortune ſhould be appointed to ſerve in
" ſuch diſtinguiſh'd offices; or otherwiſe
" for the honor of government itſelf, ſuch
" as are recalled without any notorious im-
" putation on their conduct ſhould be pre-
" ſerved from that wretchedneſs and con-
" tempt which they have been but too fre-
" quently permitted to fall into, for want
" even of a proper ſubſiſtance."----The means of avoiding this wretched iſſue of their ſervice, by making up a fortune to live on when they ſhall be recalled, is a tempta-tion which ought to be removed from this ſituation, by thoſe who regard the King's ſervice, even if they have no feelings of compaſſion for his ſervants.---A ſmall pit-
tance

tance would pay this, and that very sum might engage the services of these half pay officers in a way not unuseful to government.---They might, in consideration of this pay, be directed to attend the Board of trade or whatever board or officer was for the time being, the acting minister for the business of America, in order to give explanations, or opinions, as they should be required; or even to report, if ever they should be thought worthy to have any matter, requiring a report, refer'd to them; they might be formed into a kind of subordinate board for this purpose.---The benefit of such a measure needs not to be expatiated upon, and to explain the operation of it would be too minute a detail for the cursory mention which I here make of it.

It is a duty of perfect obligation from government towards the colonies, to preserve the liberty of the subject, the liberty of the constitution: It is a duty also of prudence in government towards itself, as such conduct is the only permanent and sure ground, whereon to maintain the dependance of those countries, without destroying their utility as colonies.

The constitutions of these communities, founded in wise policy, and in the laws of the British constitution, are established by their several charters, or by the King's commission to his governors, being in the nature of a charter of government. In these, all the just powers of government are described and defined, the rights of the subject and of the constitution declared, and the modes of government agreeable thereto established. As these pass under the great seal, no jurisdictions or offices will be inserted in the powers granted, but what are agreeable and conformable to law, and the constitution of the realm. Although the King's commission is barely a commission during pleasure, to the person therein named as governor, yet it provides for a succession without vacancy, or interregnum, and is not revoked but by a like commission, with like powers: It becomes the known, established constitution of that province which hath been established on it, and whose laws, courts, and whole frame of legislature and judicature, are founded on it: It is the charter of that province: It is the indefeasible and unalterable right of those people: It is the indefeasible right by which those colonies thus established, are the colonies of Great Britain, and therefore not to be altered; but by such means as any reform or new establishment may take place in Great Britain: It cannot, in its essential parts, be altered or destroyed

by

by any royal inſtructions or proclamation; or by letters from ſecretaries of ſtate: It cannot be ſuperceded, or in part annulled, by the iſſuing out of any other commiſſions not known to this conſtitution.

In theſe charters, and in theſe commiſſions, the crown delegates to the governor for the time being, all its conſtitutional power and authority civil and military—the power of legiſlation ſo far as the crown has ſuch.---its judicial and executive powers, its powers of chancery, admiralty juriſdiction, and that of ſupreme ordinary.—All thoſe powers, as they exiſt and reſide in the crown, are known by the laws and courts of the realm, and as they are derived to the governors are defined, declared, and *patent*, by the charters and commiſſions *patent*. It is therefore the duty and true intereſts of the Coloniſts to maintain theſe rights, theſe privileges, this conſtitution: It is moreover the duty and true intereſt of King, Lords, and Commons, to be watchful over, to ſupport and defend theſe rights of the colonies: It is the duty of adminiſtration to have conſtant regard to the exerciſe of them, otherwiſe it will be found a dangerous thing to have given ſo much of civil power out of the King's hands, and to have done ſo little to maintain thoſe into whoſe hands it is entruſted. How far the eſta-

establishment of the office and power of a military commander in chief, not subordinate but superior to these constitutional commanders in chief, how far the superceding of the *Consular* power of the Governors, by establishing, not for the time of war only, but as a settled system, this *Dictatorial* power, with a jurisdiction extending over the whole of the British empire in America, is conformable to law, to prudence, or sound policy, is matter of very serious consideration to those who regard the liberties of the constitution.

All military power whatsoever, as far as law and the constitution will justify the establishment of such, is resident in the established office of governor, as Captain general and commander in chief. There is no power here granted, but what is specified and defined by the nature of the constitution. The subject and state is duly guarded against any extensions of it, by the several laws which the legislatures of the several colonies have provided to limit that power; and it can be exercised by none but such persons as are within the jurisdiction of the province, who deriving their powers from the supream powers are amenable to the laws of the province; and to the governor, who is himself specially responsible for the trust. This power thus limited becomes part of the constitution of the province, and unless thus limited,

limited, and thus considered as part of the constitution of the government, it may be matter of great doubt, whether the crown would be advised to erect any military powers whatever. But under such limitations, and as a known established part of the constitution, the crown may safely grant these powers, and the people safely live under them, because the governor is " required
" and commanded to do and execute all
" things in due manner, that shall belong
" unto *the trust* reposed in him, according
" to the several powers and authorities men-
" tioned in the charter." That is to say, according to those powers which in charter governments are expressly part of the constitution; and which from the very nature of the *commission patent* in such constitutions as are called King's governments, are likewise to be considered in the same light.—When this military branch of the governor's office is established and received as part of the constitution, the King may safely grant, and the people safely act under " a power
" to levy, arm, muster, command, and
" employ all persons whatsoever residing
" within such province; to resist and repell
" both at land and sea, all enemies, pirates,
" and rebels, and such to pursue in or out
" of the limits of the province: to erect and
" build forts, to fortify and furnish, and to

" commit

" commit the command of the same to such
" person or persons as to such governor shall
" seem meet—and the same again to dis-
" mantle or demolish: and to do and execute
" all and every other thing which to a cap-
" tain general doth or ought of right to be-
" long, as fully and amply as any other the
" King's captains general doth or hath usual-
" ly done, according to the powers in the
" commission and charter granted." It be-
comes hence a question of the highest import, and leading to the most dangerous consequences—Whether, after the constitutions and offices of a colony or province are thus established, the King himself can dismember the same, so as to grant to any office or officer not known to the constitution, any part whatsoever of those powers, as he cannot disfranchise a people having such powers, under such charters, of any the least right or privilege included in, or as derived from, the establishment of their constitution of government? This is a question that it would behove the crown lawyers well to consider, whenever it shall be referred to their consideration. If every military power that can legally be included in any commission which the crown will be advised to issue, is already included in the office of governor, as part of the constitution of these provinces and colonies, what commission can supercede

the

the same, or give power to any other officer than the governor to exercise these powers within such province? It was suggested by the writer of these papers at the beginning of the late war, that *if the necessity of the case in time of war* urged to the appointing a military commander in chief of all North America, who should command all military operations, and preside in general over all military establishments for the general service, independent of, and superior to, the powers and authorities already granted to the governors and captains general of the provinces,—it was suggested, that no commissions under the private seal and sign manual could supercede, revoke, or take precedence of these powers granted by letters patent under the great seal, and it was determined accordingly, that the military commander in chief must have his commission patent under the great seal. But when it came to be considered what powers should be granted in this commission, the wisdom and prudence of the great statesman and lawyer who was then entrusted with that seal, issued the commission for the commander in chief, in general and indefinite terms, " to have,
" hold, exercise, and enjoy the said office dur-
" ing pleasure, together with all the powers,
" authorities, rights and privileges, thereunto
" belonging, subject however to such restric-
" tions, limitations, and instructions, as are
" given, or to be given, from time to time,
" under

" under the royal sign manual, and charging
" and requiring all the governors, lieutenant
" governors, deputy governors, and presi-
" dents of the council of the respective co-
" lonies and provinces of North America,
" and all other officers civil or military with-
" in the same, to be aiding and assisting in
" this command." These general powers undefined and unknown, and such as no minister who advises the issuing such commission will venture to describe, these general words, power and command, either mean nothing, or suppose every thing, when a justifiable occasion, or perhaps a colourable pretext calls for the exercise of them. It was seen that these general descriptions were either dangerous or nugatory, and therefore the commander in chief had at the same time, another commission under the private seal and sign manual, in which were inserted all the powers for governing the forces, &c. which were not thought proper to be included and granted by letters patent under the great seal. I am no lawyer, and do not therefore presume to give an opinion of decision, but venture to affirm, that it ought well to be considered, Whether if this commission be *now in time of peace* interpreted to extend to any one purpose at all, it must not extend to much more than can be justified by either law or the constitution? Whether (the constitutions of the provinces and colonies remaining)

maining) the office of a commander in chief exercising such powers as are supposed necessary *to the execution of that command,* can be established over all North America? These military powers, as they exist in the governor's commission, exist and must be exercised under the civil limitations and regulations of the constitution, nor can any law martial, or any other military ordonnances be published, without the concurrence of the other branches of the legislature. But the difference of this *dictatorial power* of a military commander in chief, and the *consular* power of the provincial governor, can not be better described than in the following passage: *Ea potestas (scilicet dictatoria) per senatum more Romano magistratui maxima permittitur, exercitum parare, bellum gerere, coercere omnibus modis socios atque cives: domi militiæque imperium atque judicium summum habere: aliter sine populi jussu nullius earum rerum consuli jus est* *.

If it should upon consideration and advice, of which I am no judge, be found that the dictatorial power and command of a military commander in chief, superior to the provincial governors (however necessity, in time of war, might justify it, *ne quid respublica detrimenti capiat)* is not agreeable and conformable to law, and to the constitution ei-

* Sallust, Bellum Catilinarium.

ther of Great Britain or of the colonies in time of peace; it may be supposed that such will not be continued in time of peace, and that as soon as the * hostile state of Indian affairs ceases, this power will be made to cease also.

In the considerations above, I have suggested the doubt; whether this commission may be right as to law and the constitution. But if there be only a doubt of its legality, and there no longer remains an absolute necessity for the continuance of it; I think it may be fairly made to appear, that neither prudence nor sound policy can justify it.

Such powers with such a command may be dangerous to the liberty of the subject, to the liberties of the constitution of the colonies on one hand: And on the other hand, there are no people in the whole world, when their liberties shall become infected and undermined, so liable to become the instruments of dominion, as a people who have lived under a free and popular government. This has been the fate of the free states of Greece and Italy; this the fate of Rome itself:—But may heaven avert, that this ever becomes the state of the British colonies.

* The first edition of this book was published during the continuance of the hostilities of the Indians, after the General Peace amongst the Europeans. That hath ceased.

There is not, there cannot be any danger in this power at prefent in any degree;---but thus planted when it comes to grow, *occulto velut arbor ævo,* when it has taken root, and has fpread its branches through the land, it will foon overtop and overfhadow all the weaker, humbler fhoots of civil liberty. Set once this lord of the foreft on a permanent footing, it will foon have, as Mr. Harrington fays, " Toes that have roots, and arms that " will bring forth what fruit you pleafe."

It is a common obfervation, but it is as trivial as common, which fuppofes the danger of the colonies revolting, and becoming independent of the mother country. No one colony can by itfelf become fo—and no two under the prefent ftate of their conftitutions, have any poffible communion of power or intereft that can unite them in fuch a meafure; they have not the means of forming fuch; they have neither legiflative nor executive powers, that are extended to more than one; the laws of one extend not to the other; they have no common magiftracy, no common command, in fhort, no one principle of affociation amongft them: On the contrary, as I have faid elfewhere, the different manner in which they are fettled, the different modes under which they live, the different forms of charters, grants, and frame of government which they poffefs,

the

the various principles of repulsion that these create, the different interests which they actuate, the religious interests by which they are actuated, the rivalship and jealousies which arise from hence, and the impracticability, if not impossibility, of reconciling and accommodating these incompatible ideas and claims, will keep the several provinces and colonies perpetually independent of, and unconnected with each other, and dependent on the mother country. The particular danger here meant to be pointed out, is that of furnishing them with a *principle of union*, disunited from the civil constitution, by establishing a military commander in chief over the whole. If ever the colonies revolt, and set up an empire in America, here begins the history of it; from this period as from the first dynasty, will future historians deduce their narrative. The Romans, as long as they governed their provinces by the vigour of policy, preserved their dependence, and see what that policy was.---I will produce two instances, one in Italy, the other in Greece; *Cæterùm habitari tantùm, tanquam urbem, Capuam, frequentarique placuit: corpus nullum civitatis nec senatûs, nec plebis concilium, nec magistratus esse, sine consilio publico*, sine imperio, *multitudinem nullius rei inter se sociam ad* consensum inhabilem fore[*].

[*] Liv. lib. 26. § 16. lib. 45. § 30.

The other is as follows, after the Romans had entirely overcome Perseus, and reduced all Macedonia, they restore it to its liberty; but to disarm that liberty of all power of revolt, they divide Macedon into four regions or provinces, not barely by boundary lines, and geographical distinctions, but by dissevering and separating their interests; *divisæ Macedoniæ, partium usibus separatis, et regionatim commerciis interruptis* ‡.

Under this policy they preserved their provinces and maintained the empire of Rome; but when they took up the false policy of establishing and continuing, in time of peace, military commanders in chief in their provinces, the people of the provinces became an army, and that army subverted the empire. "By how much the more remote (says Machiavell) their wars were, by so much they thought those prorogations more convenient, by which it happened that the commander might gain such an interest in the army, as might make it disclaim the

‡ I beg that it may be here understood, that while by this example, I mean to point the danger of giving any principle of union amongst the several colonies, and the sure wisdom of keeping this disunion of council and imperium amongst them, I do from principles of policy as well as those of strict justice, invariably recommend the preservation of their respective constitutions, in the full use and exercise of all their rights and privileges.

power

power of the senate." Publius Philo was the first to whom his military commission was prolonged, and this precedent once settled, we hear next of the soldiers in Spain declaring L. Marcius imperator in the field. *Res mali exempli imperatores legi ab exercitibus et solenne auspicatorum comitiorum in* castra et provincias, *procul ab legibus magistratibusque, ad militarem temeritatem transferri* †. "This "it was that enabled Marius and Sylla to "debauch the army; this it was that en-"abled Cæsar to conquer his native country. "It may be objected, that their great affairs "could not have been managed at so great "a distance, without such commands.—It "is possible indeed, that their empire might "have been longer before it came to that "height, but then it would have been "more lasting; for the adversary would "never have been able to have *erected a* "*monarchy* and destroyed their liberty so "soon."—This power, monarchical from its very nature, may have been dangerous to a commonwealth, and have ruined the republic by establishing a monarchy upon it; but it will be asked, How can this ever be the case in a regulated monarchy? Can it be supposed that any future King can ever wish to change that constitution in which his power is established? Can it be supposed that

† Lib. 26. § 2.

a free people could ever be so wild as to put themselves under an unbounded military power, in order to become independent of a limited and civil power? What may be the turn of future events, Heaven only knows; yet experience has taught us that former Kings have thus mistaken their real interest, and former people have been driven to this distraction: And if, on any such future occasion, there should be found established by repeated and continued custom, by unresisted precedents, the office of commander in chief of all North America, not only in the possession, but in the actual exercise of these powers:—*Exercitum parare—bellum gerere—coercere omnibus modis socios atque cives—* He might like another Monck, in such critical situation, give the turn to the balance, and negotiate, either with the prince, or the people, as his inclinations and interests lead him, for the liberties of Great Britain.— If in any future period of events the fate of war should reduce Great Britain to struggle for its rights, its power, perhaps, its safety, on terms hardly equal, with all its force, to its support in Europe: And in the course of that struggle, there be established in North America a commander in chief, with an army at his command; with a degree of authority presiding over the civil power, and civil governors; with an extent of command capable of affociating and uniting a number of powers, otherwife, incapable of fuch union; if fuch a man, at fuch a crifis, fhould have ambition enough to wifh, and fpirit enough to dare to fet up an independent empire in America, he could want, in fuch crifis, no fupport that a wife and artful enemy to Great Britain would not give him: *Nunc illud effe tempus occupandi res dum turbata omnia novâ atque inconditâ libertate effent, dum regis ftipendiis paftus obverfaretur miles, dum ab Annibale miffi duces affueti militibus juvare poffent incepta**. The enemy could not wifh better ground, than fuch an eftablifhment fo circumftanced at fuch a crifis, nor could take a more effectual meafure for the ruin of Great Britain, than fetting up and fupporting an American empire; for there could be no doubt of the fuccefs of the meafure, and no doubt of its effect.

The prefent government found already eftablifhed, from the neceffity of things in the ftate of the laft war, fuch a power—and as the effects of that war in America can not be faid wholly to ceafe, † while the Indian affairs wear fuch an hoftile appearance, this power is for the prefent continued: But we may confide in the true genuine principles of

* Liv. lib. 24. § 24.
† This is not the cafe now, 1768.

liberty,

liberty, which animate the royal breast; we may trust in the wisdom and prudence of the King's ministry,—that no such officer as that of a military commander in chief, presiding over all North America, and preceeding in military matters, and in the power *necessary to the execution of that command*, the constitutional power of governor; we may trust, * I venture to say, that no such office will ever be made an establishment *in time of peace*. Regular troops are in the same manner and degree necessary in North America, as in Britain or Ireland;—but we shall see them established there under the same relations to the civil power as in Ireland; we shall see again the civil governments, as established under commissions patent, and charters, predominate. If I, a private person, and wholly removed from all advice or consultation with ministry, might be permitted to indulge a conjecture, I would suppose, from some leading measures which are already taken, of dividing the American army into commanderies, and putting a stop to draughts on general contingencies, that the danger and expence of the office of commander in chief, will soon cease: and that the several commandants of the troops appointed, each to their respective districts, having every power necessary for the dis-

---

* I could venture to say so much when this was first written, and had grounds for what I said.

cipline and government of the regular forces under their command, will be established in the same relation and subordination to the civil power of that government, within which their command lies, as the commander in chief in Ireland stands to the supream civil power of Ireland :—and that as a commander in chief of those forces may in case of the commencement of hostilities, or of actual open war, be again necessary ;—if such necessity appears first here in Europe, his Majesty will immediately appoint such, and that if such necessity should appear first in America, there will be proper provision and regulations made for the giving effect to such necessary powers, *without leaving it to the judgment or will of the army to say when that is necessary, or what powers in such case, are necessary.*—The several governors of the colonies should have instructions, in case of such emergency, to meet, and in council to give effect to this command, with such powers as they shall judge necessary and safe to a General commanding in chief, until his Majesty's pleasure can be known ; that is to say, power of engaging in general expences, of ordering embargoes, of demanding vessels and carriages, of calling upon the several governments for their aid in troops, &c. of preparing an army, of taking possession of all posts, forts, and castles, (which in the

ordinary

ordinary courſe of the King's charters and commiſſions patent to his governors, muſt otherwiſe be under their commands—and cannot be taken from them, unleſs the charters of the government can be ſuperceded) of having the command and diſpoſal of all military ſtores—none of which powers ought to reſide in any one office, whoſe juriſdiction extends over all North America, and preceeds the civil power of governor—unleſs in ſuch caſe of neceſſity—unleſs confirmed (until his Majeſty's pleaſure can be known) by ſuch council, and under ſuch reſtrictions as the prudence of that council would ſee proper. Under ſuch an eſtabliſhment, every caſe of ſervice that could ariſe is provided for, and every caſe of danger that might ariſe from a predominant military power, is guarded againſt.

I muſt the rather ſuppoſe that the military eſtabliſhment will have that mode given to it; as already the commander in chief, as the commiſſion now ſtands, is inſtructed in " making any ſuch preparations as ſhall be neceſſary, and are not contained in his inſtructions, that he ſhall take the opinion and aſſiſtance of the governors."

A review and ſettlement of doubted points is no where more neceſſary, than in the maxims

maxims and rules of their law, and the state of their courts. It is a rule universally adopted through all the colonies, that they carried with them to America the common law of England, with the power of such part of the statutes (those concerning ecclesiastical jurisdiction excepted) as were in force at the time of their establishment; but, as there is no fundamental rule whereby to say, what statutes are admissible, and what not, if they admit all, they admit the full establishment of the ecclesiastical jurisdiction, from which they fled to this wilderness for refuge;—if they once make a distinction of admitting some, and rejecting others, who shall draw the line, and where shall it pass? Besides, as the common law itself is nothing but the practice and determination of courts on points of law, drawn into precedents; where the circumstances of a country and people, and their relation to the statutes and common law differ so greatly, the common law of these countries, must, in its natural course, become different, and sometimes even contrary, or at least incompatible, with the common law of England, so as that, in some cases, the determinations arising both from the statute and common law *must be rejected.* This renders the judicatories of these countries vague and precarious, dangerous, if not arbitrary: This leads necessarily (let what

care

care will be taken, in forming and enacting their provincial laws) this leads to the rendering the common law of the country different, incompatible with, if not contrary to, and independent of, the law of the mother country, than which nothing can be more difadvantageous to the fubject, and nothing more derogatory from the power of the government of the mother country, and from that fundamental maxim, that the colonifts fhall have no laws contrary to thofe of the mother country.

I cannot avoid quoting here at length, a very precife and juft obfervation of the author of the hiftory of New York. "The "ftate of our laws opens a door to much "controverfy. The uncertainty with re- "fpect to them, renders property precari- "ous, and greatly expofes us to the arbi- "trary decifion of bad judges. The com- "mon law of England is generally received, "together with fuch ftatutes as were enact- "ed before we had a legiflature of our own; "but our courts exercife a fovereign autho- "rity in determining, *what parts of the* "*common and ftatute law* ought to be ex- "tended; for it muft be admitted, that the "difference of circumftances neceffarily re- "quires us, in fome cafes, to *reject* the de- "termination of both. In many inftances,
"they

" they have also extended even acts of par-
" liament, passed since we have had a distinct
" legislation, which is greatly adding to our
" confusion. The practice of our courts is
" not less uncertain than the law. Some of
" the English rules are adopted, others re-
" jected. Two things therefore seem to be
" absolutely necessary for the public secu-
" rity.

" First, *The passing an act for settling the*
" *extent of the English laws.*

" *Secondly,* That the courts ordain a ge-
" neral set of rules for the regulation of the
" practice."

From this representation of things, by an eminent practitioner in those courts, it must be seen that something is wanting, to fix determinately the judicial powers.——But from a further review made by government here, it will be found that much more is wanting.—First, to determine (I do not at all take into consideration which way it be determined, only) I say, to determine some points on this head, which are, and will otherwise remain in dispute; but which ought by no means to be suffered one moment to remain in dispute.

The

The crown directs its governor to erect courts and appoint the judges thereto.---The actual appointment of the judges is no where *directly* disputed.---But the power of erecting courts, according to this instruction, is, I believe, universally disputed; it being a maxim universally maintained by the Colonists, that no court can be erected but by act of legislature.---Those who reason on the side of the crown,---say,---that the crown does not, by erecting courts in the colonies, claim any right of enacting the jurisdiction of those courts, or the laws whereby they are to act.——The crown names the judge, establishes the court, but the jurisdiction is settled by the laws of the realm;---and " * customs, precedents, and com-
" mon judicial proceedings of a court are a
" law to the court, and the determination
" of courts make points to be law."——The reasoning of the Colonists would certainly hold good against the erection of any new jurisdiction, established on powers not known to the laws of the realm; but how it can be applied to the opposing the establishment of courts, the laws of whose practice, jurisdiction and powers are already settled by the laws of the realm, *is the point in issue, and to be determined.* It will then be fixed, beyond dispute, whether the crown can, in

* Rep. 16. 4. Rep. 53. fol. 298.

its

its colonies, erect, without the concurrence of the legislature, courts of Chancery, Exchequer, King's Bench, Common Pleas, Admiralty, and Probate or Ecclesiastical courts.——If it should be determined in favour of the reasoning, and the claims of the Colonists,—I should apprehend that the consideration of the points under this head, would become an object of government here, even in its legislative capacity.——In which view it may be of consequence to consider, how far, and on what grounds, the rights of the crown are to be maintained by courts of King's Bench, &c. and how far the revenues by courts of Exchequer, and how far the crown and subject may have relief by courts of equity.——If in this view we consider the defects which must be found in Provincial courts, those point out the necessity of the establishment of a remedial general court of Appeal; but if we view the only mode of appeal, which at present exists, we shall see how inapplicable, how inadequate that court is. I cannot, in one view, better describe the defects of the provincial courts in these infant governments, than by that very description which my Lord Chief Justice Hales gives of our county courts, in the infancy of our own government, wherein he mentions,

" *First*,

"*First*, The ignorance of the judges, who were the freeholders of the county.

"*Secondly*, That these various courts bred variety of law, especially in the several counties, for the decisions or judgments being made by divers courts, and several independent judges and judicatories, who had no common interest amongst them in their several judicatories, thereby in process of time, every several county would have several laws, customs, rules, and forms of proceedings.——

"*Thirdly*, That all the business of any moment was carried by parties and factions, and those of great power and interest in the county did easily overbear others in their own causes, or in such wherein they were interested, either by relation of kindred, tenure, service, dependence, or application."

Upon the first article of this parallel, it will be no dishonour to many gentlemen sitting on the benches of the courts of law in the colonies, to say, that they are not, and cannot be expected to be lawyers, or learned in the law. And on the second article it is certain, that although it be a fundamental maxim of colony administration, that the colonies

colonies shall have no laws contrary to the laws of Great Britain, yet, from the fluctuation of resolutions, and confusion in the construction and practice of the law in the divers and several colonies, it is certain, that the practice of their courts, and their common law, must be not only different from each other, but in the consequence different also from that of Great Britain. In all the colonies the common law is received as the foundation and main body of their law; but each colony being vested with a legislative power, the common law is thereby continually altered; so that (as a great lawyer of the colonies has said) " by reason of the di-
" versity of the resolutions, in their respec-
" tive superior courts, and of the several
" new acts or laws made in them severally;
" the several systems of the laws of those
" colonies grow more and more variant,
" not only from one another, but also from
" the laws of England."

Under the third article, I fear experience can well say, how powerfully, even in courts, the influence of the leaders of party have been felt in matters between individuals. But in these popular governments, and where every executive officer is under a dependence for a temporary, wretched, and I had almost said, arbitrary support to the deputies of the people,

people,---it will be no injuftice to the frame of human nature, either in the perfon of the judges, of the juries, or even the popular lawyer to fuggeft, how little the crown, or the rights of government, when oppofed to the fpirit of democracy, or even to the paffions of the populace, has to expect of that fupport, maintainance, and guardianfhip, which the courts are even by the conftitution fuppofed to hold for the crown---Nor would it be any injuftice to any of the colonies, juft to remark in this place, how difficult, if ever practicable it is in any of their courts of common law to convict any perfon of a violation of the laws of trade, or in any matter of crown revenue. Some of our acts of parliament direct the profecution and punifhment of the breach of the laws of trade, to take its courfe in the courts of Vice-admiralty: And it has been thought by a very great practitioner, that if the laws of trade were regulated on a practicable application of them to the ftate of the colony trade, that every breach of them fhould be profecuted in the fame way. That there fhould be an advocate appointed to each court from Great Britain, who, having a proper falary independent of the people, fhould be directed and empowered to profecute in that court, not only every one who was an offender, but alfo every officer of the cuftoms, who

through

through neglect, collusion, oppression, or any other breach of his trust became such.— Here I own, was it not for the precedent already established by some of the laws of trade, I should doubt the consistency of this measure with the general principle of liberty, as established in the trials by a jury in the common law courts. If these precedents can reconcile these proceedings to the general principles of liberty, there can be no more effectual measure taken; yet such precedents should be extended with caution: The defect in most, and actual deficiency in many of the colonies, of a court of equity, does still more forcibly lead to the necessity of the measure of some remedial court of appeal and equity.——In all the King's governments so called,—the governor, or governor and council are the chancellor, or judges of the court of chancery.——But so long as I understand that the governor is, by his general instruction, upon sound principles of policy and justice, restrained from exercising the office of judge or justice in his own person, I own I always considered the governor, taking up the office of chancellor, as a case labouring with inexplicable difficulties. How unfit are governors in general for this high office of law; and how improper is it that governors should be judges, where perhaps the consequence of the judg-

ment

ment may involve government, and the administration thereof, in the contentions of parties. Indeed the fact is, that the general diffidence of the wisdom of this court thus constituted, the apprehension that reasons of government may mix in with the grounds of the judgment, has had an effect that the coming to this court is avoided as much as possible, so that it is almost in disuse, even where the establishment of it is allowed. But in the charter governments they have no chancery at all. I must again quote the opinion of a great lawyer in the colonies,—
" there is no court of chancery in the char-
" ter governments of New England," [and I
believe I may add also in Pensylvania] " nor
" any court vested with power to determine
" causes in equity, save only that the jus-
" tices of the inferior court, and the justices
" of the superior court respectively, have
" power to give relief on mortgages, bonds,
" and other penalties contained in deeds; in
" all other chancery and equitable matters,
" both the crown and the subject are with-
" out redress. This introduced a practice
" of petitioning the legislative courts for re-
" lief, and prompted those courts to inter-
" pose their authority. These petitions be-
" coming numerous, in order to give the
" greater dispatch to such business, the le-
" gislative courts transacted such business by
" orders

"orders or resolves, without the solemnity
"of passing acts for such purposes; and
"have further extended this power by re-
"solves and orders, beyond what a court of
"chancery ever attempted to decree, even
"to the suspending of public laws, which
"orders or resolves are not sent home for
"the royal assent. The tendency of these
"measures is too obvious to need any ob-
"servations thereon." Nor do I see how this measure of proceeding can be ventured upon in the colonies, or suffered to continue by the government here, if it be supposed that by 1 Hen. 4. 14. " it is accorded, and
" assented, that no appeal be from hence-
" forth made, or in any wise pursued in
" parliament in time to come." The general apprehension of these defects occasioned, that at the first planting of the colonies, the King in council here in England was established as a court of appeals from the provincial judicatories.——At the time of settling these colonies, there was no precedent of a judicatory besides those within the realm, except in the cases of Guernsey and Jersey, the remnants of the dutchy of Normandy, and not united within the realm: according to the custom of Normandy, appeals lay to the Duke in council; and upon this ground, appeals lay from the judicatories of these islands to the King here, as Duke in council; and upon

upon this general precedent (without perhaps attending to the peculiar case of the appeal, lying to the Duke of Normandy, and not to the King) was an appeal from the judicatories of the colonies to the King in council settled.——But, besides the inapplicableness of such appeal to the modes of the English law; besides, that this appeal does not actually take place in general, and is in some of the charter colonies actually excluded, except in personal actions, wherein the matter in difference exceeds 300 *l.* sterling;——besides the difficulty of this appeal, and inefficiency of this redress,—the King in council never being, by the constitution, in any other case, between subject and subject, formed as such a court of appeal. This body scarce ever, in the temporary and occasional sittings, looks like a court; but is rather accidentally or particularly, than officially attended.

These general apprehensions and reasonings, upon experience, have led many very knowing and dispassionate men in the colonies, into a conviction of *the necessity of some established and constitutional court of appeal* and redress: and the following measure has not only been suggested, but even taken up as matter of consideration by some of the ablest lawyers in that country;---namely, the

esta-

establishment of a supreme court of appeal and equity, not confined to any one government, but circuiting through a certain district of governments; perhaps as follows; one to Nova Scotia and New England; one to New York, New Jerseys, Pensylvania, and Maryland---one to Virginia, the Carolinas, and Georgia. It has been imagined, that this court should be established by a commission issued to two or more persons for each district, learned in the law, not only of the mother country, but of the several governments in its said district: that this commission should give full powers of a court of chancery, with power also of judging on matters of law, to be brought before this court, by writ of error, from the several superior courts of the district, which this extended to. Such court would become an established court of appeals and redress, would regulate all the courts of law, so that they could not exceed their jurisdiction; would have a general superintendency over all inferior courts; would tend to establish some regularity, and introduce a conformity, not only amongst the courts themselves, of the different colonies, but a conformity also to the courts of the mother country, in the construction and dispensation of law: such court would, more than any other measure, not only tend to preserve the laws, and practice of law in the colonies,

colonies, under a constitutional conformity to the laws of the mother country; but would also maintain that dependency therein, which is of the essence of colony administration.

There are gentlemen on this side the water, who seeing that this measure is not without defect, and not seeing the necessity of a court of chancery at all, as there is nothing contrary to the fundamentals of law, that these law-courts already established should equatize; (if I may so express myself)---think, that instead of establishing any new courts of chancery,---it would be very proper to abolish even those already established, extending the power which the law-courts already take in chancering bonds, *&c.*——by impowering them to equatize: and after that to take such measures as may best establish a fixt and constitutional court of appeals here in England.

Sensible of the danger of innovations, and abhorrent from tampering in experiments of politics, I mention the following rather as a matter of speculation, than to recommend the trial: yet I cannot but observe, that while the constitutions of the governments of the colonies take so exactly the model of the British constitution, it always struck me as a strange deviation in this one particular, that the governor's council of state, although a distinct, and I had almost said, an incompatible board,—with the council, one branch of the legislature, is yet always constituted of the same persons, in general nominated and liable to be suspended by the governor.——One may see many advantages, besides the general conformity to the government of the mother country, in having these boards distinct in their persons, as well as their office. If the council of state remaining under the same constitution as at present, was composed of men of the best experience, fortune, and interest in the colony, taken in common from the legislative council, the house of representatives, or the courts, while the members of the legislative council, independent of the governor for their existence, had all and only those powers which are necessary to a branch of the legislature, much weight would be added to administration in the confidence and extent of interest that it would thereby obtain; and to the legislature a more true and political distribution of power, which, instead of the false and artificial lead, now held up by expedients, would throw the real and constitutional balance of power into the hands of government.

There is a matter which at first or last will be found absolutely necessary to be done, and I would wish to recommend it at this time; that

that when the Lords of council shall take under consideration the general state of the administration of the King's delegated powers in America, they would order a general revision of the several powers granted by the several boards here in England, to the officers of different kinds, under their respective departments: If upon such revision they shall find that these powers are given and granted without any general concert, or any reference to that union which they ought to have, as parts of the one power centering in, and derived from the crown ; if they shall find that the several officers and offices in America, though all branches of the one united power of the crown, are by mischievous rivalship of departments, perpetually crossing and obstructing each other ; if they shall find them alternately labouring to depress and to depreciate that part of the crown's power, which does not fall within their own delegation; if they shall find that while the several powers of the crown are thus by parts impeached, and rendered contemptible in the eyes of the people, the whole cannot long remain with that authority which should be able to exert an equal and universal administration throughout the colonies: if this disconcerted delegation of powers, accompanied with this distraction in the exercise of them, should be found to lead to such con-

sequence,

sequence, it will be found, as I have repeatedly said elsewhere, " That it is a dangerous thing to have trusted so much of civil power out of the hands of the crown; and to have done so little to maintain those to whom it is intrusted." If this should be found to be the state of things, and there should arise a serious intention of putting the administration of the colonies on a practicable footing, their Lordships will advise, that these powers of the crown, delegated through the powers of the several boards and offices in England, shall be so granted as not to interfere with each other; so granted as not to serve the power or purposes of individuals, either board offices, or officers; but in such manner as shall unite, strengthen, and maintain the powers of the crown, in the true and constitutional establishment of them; and in such manner as shall render the administration of them in the colonies, uniform, equable, and universal, the common blessing and protection of the whole.

Having thus far examined into the principles of the constitutions of the colonies in that relation, by which they stood connected with the King, as Sovereign: and having reviewed those points of colony administration which derive from thence, marking, in the course of that review, such

matters

matters as seem to require the more immediate attention of government: I will proceed to examine those constitutions, in that relation, by which the colonies have become connected to the parliament, to the Empire, not only of the King, as Sovereign, but to the Empire of King, Lords, and Commons, *collectively taken*, as having the whole supream power in them, have become connected to the Realm. In whatever predicament the colonies may stand, as to their allegiance to the King, which must mark out the mode of administration, by which they should be governed; yet the precise settlement of this relation and connection, is what must decide and determine those points, which have come into dispute between the government of Great Britain, and the people of the colonies.

And first, how much soever the colonies, at their first migration, may be supposed to have been, or were in fact, without the Realm, and separated from it: Yet, from the very nature of that union of the community, by which all civil society must subsist, they could not have migrated, and been absolved of their communion and connection to the Realm, without leave or licence; they had such leave, according to the then forms of the constitution, and the terms were, that the society, community, or government which they should form, should neither act nor become any thing repugnant or contrary to the laws of the Mother Country. Here therefore is an express subordination to a certain degree—The Colonists allowed the subordination, but held their allegiance, as due only to their sovereign Lord the King.---The direct and necessary consequence of this subordination must be, that the legislature of England (afterward Great Britain) must have power to make laws which should be binding upon the Colonies; contrary or repugnant to which the Colonies could not act, either in their legislative, or executive capacity---contrary to which they could neither settle nor trade.

In the first attempts, indeed, which parliament made to exercise this power, in asserting the right which the people of the realm had, to the use of certain possessions in America, against the exclusive claim, which the King assumed in the property of it---They were told, that it was not proper for them to make laws about America, which was not yet annexed to the realm, but was of the King's foreign dominions, in the same manner, as Gascoigne or Normandy were, that they had no jurisdiction
over

over those dominions; and the attempt was dropt. In a second attempt, wherein they took up the petition of some settlers of Virginia, upon the Speaker's reading a letter from the King, the petition was withdrawn,——and we find no more of the parliament, as the constitutional legislature of the kingdom, interposing in these affairs until after the restoration.

In the year 1643, when the two Houses of Lords and Commons, had assumed the sovereign executive power of government, and were, in fact, the acting sovereign, they made an ordinance Nov. 2. * "Where-
" by Robert Earl of Warwick is made
" Governor in Chief, and Lord High-
" Admiral of those Islands and other plan-
" tations, inhabited, planted or belonging
" to any, his Majesty's the King of Eng-
" land's subjects, within the bounds, and
" upon the coasts of America." At which time, a † committee was appointed, for *regulating the Plantations*. The colonies indeed, by this ordinance, changed their Sovereign. But the sovereignty was exercised over them in the same manner, and

* Scobel's Acts, and Journals of the House of Commons, Nov. 2.
† Journals of the House of Commons, Nov. 2.

in the same spirit as the King had attempted to exercise it, by his commission of 1636, for regulating the Plantations.—That is the parliament, not as legislature, but as sovereign, assumed the same power of making laws, ordinances, &c. for the Plantations: nay, went one step further, in 1646, and charged them with a tax by excise. In 1650 this patent, or commission, was revoked, and the same power was lodged in the council of state, who had power ‡ " to grant commission or com-
" missions to such person or persons as they
" shall think fit, with power to enforce all
" such to obedience, as do or shall stand in
" opposition to the parliament, or their
" authority; and to grant pardons, and to
" settle governors in all, or any of the said
" islands, plantations and places, and to do
" all just things, and to use all lawful
" means to settle and preserve them in
" peace and safety, until the parliament
" shall take further, or other order therein,
" any letters patent, or other authority,
" formerly granted or given, to the con-
" trary notwithstanding."

During the administration of this so-

‡ Scobell's Acts.

vereignty,

vereignty, an * act passed in 1646, exempting the plantations from all customs, subsidies, taxation, imposition, or other duty, *except the excise: provided*, their trade was carried on in English bottoms, *otherwise*, they were made liable to all these duties. Also, in * 1650, when the Islands of Barbadoes, Bermudas, and Antego, and the country of Virginia, continuing to hold for the King, were considered as in rebellion; all commerce with them was prohibited. At which time also, in the same act, " all
" ships of foreign nations, were forbid and
" prohibited to come to, or trade in, or
" traffic with any of the English plantations
" in America, or any islands, ports, or
" places thereof, which are planted by, or
" in the possession of the people of this
" commonwealth, without licence first
" had or obtained from the parliament,
" or council of state."

If we consider the parliament acting here, as the sovereign, not the legislature, if we could look upon it as lawful, or de facto sovereign for the time being, yet we should

* Note, These acts or ordinances became the ground-work of that act of parliament, after the restoration, which was called the navigation act, of which we shall take notice, in its proper place.

certainly

certainly view every exertion of its power, in the same light, and should examine it by the same principles, as we did those of the King, as sovereign, exercised in the issuing his grants, charters, or commissions. And if we doubt whether the King, as lawful sovereign, could legally himself, exercise or commission other persons to exercise those powers, assumed in his commission of 1636, of making laws, ordinances and constitutions for the plantations; considering the inherent, natural and established rights of the colonists,—we may *à fortiori* by much more powerful objections, doubt the right of these powers in the two houses called then the parliament acting as sovereign.—No precedent therefore can be drawn from this period.—

We have seen above how at one time the King as sovereign, without the intervention of the parliament, assumed a right, both administrative and legislative, to govern the colonies.—We have seen how the parliament, without the intervention of the King's commission, assumed as sovereign the same powers. But whatever the natural or established rights and liberties of the colonies were, at their first migration, they could not be said, to be legally suspended, ed, abridged or altered by these assumptions of power.

Upon the restoration of the monarchy, when many of the rights of the subject, and of the constitution were settled, the constitution of the colonies, received their great alteration: the King participated the sovereignty of the colonies with the parliament, the parliament in its proper capacity, was admitted to a share in the government of them: The parliament then first, taking up the idea, indeed very naturally, from the power they had exercised during the commonwealth, that all these, his Majesty's foreign dominions, and " all these, " his Majesty's subjects," were of or belonging to the realm, then first, in the proper capacity of legislature, supreme legislature of the realm, interposed in the regulation and governing of the colonies.---And hence forward, from time to time, sundry acts of parliament were made, not only 1st, for regulating the trade of the colonies, but also 2dly, for ordering and limiting their internal rights, privileges and property, and even 3dly, for taxing them.---In the course of which events, while the Colonists considered this principle, that they were to be ruled and governed only by acts of parliament, together with their own laws, not contrary

contrary to the laws of England, as the palladium of their liberties, the King from time to time, by his ministers, called in the aid of parliament to enable him to regulate and govern the colonies.—The British merchants at times applied to parliament, on the affairs of the colonies, and even the West India Planters applied to the same power, to carry a measure against the continent of North America. Hence we find enacted,

I. The navigation act, the sugar and other acts for regulating and restraining the trade of the colonies.

II. Also Acts, 1. altering the nature of their estates, by treating real estates as chattels. 2. Restraining them from manufactures. 3. Regulating their money. 4. Altering the nature of evidence in the courts of common law, by making an affidavit of a debt before the Lord mayor in London, &c. certifyed in writing, an evidence in their courts in America. 5. Dissolving indentures, by discharging such of their servants as should enlist in the King's service.

III. Also Acts, fixing a tax upon American sailors, payable to the Greenwich Hospital.

pital. 2. Likewise imposing taxes, by the several duties payable on sundry goods, if intended as materials of trade, to be paid *within the province*, or colony, *before* they can be put on board, for exportation. 3. Also, the revenue arising from the *duties* payable on the postage of letters. 4. Also, the tax of quartering soldiers, and supplying them in their quarters. Lastly, establishing the claim which Great Britain makes, of taxing the colonies in all cases whatsoever, by enacting the claim into a declared right, by act of parliament.

From the uncontroverted, and universal idea of the subordination of the colonies to the government of the mother country, this power, by which the parliament maketh laws that shall be binding on the colonies, hath been constantly exerted by the government of England, (afterwards Great-Britain) and submitted to by the colonies. The fundamental maxim of the laws of those countries, is, that 1st, the common law of England, together with such statutes (the ecclesiastical laws and canons excepted) as were enacted before the colonies had a legislature of their own. 2dly, The laws made by their own legislature; together with 3dly, such acts of parliament, as by a special clause are extended to America, since that

that time, are the laws of each province or Colony. The jurisdiction and power of every court established in that country; the duty of every civil officer; the process of every transaction in law and business there, is regulated on this principle. Nay further, every * act of parliament passed since the establishment of the colonies, *which respects the general police of the realm, or the rights and liberties of the subjects of the realm*, although not extended by any special clause to America by parliament, although without the intervention, or express consent of their own respective legislatures or representatives, hath been considered, and I may venture to say, adopted as part of the law and constitution of those countries; but by what principle of our constitution, by what maxim of law, this last practice hath been established, is not so easy to ascertain, any more than it will be easy to fix any rule, when the colonies shall adopt, or when they may refuse those kind of laws of the mother country. This arises, as I have said, from some vague indecisive idea--- That the colonies are of, or some parts of, the realm; but how or what parts, or whether any parts at all, has never yet been thoroughly examined.—

* As the bill of rights, the 7th Wil. 3. &c.

We have seen what was, in reality, the dependance and subordination of the colonists to the King, while they were supposed to be subject to him in a seignoral capacity.——We have seen what must have been the same subordination, while they were supposed to be subject to the two houses of Lords and Commons, as sovereign in the same capacity.

Let us take up the next idea, that while they are not of the body of the realm, are no parts or parcel of the same, but bodies corporate and politick, distinct from and without the realm : * " They are nevertheless, and
" of right ought to be subordinate unto, and
" dependant upon the imperial crown of
" Great Britain ; [i. e. the realm,] and that
" the King's Majesty, by and with the ad-
" vice and consent of the Lords spiritual
" and temporal, and Commons of Great
" Britain assembled in parliament, had, hath,
" and of right ought to have full power
" and authority to make laws and statutes
" of sufficient force and validity, to bind
" the colonies and people of America, sub-
" jects of the crown of Great Britain, in all
" cases whatsoever."—In this idea we have a very different state of the relation, namely, the imperial crown of Great Britain, the

* 6 Geo. III. c. 12.

King,

King, Lords and Commons, collectively taken, is stated *as sovereign,* on the one hand, and *the Colonists as subjects* on the other.——

There is no doubt, but that in the nature, reason, justice and necessity of the thing, there must be somewhere, *within* the body politic of every government, an absolute power. The political freedom of Great Britain, consists in this power's being lodged no where but in King, Lords and Commons in parliament assembled. This power is absolute throughout the realm,—and yet the rights and liberties of the subject are preserved, as the *Communitas Populi* is the *body,* of which this *Imperium* is the soul, reasoning, willing, and acting, in absolute and intire union with it, so as to form one political person.

There can be no doubt but that this power is absolute throughout the dominions of the realm; yet in the exercise of this power, by the imperial crown of Great Britain, that is, by the King's Majesty, with the Lords and Commons in parliament assembled---towards the colonies, if they are not of this body of the realm, but are still to be considered as distinct bodies, foreign, or extraneous parts without the realm and the jurisdiction of this kingdom *.——There

* Blackstone, B. 1. c. 5.

is surely some attention due to the nature of this absoluteness in this case.

If the people of the colonies are no part of the people, or of the body, of the realm of Great Britain,---and if they are to be stated in the argument, as subject to the King, not as the head of that compound political person, of which they are in part the body, *sed ut caput alterius populi*, as wearing the imperial crown of Great Britain, as the head to which the realm of Great Britain is the body, and of which body the parliament is the soul, but of which the colonies are no part; then this imperial supreme magistrate, the collective power of King, Lords and Commons, may be stated as sovereign on the one hand, while the people of the colonies stand as subjects on the other.---

Taking the relation of the colonies to the mother country in this view, when the argument is stated in this manner, we surely may say with exactness and truth, that if the colonists, by birthright, by nature or by establishment, ever were entitled to all the rights, privileges, liberties and franchises of an Englishman, the absolute power of this sovereign must have some bounds; must from its own nature, from the very nature of these rights of its subjects, be limited in its extension and exercise.

(132)

Upon this state of the case, questions will necessarily arise; which I will not take upon me to decide, whether this sovereign can disfranchise subjects, so circumstanced, of their rights because they are settled beyond the territorial limits of the realm; whether these subjects, thus circumstanced can, because they are supposed not to be of the realm, lose that interest in the legislative power, which they would have had if they were of, or within the realm.——Whether this natural right which they have to personal liberty, and to political freedom is inherent in them " to all intents and pur- " poses, as tho' they had been born within " the realm:" Or whether " * it is to be " understood, with very many *and very* " *great restrictions.*" Whether these people, from the nature of these inherent rights and liberties, are intitled to have, and have a right to require a constitution of the same political liberty as that which they left; or whether ‡ " the whole of their constitutions " are liable to be new modelled and re- " formed,"---at the will of this sovereign. Whether the legislative part of their constitution is, they being distinct, altho' subordinate, dominions, and no part of the mother country, an inherent right of a body of Englishmen, so

* Blackstone, Introduction § 34.
‡ Ibid.

cir-

circumstanced, or whether it can be suspended, or taken away at the will of this sovereign. In stating these doubts I do not here add the question, which in time past hath been raised, on the right which this sovereign hath, or hath not, to impose taxes on these subjects, circumstanced as above stated, without the intervention of their own free will and grant.—Because, let these other questions be decided how soever they may, this stands upon quite other ground, and depends upon quite other principles.

So long as the government of the mother country claims a right to act under this idea, of the relation between the mother country and the colonies; so long as the colonies shall be esteemed in this relation, as " *no part of the mother country* ;" so long will the colonists think they have a right to raise these questions ; and that it is their duty to struggle in the cause, which is to decide them; and so long will there be faction and opposition instead of government and obedience.

But the matter of perplexity is much stronger, in the questions which have been raised, as to the right of imposing taxes on the subject, so stated.

In the same manner as in the act of granting a general pardon, the King alone is the originating and framing agent; while the other two branches of the legislature, are only consenting thereto, that it may be an act of parliament: so in the same manner in the act of granting supplies, by imposing taxes on the people, the house of commons is the sole originating and framing agent, " as to " the matter, measure and time;" while the King and lords act only as consentients, when it becomes an act of parliament. In one case the King acts as chief magistrate, representing and exercising the collective executive power of the whole realm: in the other, the commons act, as " granting for the counties, cities and " boroughs whom they represent *."

If in the act of taxing, the parliament acted simply in its capacity of supream legislature, *without any consideration had to the matter of representation* vesting in the commons, I know of no reason that can be assigned, why the resolve to give and grant should not originate from, and be framed or amended by another branch of the legislature as well as by the commons. The only reason that I find assigned, and the only one I venture to rely upon, for explaining that right of the commons to originate,

* Comm. Journ. 1672.

and

and form the resolve of giving and granting; and to settle the mode of charging, and imposing taxes on the people, to make good those grants; and to name commissioners, who shall actually levy and collect such taxes; " as a fundamental constitution," is that which the commons themselves have given, that " the commons grant for the " counties, cities and boroughs *whom they* " *represent*,"—and that the word " grant," when spoken of the lords, " must be un-" derstood only of the lords assent, to what " the commons grant; because the form of " law requires, that both join in one bill, to " give it the force of law."——Therefore, previously inserting this caution, that I do not presume to form an opinion, *how* they represent the property of, or grant for the lords; and without reasoning on *this mode* of the right: " for it is a very unsafe thing " in settled governments, to argue the rea-" son of the fundamental constitutions!" The fact is, that this right is ab initio, a fundamental constitution, in that the commons grant for the counties, cities and boroughs whom they represent; and that they do, in fact, represent the property of the realm; although copyholders, and even freeholders within the precincts of boroughs, or within the counties of cities, not being freemen or burgesses in such boroughs, have no vote in

the

the election of them:——For the property of the copyholder is represented by it's lord; and the property within the borough or city, is actually represented by the corporation or body of freemen in such borough or city, who chuse the member of parliament.

Although it should be willingly acknowledged without dispute, by the Americans, even upon this stating of the case, that the legislative power of parliament extends throughout America in all cases whatsoever; yet, as to the matter, measure and time, in the article of taxes, originating with, and framed by the commons; "granting for the counties, cities and boroughs whom they represent;" it would greatly relieve the perplexity and doubts, which have raised questions, much agitated, if any one could, according to this state of the case, and according to this reasoning, show how the commons do represent the property in America, when stated as being without the realm; and no part of any county, city or borough of the same: and how the freeholders of that property are represented, even as the copyholder and landholder within a borough or city is represented. For, so long as the case shall be so stated, that the Colonies are neither within the realm, nor any part of it; or of any county, city

or

or borough within the same; until it can be positively demonstrated, either that in granting supplies, by imposing taxes, the commons *do not act in virtue of their representing* the counties, cities and boroughs for whom they grant; or that in granting for the counties, cities and boroughs whom they represent, they do also represent the property of America; the people of America will distinguish their not acknowledging the power of the commons of Great Britain in the case of granting for them, as a very different case, from that under which they acknowledge their subordination to the legislative power of parliament.—Nay, further, every reason which the commons give for that fundamental right of granting supplies, and imposing taxes on the counties, cities and boroughs whom they represent; and every precedent which the commons alledge for the exercise of this right; the people of America will use, and alledge for and apply to their own special case, in a way that may be very perplexing, unsafe and dangerous to fundamental constitutions. But all this perplexity and danger arise from stating the Colonists as subjects of the realm, at the same time that the Colonies are stated as being no part of the realm, as no otherwise connected to it than by their subjection.

On

On the other hand, let us review the state of this matter as it seems actually to have stood. If the state of it which we shall represent, cannot and must not be supposed right in law; may we be permitted to state it, at least, as an hypothesis.

The Colonies, from their remote distance, and local circumstances, could not have been incorporated into any county, city or borough; at least so it is said: and yet, at the same time, they are supposed to be, and considered as, within the diocess of London. The Colonists were considered as having gone forth from, and having *quitted the realm*; as having settled on lands *without the realm*.

The Colonies thus remote and separate from the realm, were formed, and incorporated into distinct communities; were erected into provinces; had the jura regalia granted to them; were, in consequence thereof, to all intents and purposes, *counties palatine*, in like and as ample manner as the county palatine of Durham was, some matters of form excepted. They were dominions of the King of England; although, according to the language of those times, " not yet annexed to the crown." They were under the jurisdiction of the King,

upon

upon the principles of fœdal sovereignty: although considered " * *as out of the jurisdiction of the kingdom.*" The parliament itself doubting, at that time, whether it had jurisdiction to meddle with those matters, did not think proper to pass bills concerning America.——The Colonies had therefore legislatures peculiar to their own separate communities; subordinate to England, in that they could make no laws contrary to the laws of the mother country; but in all other matters and things, free uncontrouled and compleat legislatures, in conjunction with the King or his deputy as part thereof.

When the King, at the restoration, participated this sovereignty over *these his foreign dominions,* with the lords and commons, the Colonies became *in fact,* the dominions of the realm——became subjects of the kingdom.——They came, in fact, and by an actual constitutional exercise of power, under the authority and jurisdiction of parliament. They became connected and annexed to the state: By coming as parts of the British realm, not as a separate kingdom, (which is the case of Ireland) under subjection to the parliament, they became par-

* Blackstone, B. 1. c. 5.

ticipants

ticipants of the rights and liberties on which the power of parliament is founded. By the very act of extending the power of parliament over the Colonies, the rights and liberties of the realm must be also extended to them, for, from the nature of the British constitution, from the constitution of parliament itself, they, as parts, can be subject by no other mode, than by that in which parliament can exercise its sovereignty; for, the nature of the power, and the nature of the subjection must be reciprocal. They became therefore *annexed*, although perhaps *not yet united parts* of the realm. But to express all that I mean, in a proposition that can neither be misunderstood nor misinterpreted; they from that moment (whatever was their prior situation) stood related to the crown and to the realm literally and precisely in the same predicament, in which the county Palatine of Durham stood; that is, subject to be bound by acts of parliament in all cases whatsoever; and even " liable " to all rates, payments and subsidies granted " by parliament;" although the inhabitants of these countries, " have not hitherto had " the liberty and privilege of sending " knights and burgesses to parliament of " their own election." And, in the same manner also, because in that, the inhabitants of the county Palatine of Durham were liable

liable to all rates, payments and subsidies granted by parliament; and were therefore concerned, with others the inhabitants of this kingdom, to have knights and burgesses in parliament, *of their own election*; to represent the condition of their country, as the inhabitants of other countries had,——it was by act of parliament enacted, that they should have such: in the same manner, I say, whenever these colonies shall be considered in parliament, as objects of taxation, and be rendered liable to rates, payments and subsidies granted by parliament out of their property——they will become concerned equally with others the inhabitants of this kingdom, to have knights and burgesses in parliament, *of their own election*, to represent the condition of their country, as the inhabitants of other countries have,——and of right ought to have; although a right in parliament, to make laws for governing, and taxing the Colonies, may and must, *in the order of time*, precede any right in the Colonies, to a share in the legislature: yet there must arise and proceed pari passu, a right in the Colonies to claim, by petition, a share in the representation, by having knights and burgesses in parliament, of their own election; to represent the condition of their country. And as in such circumstances, this right shall arise on one hand,

so

so on the other, it may become a duty in government, to give them power to send such representatives to parliament; nay, could one even suppose the Colonies to be negligent in sending, or averse to send such representatives, it would, in such case, as above settled, become the duty of government to require it of them.

Although from the spirit and essence of our constitution, as well as the actual laws of it, " the whole body of the realm, and " every particular member thereof, either " in person, or by representation, (upon " their own free election) are, by the laws " of the realm, deemed to be present in the " high court of parliament †." Yet as the circumstances of the several members of this body politic must be often changing; as many acquisitions and improvements, by trade, manufactures and Colonies, must make great changes in the natural form of this body; and as it is impossible, both from the gradual nature of these changes, and from the mode of the representative body, that this representative body can, in every instance and moment, follow the changes of the natural passibus æquis; it must necessarily at times, from the nature

† 1 Jacobi I.

of

of things, *not be an actual representative.*—
Although, from the nature of the constitution of government, it must, in the interim, continue to be a just and *constitutional representative.* And hence, from the laws of nature, as well as from the nature of our own laws and constitution, arises the justice and right, which parliament always hath had to render several members of the realm liable to rates, payments and subsidies, granted by parliament; although such members have not, as yet, had the liberty and privilege to send knights and burgesses to parliament, of their own election. Yet on the other hand, as the principle, that no free people ought to be taxed, but by their own consent, freely originating from, and given by themselves or their representatives, is invariable, absolute and fixed in truth and right, so the mode of the representation in parliament, hath from time to time, altered, so as to extend to, and to suit the mode, under which the represented were, from time to time, found to exist. Hence it was, that many towns, boroughs, counties, and even dominions, which from any thing that did exist, or was to be found in their antiquas libertates, and liberas consuetudines, were not previously represented by members of parliament of their own election; have, as they acceded to the realm, or encreased

within

within the realm, so as to be equally concerned, to have knights, and burgesses in parliament of their own election, to represent them equally as other inhabitants of the realm have, according to such modes as were at the time admitted to be legal and constitutional, been called to a share in the common-council of the realm. Hence it was that the county Palatine of Durham, after many tryals, and a long struggle, was admitted to the privilege of sending knights and burgesses to parliament;—but of this case enough has already been said.

In the time of King Henry VIII, we find parliament *reasoning and acting* upon this very principle in the case of the county of Chester. —The *reasoning of parliament* sets forth †, " that the King's county Palatine of Ches-
" ter, had hitherto been excluded out of
" his high court of parliament, to have any
" knights within the said court.—By rea-
" son whereof, the inhabitants had sus-
" tained manifold disherisons, losses and da-
" mages, as well in their lands, goods and
" bodies, as in the good, civil and politic
" government of their said county.——
" That forasmuch as they have alway hi-
" therto *been bound by the acts and statutes,*

† 34 and 35 of Henry 8.

" made

" made and ordained by the King, by au-
" thority of the said court, as far forth as
" other counties who had knights and bur-
" gesses in parliament;——and yet had nei-
" ther knights nor burgesses:—The inhabi-
" tants for lack thereof have been often times
" grieved with acts and statutes, made within
" the said court derogatory to their ancient
" privileges and liberties, and prejudicial to
" the common-wealth, quietness, rest and
" peace of the King's bounden subjects in-
" habiting within the same. For remedy
" whereof, the parliament *acts*—and it is
" enacted, that the county of Chester
" should have two knights, and the city
" two burgesses, which knights and bur-
" gesses are to have the *like voice and autho-
" rity*, to all intents and purposes,——the
" like liberties, advantages, dignities, pri-
" vileges, &c. with other knights and bur-
" gesses."

Hear also, *the reasoning*, and view the *acts* of parliament, in the case of the acquisition of the dominions of Wales*, subject to the imperial crown of, although not yet incorporated or annexed to, the realm.——The reasoning sets forth, that Wales ever had been united and subject to the imperial

* 27th of Hen. 8. cap. 6.

crown of the realm, and to the King, *its very Head, Lord and Ruler*.——That the principality and *dominions* had rights, laws and customs, different from the laws, &c. of *this realm*.

That the people of *that dominion* had a speech different from the tongue used in *this realm*.

——Thence some *ignorant people made a distinction* between the King's *subjects of the realm*, and *his subjects of the principality*.— His Highness, therefore, out of love to his subjects of the principality, and to bring *his subjects of the realm* and *his subjects of the principality* to *concord and unity*, by advice of Lords and Commons, and by authority of the same hath enacted, that henceforth and for ever, his said *country and dominion of Wales*, shall be incorporated, united and annexed to *this realm of England*; and that all, singular person and persons, born, and to be born in the said principality of Wales, shall have, and enjoy all the same freedoms, liberties, rights, privileges and laws within this his realm, and *other* the King's dominions, as other the King's subjects, naturally born within the same, have, enjoy and inherit; and that knights and burgesses shall be elected, and sent to represent them in parliament, with all the like dignity, pre-eminence and privilege as other knights and burgesses of the parliament have and be allowed.

We also find, upon the acquisition of Calais to the King's dominions, that King Edward turned all the French inhabitants out of it; planted *an English Colony there*, with all the rights, freedom, privileges, &c. of natural born subjects within the realm, and that *this Colony sent burgesses* to parliament.

Seeing then how exactly, and to the minutest circumstance, similar the case of the *Colonies erected into provinces*, is to these counties Palatine, to those acquired and annexed dominions; can the statesman, whether in administration or in parliament, reason or act towards the Colonies in any other mode, or by any other acts, than what the foregoing give the wisest and happiest examples of?

It is a first and self-evident truth, without which all reasoning on political liberty is *certâ ratione insanire*. That a free people cannot have their property, or any part of it, given and granted away in aids and subsidies, but by their own consent; signified by themselves

selves or their legal reprefentatives. It is alfo (as hath been marked before) an undoubted principle and law of our conftitution, that the whole body of the realm, and every particular member thereof, either in perfon, or by reprefentation, (upon their own free elections) are deemed to be perfonally prefent in the high court of parliament: And, that the King, Lords and Commons affembled in parliament, are the commune concilium, the common-council of the realm;——the legal and conftitutional reprefentative of the whole body of the realm, and of every particular member thereof: having perfect right, and full power and authority to make laws and ftatutes of fufficient force and validity to bind the Colonies and people of America, fubjects of the crown, in all cafes whatfoever.——But as various external acquifitions and dominions, may accede to this body, ftill remaining without the realm, out of its jurifdiction; not yet annexed, united and incorporated with the realm:—As various and divers new interefted individuals, may arife and increafe within the realm; which, although *conftitutionally reprefented* in parliament, cannot be faid to have there *actually* reprefentatives of their own free election.— Let us look and fee how government, to be

con-

confistent with itself and its own principles, hath acted in such cases.

Parliament hath never ceased to be deemed the constitutional representative of the whole dominions of the realm: Hath never ceased to act as the commune concilium, both in the case of making laws, which did bind these subjects under this predicament; as also, in the case de auxilio assidendo; and render'd them liable to all rates, payments and subsidies granted by parliament: Yet on the other hand, parliament (these subjects being equally concerned to have representatives in parliament, of their own election, equally as other inhabitants of the realm) hath always given them power to send such; as they have arisen to an importance and a share of interest in the state, which could justify the measure. On this principle, and by this proceeding, has the number of representatives in parliament, increased from between two and three hundred, to above five hundred.

In other cases, as in the case of the American Colonies, where these acquisitions in partibus exteris, have been deemed so far separate from the kingdom; so remote from the realm, and the jurisdiction thereof; that they could not have been incorporated into any county, city or borough within the realm; that the state and condition of their country could scarcely be said to be within the actual cognizance of parliament: Where the local internal circumstances of their property could scarce fall within the ways and means adopted by parliament for taxes;—where the peculiar nature of their establishment required the constant and immediate presence of some power to make orders, ordinances and laws for the preservation and well government of those countries: There government hath constantly and uniformly established and admitted the governor, council and representatives of the freeholders of the country assembled, to be a full and perfect legislature, for the making laws and imposing taxes in all cases whatsoever, arising within, and respecting the body of that community;—full and perfect within itself, to all the purposes of free debate, free will, and freedom of enacting;——although subordinate to the government of the mother, as being bound by its laws, and not capable to act, or to become any thing contrary or repugnant to it. Although parliament hath, in some cases, as before recited, imposed taxes, arising from customs and duties, paid by the trade and intercourse of the inhabitants of the Colonies: Yet, from the first moment that they have been considered as

capable

capable of paying a certain quota to the extraordinary services of government, and as being in circumstances proper to be required so to do;———government fixed the mode, and hath hitherto invariably continued in the same, of doing this by requisition from the crown, to be laid before the assembly by his Majesty's commissioner the governor.—

If it be the spirit and sense of government, to consider these Colonies still as thus separate unannexed parts; as incapable, from their local circumstances, of having representatives of their own election, in the British parliament;—the same sense and spirit will, I suppose, continue to the Colonies this liberty*; " which, through a tender-
" ness in the legislature of Great Britain, to
" the rights and privileges of the subjects
" in the Colonies, they have hitherto al-
" way enjoyed; the liberty of judging, by
" their representatives, both of the way and
" manner in which internal taxes should be
" raised within the respective governments,
" and of the ability of the inhabitants to pay
" them:" will think it wise, if not just also, from its having become, I had almost said, a constitutional mode of administration,

* Petition of the general assembly of the Massachusett's-bay.

through the establishment and invaried continuance of the precedent, to raise the Provincial quota of taxes, by making, in each case, a requisition to the assemblies, to grant subsidies, adequate to the service of government, and in proportion to the circumstances of the Colony or province which they represent.

This is the alternative, either to follow the sober temper and prudence of this established mode, or to adopt the wisdom, justice and policy of the reasoning and acts of parliament, in the cases of Chester, Wales and Durham. There is no other practicable or rational measure.

If these external circumstances of our American dominions, and the internal circumstances of our police and parties, lead administration to this measure, of continuing to derive aids and subsidies from the Colonies by the establishment of general assemblies of the states in each Colony, upon the precise model of the parliament in the mother country: It may be very well justified by example, and from precedent, in the government of the Roman Colonies.

Although the Romans governed their provinces by an absolute imperium, which superceded all civil government, properly so called;

called; yet the inhabitants of their *Colonies* were, in their civil conſtitution *, divided into Senate and People, exactly according to the conſtitution of the city itſelf: And conform exactly to the model of the ſovereign ſenate. As the order of the patres conſcripti were the conſtituents of that body,—ſo the order of the decuriones, the tenth part from amongſt the people were, for the purpoſe of forming a like council, enrolled by the triumvirs whom the Roman ſtate had created, to lead out Colonies either of Citizens or Latins.—By this eſtabliſhment, a ſenate, for this council is literally ſo called in the Pompeian law de Bithynis, was formed in every Colony—and latterly, in every municipal corporation alſo.—

As the ordinary ſupply of the ſenate in the city, was from the annual election of magi-

---

* Conſtituendum eſt ad urbis inſtar, in Coloniis Plebem a Patribus diſcriminatum; & ad exemplum Senatus ampliſſimi ordinis, decurionum ordinem (quem et Senatum dictum in Pompeia lege de Bithyniis Plinius ſcribit) in civitatibus orbis Romani ex decima parte Colonorum, concilii publici gratiâ, conſcribi ſolitum fuiſſe a triumviris quos S P Q R creabat ad Colonias aut latinorum aut civium ducendas; cumque in Coloniis veluti in ſpeculo effigies Repub. Rom. cerneretur ſimulachrum quoddam Senatûs in illis, & demum in municipiis ex decurionum ordine fuit.

Marcus Vetranius Maurus de jure liberorum. Cap. 8.

ſtrates,

ſtrates, who, in conſequence of their having been inveſted with ſuch magiſtracy, acquired a ſeat there; as the extraordinary ſupply of ſenators, was by Kings, Conſuls, Cenſors, or Dictators (according to the different times and periods of the Roman government) propoſing good and true citizens to the people,—of whom thoſe, who were approved, were enrolled Conſcripti, Senatores, juſſu populi: So the ordinary ſupply of the members of this Colony ſenate or curia was from the decuriones, the magiſtracy of that community,—while the extraordinary ſupply was by the triumvirs enrolling, in like manner, the ſenator at the firſt eſtabliſhment, or the ‡ governors, upon extraordinary caſes, which might afterwards ariſe,——propoſing honeſt and honourable men, from whom the people choſe thoſe who were enrolled.—Both council and reſult were left to the community.——The council in the ſenate, the reſult in the people;—who made, and were governed by their own laws, ſubordinate to the laws of the empire; who created, and were governed by their own magiſtrates.—

When this iſland was itſelf, in a provincial ſtate, under the empire of Rome, ſeve-

‡ Vide Plinii Epiſt. et Trajani Reſp. lib. x. Epis. 80 and 81.

ral

ral Colonies and municipal districts within the same, were happy under this very constitution of being governed by a representative, magistracy, and legislature,—which the British Colonies now contend for. The manuscript of Richard of Cirencester, lately discovered, tells us which they were.—— The Colonies were, London, Colchester, Sandwich with Richborough, Bath, Caërleon in Wales, West Chester, Gloucester, Lincoln and Chesterford. The municipal districts, York and St. Albans. To which perhaps we may add, from the same list, as Civitates, Latio jure donatæ, Old Sarum, Cirencester, Carlisle, Burton north of Lancaster, Caster by Peterborough, Alkmanbury and Catteric in Yorkshire, Perth, Dunbritton and Inverness.

If this mode of administration for the Colonies be adopted by government, especially in the article of taxation—It will behove administration, to be thoroughly informed of, and acquainted with the circumstances of the Colonies, as to the quota or share of the taxes which they are capable to bear, and ought to raise, not only in proportion to those raised by the mother country, but amongst themselves: It will become the duty of ministry, to endeavour to persuade the Colonies to establish, *as far as their circumstances will*

will admit of it, the same mode of taxation, by stamp duties, excises and land tax, as is used in this country:—That the property and manufactures of the Colonies may not, by an exemption from these, have a preference and advantage over the property and manufactures of the mother country. It will require all the wisdom and interest, all the firmness and address, of a thoroughly established ministry, to carry these points:—As the Colonies, no doubt, will keep off such incumbrances as long as they can; and as the assemblies of the Colonies, will, under this constitution, reasonably argue, that as to the matter, extent, mode and time of taxes, they, the representative of the people for whom they grant, are the only proper and constitutional judges.

Government ought at all times to know the numbers of the inhabitants, distinguishing the number of the rateable polls.

2. The number of acres in each province or Colony, both cultivated and lyeing in waste.——The number of houses—and farms, &c.

3. The numbers and quantity of every other article of rateable property, according to the method used by the provinces themselves, in rateing estates, real and personal.

4. Go-

4. Government ought alway to know what the annual amount of the several province taxes are, and by what rates they are raised, and by what estimate these rates are laid.

From whence, by comparing the estimation with the real value, for the time being, of each article, they may alway collect nearly the real value of the property of such province or Colony. All which, compared with the prices of labour, provisions and European goods imported, with the value of their manufactures, the interest of money, and their exports, will fully and precisely mark their abilities to bear, and the proportion which they should bear, of taxes, amongst one another, and with the mother country.

The following estimates of the provinces, Massachusett's-Bay to the northward, of South-Carolina to the southward, and of New Jersey in the center, are founded in the tax-lists of each province; which tax-lists, being of * ten years standing, must, in encreasing countries as the Colonies are, fall short of the numbers and quantity which

* That is ten years back from the time of the publication of the first edition of this book.

would

would be found on any tax-lift faithfully made out at this time. The estimates which I have made thereon are in general at such an under-valuation, that I should think no man of candour in the provinces will object to them; although they be, in some articles, higher than the valuation which the legislatures directed so long ago to be made, as the fund of the taxes that they order to be levied on them. This valuation of the estates, real and personal, gives the gross amount of the principal of the rateable property in the province. I think I may venture to affirm, that no man, who would be thought to understand the estimation of things, will object that I over-rate the produce of this property, when I rate it at six *per cent.* only of this moderate valuation; when he considers that money, in none of those provinces, bears less than six *per cent.* interest; and that under loans of money, at five *per cent.* most of the best improvements of the country have been made.

The valuation of the provinces, New-York and Pensylvania, lying on each side of New-Jersey, are calculated in a different manner, by taking a medium between the supposed real value and the very lowest rate of valuation. Without troubling the reader, or encumbering the printer with the detail
of

of these tax-lists, and the calculations made thereon, I will insert only the result of them, as follows.

The provinces under-mentioned could annually raise, by one shilling in the pound on the produce of the rateable property, estates real and personal in each province:

	£.	s.	d.
Province Massachusett's-Bay,	13172	7	11
New-York, - -	8000	0	0
New-Jersey, - -	5289	17	0
Pensylvania, - -	15761	10	0
South-Carolina, -	6971	1	11
Sterling, £.	49395	16	10

Suppose now the rest of the colonies to be no more than able to double this sum:

The sum-total that the colonies will be able to raise, according to their old tax-lists, and their own mode of valuation and of rating the produce of estates, real and personal, will be, at one shilling in the pound on the produce, *per annum.* - - } 98791 13 8

In juftice to the reft of the provinces, particularized above, I ought to obferve that, by the equalleft judgment which I can form, I think that the province of South-Carolina is the moft under-rated.

I fhould alfo point out to the American reader, that, as the calculations and lifts above referred to, are taken from the private collections of the writer of thefe papers, without any official communication of fuch papers as miniftry may be poffeffed of, I defire him to give no other credit to them, than fuch as, by referring to his own knowledge of the ftate of things in the Colonies, he finds to be juft and near the truth. I fhould, on the other hand, inform the Englifh reader, that thefe were collected on the fpot, and communicated by perfons leading, and thoroughly converfant in the bufinefs of their refpective provinces.

Another remark is neceffary, That, except what relates to Penfylvania, thefe collections were made nine years ago; fo that, wherever any difference may arife, from the different proportion in which thefe provinces have encreafed, that ought to be carried to account; at the fame time, that a certain addition may be made to the whole from the certain encreafe of all of them.

If

If this moderate tax, raised by the above moderate valuation, be compared with the internal annual charge of government in the respective provinces, that charge will be found much below the supplies of this fund. The whole charge of the ordinary expence of government in the province of Massachusett's-Bay, which does, by much, more to the support of government, and other public services than any other province, is, in time of peace, sterling 12937 *l.* 10 *s.* whereas that of New-York is not more than about, sterling, 4000 *l.* annually.

When these points shall be settled, there cannot be a doubt but that the same zealous attention, which all parties see and confess to be applied in the administration of the British department to the public revenue, will be applied to the establishing and reforming that of America.

A proper knowledge of, and real attention to, the Crown's quit-rents in America, by revising the *original defects*, by remedying the almost insurmountable difficulties that the due collection of them is attended with, may render that branch a real and effective revenue, which at the same time will be found to be no inconsiderable one.

M   By

By proper regulations for securing the Crown's rights in waifs and wrecks, in fines and forfeitures, and by proper appropriations of the same, that branch of revenue may be made effective: But, whenever it is taken up in earnest, whenever it shall be resolved upon to give a real official regard to the revenue in America, the office of *Auditor General of the Plantations* must cease to be a mere sinecure benefice, and be really and effectively established with such powers as will carry the duty of it into execution, yet under such cautions and restrictions as shall secure the benefit of its service to the use of the crown.

If it should be thought difficult and hazardous, to extend the legislative rights, privileges and preeminences, the true Imperium of government, to wheresoever the dominions of the state extend,—the administration must be content to go on in this ptolomaïc system of policy,—as long as the various centers and systems shall preserve their due order and subordination: Or to speak in a more apposite idea ;—if we would keep the basis of this realm confined to this island, while we extend the superstructure, by extending our dominions: We shall invert the pyramid (as Sir William Temple expresses it) and must in time subvert the

the government itself. If we chuse to follow the example of the Romans, we must expect to follow their fate.

Would statesmen, on the other hand, doubt for a while, the predetermined modes which artificial systems prescribe; would they dare to look for truth in the nature of things; they would soon adopt what is right, as founded upon fact.——They would be naturally led into the true system of government, by following *with the powers of the state,* where the actual and *real powers of the system of things* lead to. They would see, that by the various and mutual interconnections of the different parts of the British dominions, throughout the Atlantic, and in America; by the intercommunion and reciprocation of their alternate wants and supplies; by the combination and subordination of their several interests and powers; by the circulation of their commerce, revolving in an orbit which hath Great Britain for its center: That there does exist, in fact, in nature, a real union and incorporation of all these parts of the British dominions, *an actual system of dominion;* which wants only to be avowed and actuated by the real spirit in which it moves and has its being: By that spirit, which is the genuine spirit of the British constitution: By that spirit from which the British government hath arisen to what it is: By the spirit of extending the basis of its representative legislature, through all the parts to wheresoever the rights, interest or power of its dominions extend; so as to form (I cannot too often inculcate the idea) A GRAND MARINE DOMINION, CONSISTING OF OUR POSSESSIONS IN THE ATLANTIC, AND IN AMERICA, UNITED INTO A ONE EMPIRE, IN A ONE CENTER, WHERE THE SEAT OF GOVERNMENT IS.

This measure has been, and I dare say will be generally treated as impracticable and visionary *. I wish those declarations of power, with which we mock ourselves, may not be found the more dangerous delusion. Such is the actual state of the really existing system of our dominions; that neither the power of government, over these various parts, can long continue under the present mode of administration; nor the great interest of commerce extended thro'-out the whole, long subsist under the present system of the laws of trade: Power,

* On repealing the stamp-act, an act pass'd, declaring the power of parliament to bind these Colonies in all cases whatsoever: This, however, was only planting a barren tree, that cast a *shade* indeed over the Colonies, but yielded *no fruit*. Pensylvania Farmer's Letters, Letter 10th.

when ufed towards them, becoming felf-deftructive, will only haften the general ruin.

To this meafure, not only the Briton but the American alfo *now* objects, that it is unneceffary, inexpedient and dangerous: But let us confider their feveral objections.

The Briton fays that fuch meafure is unneceffary, becaufe the power of parliament extends to all cafes and purpofes required.—Be it allowed, that this power does, in right and theory, thus extend: Yet furely the reafoning, the precedents, the Examples, and the practice of adminiftrations do fhow, that fomething more is neceffary in this cafe.

The American fays it is unneceffary, becaufe they have legiflatures of their own, which anfwer all their purpofes.———But each Colony having rights, duties, actions, relations, which extend beyond the bounds and jurifdiction of their refpective communities; beyond the power of their refpective governments: The colonial legiflature does certainly not anfwer all purpofes; is incompetent and inadequate to many purpofes: Something therefore more is neceffary, *either a common union amongst themfelves;* or a one common union of fubordination, under the one general legiflature of the ftate.

The Briton says that it would be inexpedient to participate with, and communicate to the Colonists, the rights and privileges of a subject living and holding his property within the realm; to give these rights to people living out of the realm, and remote from it, whose interests are rival and contrary, both in trade and dominion, to those of this realm. But the scheme of giving representatives to the Colonies, annexes them to, and incorporates them with the realm. Their interest is contrary to that of Great Britain, only so long as they are continued in the *unnatural artificial* state of being considered *as external provinces*; and they can become rivals only by continuing to increase in this separate state: But their being united to the realm, is the very remedy proposed.

The American says, that this measure is inexpedient; because, if the Colonies be united to the realm; and have participation in the legislature, and communication of the rights and privileges of a subject within the realm: They must be associated in the burden of the taxes, and so pay a share of the interest and principal of the national debts, which they have no concern in.——This is literally the objection which was made by the Scots, at the proposal of the union of the two kingdoms; and came indeed with

reason

reason and propriety, from an independent sovereign kingdom, which had no concern in the debts of England. But the like objection can never be made with propriety, reason or justice, by Colonies and provinces which are constituent parts of a trading nation, protected by the British marine. Much less can it be said, that they have no concern in these debts, when they are debts contracted, by wars entered into, the first for the preservation of the protestant interest and independency of the sovereignty of the mother country; the two latter, solely in defence, and for the protection of the trade and actual existence of the Colonies. However, if the Colonies could, on any reasonable grounds of equity or policy, show any inequality, or even inexpediency in their paying any part of the taxes, which have a retrospect to times, before they were admitted to a share in the legislature.—There is no doubt but that the same moderation and justice which the kingdom of England showed towards Scotland, in giving that *an equivalent*, would be extended to the Colonies, by the kingdom of Great Britain. And I cannot but think, that it would not be more than such equivalent, that the government should grant them a sum of money sufficient to pay off all their debts, which were contracted, in consequence of the laſt war, and were ſtill out-ſtanding; unleſs Great Britain engaged from henceforth to conſider theſe as the debts of the ſtate in general. I cannot but think that it would not be more than ſuch equivalent, that the crown ſhould give up all its right to quit rents; and that every act, whereby any ſpecial revenue was raiſed upon the Colonies, ſhould be repealed.

The Briton ſays, that this meaſure would be *dangerous*; as it might prove a leading ſtep, to the finally removing of the ſeat of Empire to America.——To which the true anſwer is, that the removing of the Seat of the Empire to America or not, depends on the progreſſive encreaſe of the territories, trade and power of the American Colonies; if continued in the ſame unnatural ſeparate rival and dangerous ſtate, in which they are at preſent.—That this is an event not to be avoided.—But this meaſure of uniting the Colonies to the realm, and of fixing the legiſlature here in Britain, is the only policy that can obviate and prevent this removal. For, by concentring the intereſt and power of the ſeveral parts in this iſland, the Empire muſt be fixed here alſo.—But if this removal cannot finally be prevented,—is it better that a new Empire ſhould ariſe in America, on the ruins of Great Britain; or that

that the regalia of the British Empire extending to America, should be removed only to some other part of the dominions, continuing however in the same realm?

The American says, that this measure might be dangerous to their liberties; as this calling the American representatives to a parliament, sitting in Great Britain, would remove their representatives at too great a distance from their constituents, for too long a time; and consequently from that communication and influence, which their constituents should have with them; and therefore transfer the will of the Colonies out of their own power, involving it, at the same time, in a majority, against which their proportion of representatives would hold no ballance. This objection, if it hath any ground for its fears, is a direct answer to the British objection last mentioned:—But it proves too much; as, according to this argument, no remote parts of a state ought to send representatives, as the seat of Empire is also remote; the truth and fact is, that the mutual situation of Great Britain and America, very well allows every communication, which a member of parliament ought to have with his constituents; and any influence beyond that, is unparliamentary and unconstitutional.

As

As to all objections which arife from apprehenfions of what effect fuch an additional number of members, acceding all at once to the Houfe of Commons, might have on the politics, conduct and internal management of that body.—They arife from an unwarranted and (one fhould hope) groundlefs fufpicion of fome undue influence operating there.—But fhould this be a fuppofition, that could ever be admitted to be true, even amongft the fœces Romuli; the contrary apprehenfions, from the different quarters, are fuch as mutually deftroy each other.—The Americans fear, that the number of reprefentatives which will be allowed to them, will have no power proportionable to their fhare of intereft in the community. That this union to the Britifh legiflature, will only involve them in the conclufions of a majority, which will thence claim a right to tax them, and to reftrain their trade, manufactures and fettlements as they pleafe. The Briton fears, that thefe reprefentatives may be an united phalanx, firmly oppofing every tax propofed to be laid upon the Colonies; and every regulation meant to keep their actions and intereft in due fubordination to the whole.——That they will be a party, a faction, a flying fquadron, alway ready, and in moft cafes capable, by uniting with oppofition to adminiftration, or with
com-

commercical factions, to distress government and the landed interest of the kingdom. The Americans again on the other hand, fear that some future British ministry, in some future days of corruption, will succeed in bribing their representatives, against which the Colonies will have no remedy, but must submit to the betraying consequences.—— These are objections which, on the very supposition, mutually counteract and destroy one another.—They are objections which have had fair trial upon experience, in the case of the Scots members,—and are directly contradicted by truth and fact.

As to all objections raised on the supposed impracticability of the measure; they are too contemptible to deserve an answer.—There is but one which hath any sense in it,—it is said, that the Colonies are too remote, upon a dissolution, to receive the writs and return their representatives within the time limited by law; and that, if the parliament should be assembled immediately on its election, the Colonies could not have their representatives in the house for some time. The portion of time limited by law, is fixed in proportion to the distance of the remotest parts concerned at present, to send members to parliament. A special time might be be fixed by law, in proportion to the special case of the distance of the Colonies. And as to their having their representatives in a new parliament, upon its being assembled immediately; in the same manner, as upon the demise of the King, the parliament, then sitting, is by law, to continue six months, unless dissolved by the successor: so the old representatives of the Colonies, might by law, be permitted to sit in the new parliament, if assembled within six months; until they were reelected or others sent in their room; the doing of which, might be limited to six months.

Notwithstanding, I know that this proposal will be considered as utopian, visionary, idle, impertinent and what not:—I will proceed to consider the justice and policy of this measure, of this invariable truth, this unavoidable consequence; that in the course and procedure of our government, there must arise a duty in government to give, a right in the Colonies to claim, a share in the legislature of Great Britain.

While we consider the realm, the government of Great Britain, as the *Sovereign*, and the Colonies as the subject, without full participation in the constitution; without participation in the legislature; bound implicitly

citly to obey the orders of government; and implicitly to *enact or register* as an act of their own, those grants which we have by our acts required them to make, as a tax imposed on them: They say that their obedience in this case, without the interposition of their own free will, is reduced to the lowest predicament of subjection, wherein they are not only required to *act*, but to *will*, as they are ordered. Yet, however too strongly they may be supposed to state their case, surely there is a species of injustice in it.

Supplies granted in parliament, are of good will, not of duty, the free and voluntary act of the giver, not obligations and services which the giver cannot, by right, refuse. Whatever therefore is given out of the lands and property of the Colonies, should some way or other, be made their own act.

The true grounds of justice whereby the parliament grants supplies, and raises them by taxes on the lands and property of themselves and their constituents, is, that they give what is their own; that they lay no tax, which does not affect themselves and their constituents; and are therefore not only the proper givers, but also, the best and safest judges,

judges, what burdens they are beſt able to bear: They do not give and grant from the property of others, to eaſe themſelves. Let the ſtateſman apply this reaſoning to the caſe of the Colonies, and he may be lead up to the true ſources of the diſcontents, murmurings, proteſts and counteractings againſt government, which divert its effect, which undermine its eſtabliſhment, and tend to its utter diſſolution.

Whereas on the other hand, we ſhall find, as hath ever been found, that univerſal participation of council, creates reciprocation of univerſal obedience. The ſeat of government will be well informed of the ſtate and condition of the remote and extreme parts: And the extreme and remote parts, by participation in the legiſlature, will, from ſelf-conſciouſneſs, be informed of, and ſatisfied in, the reaſons and neceſſity of the meaſures of government: Theſe parts will conſider themſelves as acting, in every grant which is made, and in every tax which is impoſed: This conſideration alone, will give efficiency to government; and will create that *conſenſus obedientium*, on which only, the power and ſyſtem of the Imperium of a ſtate can be founded: This will give extention and ſtability of Empire, as far as we can extend our dominions.

I could

I could here proceed to justify this proposition, as founded in fact, by showing, that *this principle of establishing the Imperium of government, on the basis of a representative legislature*, hath been, from the earliest and * first instance of the establishment of a BRITISH SENATE, under the government of Carausius, founded on its native and natural basis, a marine dominion, invariably through all times, *the spirit of this country*: The spirit of that constitution, by which government hath been alway the most surely and happily established in the British dominions. It is a native plant of this soil, which, although at various times, it hath been trodden and cut down, almost to the very roots, hath alway again broken forth with a vigour superior to all false culture and all force. Although it was suppressed for a while, under the last despairing efforts of the Roman corrupted state; yet having taken root, it revived: Although it was, in part, oppressed by the feudal system, in the latter times of the Saxons, as well as under the Normans; yet I could here show, not only how, by its native vigour, it rose again from ruin, but also mark the progress of its restoration, to the time of Henry the third.

* Anno Dom. 291.

But

But these are arguments only to those who feel their hearts united to this spirit, who revere the institutions of their ancestors, as the true sources of the original liberty, and political happiness of this country. In these days, when it is the wisdom of statesmen to raise objections to this spirit of policy; when the learned fortify their understanding against conviction of the right of it; when the love of liberty, nay, the very mention of such a feeling is become ridiculous, such arguments must of course become ridiculous also.

It would be a melancholy, and but an useless consideration, to look back to that state of political liberty, on which the British Empire hath extended itself; or to look forward to that state of political glory, liberty and happiness on which it might be extended and established. When we find bounds set to the principle of this spirit; thus far shalt thou extend and no further: When we see a system of policy adopted, under which this country must continue for a while, entangled in a series of hostile disputes with its Colonies, but must at length lose them; must be finally broken in its commercical interest and power, and sink by the same pride, and same errors, into the same insignificance and dependence, as all
other

other commercial states have done, one after another; one has only left to hope, that the ruin is not inevitable, and that heaven may avert it.

> I decus: I nostrum: melioribus utere fatis.

Let us here close this view, and let us return to the examination of matters, which form the internal administration of the Colonies. And first their money.

The British American Colonies have not, within themselves, the means of making money or coin. They cannot acquire it from Great Britain, the balance of trade being against them. The returns of those branches of commerce, in which they are permitted to trade to any other part of Europe, are but barely sufficient to pay this balance.— By the present act of navigation, they are prohibited from trading with the Colonies of any other nations, so that there remains nothing but a small branch of African trade, and the scrambling profits of an undescribed traffic, to supply them with silver. However, the fact is, and matters have been so managed, that the general currency of the Colonies used to be in Spanish and Portuguese coin. This supplied the internal circulation of their home bufinefs, and always finally came to England in payments for what the Colonifts exported from thence. If the act of navigation fhould be carried into fuch rigorous execution as to cut off this fupply of a filver currency to the Colonies, the thoughts of adminiftration fhould be turned to the devifing fome means of fupplying the Colonies with money of fome fort or other: and in this view, it may not be improper to take up here the confideration of fome general principles, on which the bufinefs of money and a currency depends.

SILVER, *by the general confent of mankind, has become a* DEPOSITE, *which is,* THE COMMON MEASURE *of commerce.* This is a general effect of fome general caufe. The experience of its degree of fcarcenefs compared with its common introduction amidft men, together with the facility of its being known by its vifible and palpable properties, hath given this effect: Its degree of fcarcenefs hath given it a value proportioned to the making it a DEPOSITE, and the certain quantity in which this is mixed with the poffeffions and tranfactions of man, together with the facility of its being known, makes it a COMMON MEASURE amongft thofe things. There are perhaps other things which might be better applied to commerce as a common

mea-

measure, and there are perhaps other things which might better answer as a deposite; but there is nothing except silver known and acknowledged by the general experience of mankind, which is a deposite and common measure of commerce. Paper, leather, or parchment, may, by the sanction of government, become a common measure to an extent beyond what silver could reach; yet all the sanction and power of government never will make it an adequate deposite. Diamonds, pearls, or other jewels, may in many cases be considered as a more apt and suitable deposite, and may be applied as such, to an extent to which silver will not reach; yet their scarcity tends to throw them into a monopoly; they cannot be subdivided, nor amassed into one concrete, and the knowledge of them is more calculated for a mystery or trade, than for the forensic uses of man in common, and they will never therefore become a common measure.

This truth established and rightly understood, it will be seen that that state of trade in the Colonies is the best, and that administration of the Colonies the wisest, which tends to introduce this only true and real currency amongst them. And in this view I must wish to see the Spanish silver flowing into our Colonies, with an ample and uninterrupted stream, as I know that that stream, after it hath watered and supplyed the regions which it passeth through, must, like every other stream, pay its tribute to its mother ocean: As this silver, to speak without a metaphor, after it hath passed through the various uses of it in the Colonies, doth always come to, and center finally in Great Britain.

The proportion of this measure, by the general application of it to several different commodities, in different places and circumstances, forms *its own scale*. This scale arises from the effect of natural operations, and not from *artificial imposition:* If therefore silver was never used but by the merchant, as the general measure of his commerce and exchange, coin would be (as it is in such case) of no use; it would be considered as bullion only. Although bullion is thus sufficient for the measure of general commerce, yet for the daily uses of the market something more is wanted in the detail; something is wanted to mark to common judgment its proportion, and to give the scale: Government therefore, here interposes, and by forming it into COIN *gives the scale*, and makes it become to forensic use AN INSTRUMENT in detail, as well as it is in bullion a MEASURE in general.

This

This *artificial marking* of this scale on a *natural measure,* is neither more nor less than marking on any other rule or measure, the graduate proportions of it: And this artificial marking of the scale, or graduating the measure is of no use but in detail, and extends not beyond the market;——for exchange restores it again in commerce. No artificial standard therefore can be imposed.

Having this idea of money and coin, I could never comprehend to what general uses, or to what purposes of government, the proclamation which Queen Ann issued, and which was confirmed by statute in the sixth year of her reign, could be supposed to extend, while it endeavoured to rate the foreign coins current in the Colonies by an artificial standard. It would seem to me just as wise, and answering to just as good purpose, if government should now issue a proclamation, directing, that for the future, all black horses in the Colonies should be called white, and all brindled cows called red. The making even a law to alter the names of things, will never alter the nature of those things; and will never have any other effect, than that of introducing confusion, and of giving an opportunity to bad men of profiting by that confusion.

The safest and wisest measure which government can take, is not to discourage or obstruct that channel through which silver flows into the Colonies,—nor to interfere with that value which it acquires there;—but only so to regulate the Colony trade, that that silver shall finally come to, and center in Great Britain, whither it will most certainly come in its true value;———but if through any fatality in things or measures, a medium of trade, a currency of money, should grow defective in the Colonies, the wisdom of government will then interpose, either to remedy the cause which occasions such defect, or to contrive the means of supplying the deficiency. The remedy lies in a certain address in carrying into execution the act of navigation;———but if that remedy is neglected, the next recourse must lie in some means of maintaining a currency specially appropriated to the Colonies, and must be partly such as will keep a certain quantity of silver coin in circulation there,— and partly such as shall establish *a paper currency*, holding a value nearly equal to silver.

On the first view of these resources, it will be matter of serious consideration, whether government should establish a mint and coinage specially appropriated for the use of the

the Colonies; and on what basis this should be established. If it be necessary that silver, which in bullion is a common measure of general commerce, should, that it may be instrumental also to the common uses of the market, be formed into coin, it should be so formed, that while it was the duty of the public to form this coin, it may not be the interest of the individual to melt it down again into bullion.

If a certain quantity of coin is necessary for the forensic uses of the Colonies, it should be so formed as *in no ordinary course of business to become the interest of the merchant to export it from thence.*

This coin should be graduated by alloy, somewhat below the real scale, so as to bear a value in tale, somewhat better than the silver it contains would fetch after the expence of melting down the coin into bullion,—somewhat better *as an instrument*, in common forensic use, than the merchant *in ordinary cases* could make of it, in applying it *as a measure* by exporting it.

I have here inserted the caution against ordinary cases only, as I am not unaware that the lowering the intrinsic worth of the coin for America, will have in the end no other effect,

effect, than to raise the price of the European goods carried thither, while the coin will be exported to Great Britain the same as if it were pure silver.

If such a necessity of an artificial currency should ever exist in the Colonies, and if such a coinage was established, the Colonists would, for the purposes of their forensic business, purchase *this instrument* either in gold or silver, in the same manner as they do now purchase copper coin for the same purposes.

There are two ideas of *a paper currency*. The one adopts a measure for establishing a bank in the Colonies, which is quite a new and untried measure; the other turns the view to the regulating the present paper money currency, which the Colonies have had experience of in all its deviations, and to the establishing the same on a sure and sufficient basis.

I have seen this plan for *a provincial bank*, and think it justice to the very knowing person who formed it, to say, that it must be because I do not understand it, that many objections arise in my mind to it. Whenever he shall think fit to produce it, it will come forth clear of all objections, with that force

force of conviction with which truth always flows from a mind in full and perfect poffeffion of it.

In the mean while, I will recommend to the confideration of thofe who take a lead in bufinefs, a meafure devifed and adminiftered by an American affembly.—And I will venture to fay, that there never was a wifer or a better meafure, never one better calculated to ferve the ufes of an encreafing country, that there never was a meafure more fteadily purfued, or more faithfully executed, for forty years together, than the loan-office in Penfylvania, formed and adminiftered by the affembly of that province.

An encreafing country of fettlers and traders muft alway have the balance of trade againft them, for this very reafon, becaufe they are encreafing and improving, becaufe they muft be continually wanting further fupplies which their prefent circumftances will neither furnifh nor pay for:—And for this very reafon alfo, they muft alway labour under a decreafing filver currency, though their circumftances require an encreafing one. In the common curfory view of things, our politicians, both theorifts and practitioners, are apt to think, that a country which has the balance of trade againft it, and is continually

nually

nually drained of its silver currency, must be in a declining state; but here we may see that the progressive improvements of a commercial country of settlers, must necessarily have the balance of trade against them, and a decreasing silver currency; that their continual want of money and other materials to carry on their trade and business must engage them in debt——But that those very things applied to their improvements, will in return not only pay those debts, but create also a surplus to be still carried forward to further and further improvements. In a country under such circumstances, money lent upon interest to settlers, creates money. Paper money thus lent upon interest will create gold and silver in principal, *while the interest becomes a revenue that pays the charges of government*. This currency is the true Pactolian stream which converts all into gold that is washed by it. It is on this principle that the wisdom and virtue of the assembly of Pensylvania established, under the sanction of government, an office for the emission of paper money by loan.

A plan of a general paper currency for America, which was intended to have been inserted in the first edition of this work, hath been witheld from publication now four years, for reasons, which, I was in hopes, might

might have led to more publick benefit, than the making it public in this work could do. I have inserted it in this edition, but first—I proceed to the consideration of the ordinary mode of making paper-money, by the legislatures of the Colonies issuing government-notes, payable at a certain period by a tax. It may be useful to give some description of this, and to point out such regulations as will become necessary in this case, should the other not be adopted.

This paper-money consists of promissory notes, issued by the authority of the legislature of each province, deriving its value from being payable at a certain period, by monies arising from a tax proportioned to that payment at the time fixed. These notes pass as lawful money, and have been hitherto a legal tender in each respective province where they are issued.

As any limitation of the USES of these notes as a currency, must proportionably decrease its value; as any insecurity, insufficiency, or uncertainty in the FUND, which is to pay off these notes, must decrease their value; as any QUANTITY emitted more than the necessities of such province calls for as a medium, must also decrease its value; it is a direct and palpable injustice,
that

that that medium or currency which has depreciated by any of thefe means from its *real value*, fhould continue *a legal tender at its nominal value.*

The outrageous abufes practifed by fome of thofe legiflatures who have dealt in the manufacture of this depreciating currency, and the great injury which the merchant and fair dealer have fuffered by this fraudulent medium, occafioned the interpofition of parliament to become neceffary:— Parliament very properly interpofed, by applying the only adequate and efficient remedy, namely, by prohibiting thefe Colony legiflatures from being able to make the paper currency *a legal tender*. And government has lately for the fame prudent reafons made this prohibition general to the whole of the Colonies. For, *when this paper-money cannot be forced in payment as a legal tender*, this very circumftance will oblige that legiflature which creates it, to form it of fuch internal right conftitution, as fhall force its own way by its own intrinfic worth on a level nearly equal to filver. The legiflature muft fo frame and regulate it as to give it *a real value.*

Thefe regulations all turn upon *the fufficiency and certainty of the* FUND, *the extent of of the* USES, and the proportioning the QUANTITY to the actual and real necessities which require such a medium.

The FUND should at least be equal to the payment of the principal *in a limited time*; and that time should be certainly so fixed, as that the legislature itself could not alter it. Where the paper currency is treasurer's notes given for specie actually lent to government, the fund whereon it is borrowed should be also capable of paying, *ad interim*, a certain interest, as is the case of treasurer's notes in the province Massachusetts-Bay.

This medium ought to be applicable to all the equitable as well as legal USES of silver money within the Colony or province, except that of being a legal tender.

The QUANTITY ought always to be proportioned to the necessity of the medium wanted; which (the *fund and uses* being fairly and absolutely fixed) may always be judged of by the rise or fall of the *value* in its general currency or exchange: for where the quantity issued is more than necessity requires, the value will depreciate: and where the fund is good, and all proper uses of the medium secured, so long as no more paper is issued than necessity does require, it will always

always hold a value near to, though somewhat less than silver. On this subject I here refer the reader to the following very judicious tract, written and given to me, several years ago, by *Tench Francis*, Esq; late attorney-general of the province of Pensylvania, conversant in these matters, both as a lawyer and a merchant. I print and publish it by leave of a near relation, and subjoin it as containing the most exact and decisive sentiments on this subject that I have any where met with. I entitle it, CONSIDERATIONS ON A PAPER-CURRENCY.

ALL value is given to things for their fitness or power to answer or procure the necessary conveniences or pleasures of human life.

This value may be considered as absolute or relative. Absolute value terminates in our esteem of any thing, without referring to any other; relative is that which it has compared with another. The latter only I shall have occasion to treat of.

Men have power to discover qualities in a thing, which shall give it value. They can by laws, customs, or fashions, greatly increase

crease that value; yet, to know or fix its worth or price, compared with other things *à priori*, has always been found beyond their reach and capacity.

This is owing to an inability to foresee, estimate, and govern exactly all the points and circumstances, on which the value of things turns, which are such as are in, or follow the nature and order of things in general, and then may be foreseen and judged of with some certainty; or which consist of the passions, prejudices, and misapprehensions of mankind, whose number and influences we cannot rate or calculate.

From the *natural* state and order of things, I think it may be affirmed, that the worth or price of any thing will always be, as the quantity and uses amongst mankind; as the uses directly, and as the quantity reciprocally or inversely. Use is the sole cause of value, and value the necessary effect of use. Abating these distinctions of cause and effect, useless and worthless, are synonymous terms. Every man must agree, that if you add to a cause, you must increase the effect; substract from it, and the contrary effect must follow. Let the quantity of any thing be as 20, and the uses as 20, and let it have a value; let the uses be increased to 30, without in-

inlarging the quantity; it is plain, the equal proportion that every man can enjoy will be as 20 divided by 30, $\frac{2}{3}$ds only. But this being lefs by $\frac{1}{3}$ than each man requires, the demand for it, and confequently the value muft rife. Subftract 10 from the ufes when 20, and then under an equal diftribution, each fhall have double the value he wants, which muft leffen the demand, and the value dependent upon it.

Governing the ufes is one of the rational powers, that men have over the value of things.

Experience teaches the meaneft underftanding, that price depends on quantity, and that they are to each other inverfely, or the more of one the lefs the other. Water is as neceffary as any thing, and a diamond perhaps as little; yet the fuperfluous plenty of one has rendered it of no worth in moft places, and the fcarcity of the other has carried it to an extravagant price.

Limiting the quantity is another rational power men have over the value of things; and I do not know a third.

From hence it appears, that increafing the ufes, and leffening the quantity, and leffening sening the uses, and increasing the quantity, must always have the same influence upon the rates and prices of things. Therefore, whenever I shew the effect of one, for brevity's sake, let it be understood, that I suppose the same consequence will attend the other respectively.

Although I affirm, that variation in quantity or use shall cause a change in the price of a thing, yet I do not say, that this change shall be in proportion equal to the variation in the quantity or use; for I think the contrary. To instance in quantity, let it be in any thing as 30, and let the use be as 30, and it shall then have a mean value. The use unchanged, let the quantity be at one time as 20, at another 40. Whoever considers the prevalence of men's appetites for a scarce commodity, under the dreads and apprehensions of wanting it, with their different abilities to procure it, on one hand, and their great contempt of useless excess on the other, must agree it is more than probable, that the difference between the means and the extremes shall not be the same in the prices, as in the quantities. Merchants, by experience, have found the truth of what I advance. I think they have observed, that lessening a commodity one third from the mean quantity, *cæteris paribus*, nearly doubles

doubles the value; adding a third, fubftracts one half from it; and that by further increafing or diminifhing the quantity, thefe difproportions between the quantity and prices vaftly increafe.

It is extremely difficult, if not impoffible, to inveftigate thefe proportions mathematically; but events fpringing from ufe and experience have equal certainty in them, and to all practical purpofes are as much to be relied and depended upon.

It is further worth obfervation, that whatever fluctuates much in quantity, and confequently in worth, will fink beneath its mean value.

Suppofe the quantity of any thing produced in every 50 years be exactly the fame: let the annual product be as *one* anfwerable to the neceffities of mankind, then the value in each year fhall be as one, and the whole equal to 50. But if the quantity of the annual product fluctuates, there will be annual fluctuations in the value; but as the proportions of the decreafe of value, from experience above ftated, will be greater than the proportions of the increafe of value, this fluctuation will caufe a deficiency in the mean value, which deficiency will always be in proportion to the greatnefs and quicknefs of the changes. This, I presume, is occasioned by the desire of mankind in general to rest on certainty, rather than rely on what is fluctuating and inconstant, though they should expect gain equal to the risque, and by the low circumstances of the majority of men, whose fortunes, in all prudence, direct to the first, rather than the latter. The case of insurances is an evident proof of this remark. If the insurers gain, which I think must be admitted, then they receive a premium beyond the value of the risque, and this again the insured pay for *certainty* against *contingent losses*.

These few rules of estimating the value of things, well applied, will, I presume, shew when it is convenient to introduce paper-money into a country, and when it will prove hurtful; what are its advantages and inconveniencies, general and particular, when introduced; of what great importance it is to prevent an excess in quantity, and to extend the uses; and nearly what its value will be in any given state.

If a nation has a quantity of money equal to its commerce, the lands, commodities, and labour of the people shall bear a middle price. This state is the best, and tends most to enrich the people, and make their happiness lasting. If they should mint paper to pass for money, the increase of quantity in the former will lessen the value of the latter, will raise the price of lands and rents, and make the labour of such a people, and the commodities, be *rated* higher than in other places. Men's fortunes will rise in *nominal, not real value*; from whence idleness, expence and poverty shall follow. Under these circumstances, their *real money*, instead of their commodities, shall be exported from them. Here the paper will be their bane and destruction. But if their commerce, or uses of money, exceed the quantity of it, their lands, labour, and commodities shall sink beneath their worth in other countries. Few purchasers of lands will be found in regard to the superior profit that must attend the use of money in trade: the *wealthy merchant shall be at the head of affairs:* with few competitions; he shall be able to grind down the farmer in the sale of his commodities, and, when those fail to support him, in the purchase of his lands. The artisan's labour shall be depreciated by the merchant who exports it, or the needy farmer that uses it. The wealthy only shall accumulate riches, the commonwealth shall decline, and in time farmers and artisans must desert the place for another, where their labour shall be better rewarded. Here the

the use of paper-money will shake off the fetters and clogs of the poor. Merchants will multiply; they will raise the price of labour, and of the fruits of the earth, and thereby the value of lands. An equal distribution of gain and profit shall succeed, and destroy the partial accumulations of wealth.

I think these marks, taken from the value of lands, labour, and commodities, compared with their worth in other countries, will be found the only infallible rules to judge of an equality, excess, or defect of money in any place wheresoever; and consequently will, at all times, unerringly shew the necessity of increasing coins, or the contrary. Had a neighbouring province well understood and weighed these points, they had not created a paper credit far exceeding all their uses for money, when they were able to supply themselves with gold equal to their trade, nor at the same time have dammed up so many uses for it, which now cover them with clouds and confusion, that no man can see his way through. The best method they can use is to sink it as fast as possible, and not let their fund lie in Britain at an interest less than 4 *per cent.* when it is worth 6 in their own country, and their paper passes 50 *per cent.* less than the nominal value. But to return: when it is found necessary to add *paper-money* to the coin of any country, to support its value ought to be the main and principal view. This will turn upon the FUND, the USES, and the QUANTITY.

All value arising from the use, I beg leave to call *extrinsick*.

Having shewn that paper-money acquires its extrinsic value from the uses, which uses apparently may be encreased or diminished; I think it would be needless and mispending the reader's time, to demonstrate, that this value must be in direct proportion to the uses; for it would really amount to no more than the proof of an axiom universally acknowledged, that the effect shall always be adequate to the cause. Therefore, in all future arguments, I shall take it for granted.

The fund ought to be as satisfactory to mankind as human wisdom can devise and furnish.

The community should become security to answer all deficiencies in the FUND; this is not only the highest justice, but the best policy. It is just, because it is a creature of
their

their own, calculated for their private utility and advantage, and is in the management of the country by their reprefentatives and officers. But when they receive an intereſt from the money, the equity of it is unanſwerable: for it ſeems wholly inconſiſtent with juſtice, that one ſhould receive the intereſt, and another run the riſque of the principal. Policy requires it, becauſe the community will certainly receive more profit from its credit under their ſupport, than, with due caution, they can probably loſe by accidents in the fund.

Our next conſideration, with reſpect to the value, turns on *what* the fund is to pay, and *when*. Theſe are arbitrary, being within the power of thoſe by whoſe authority the money is emitted. But for the preſent purpoſe: Let us ſuppoſe it is to pay ſilver money, according to the late Queen's proclamation, to the value of 1000 *l.* for ſo much of the paper, as, according to the *nominal value*, amounts to that ſum at the end of 15 years. In this ſtate the 1000 *l.* paper, *with regard to the fund alone*, at the time of its emiſſion, is worth no more proclamation money than what will produce 1000 *l.* of that money at the end of the term, at compound intereſt, under as good ſecurity.

For example, take a 1000 *l.* paper, and let it reprefent that the poffeffor fhall receive 1000 *l.* proclamation money for it at the end of 15 years, and let the ufe of money be worth 6 *per cent. per annum*; rebate 6 *per cent. per annum* with compound intereft for 15 years, and you have the value of the 1000 *l.* proclamation money in hand, which appears to be but 417 *l.* 5 *s.* 3½; more it cannot be worth, becaufe 417 *l.* 5 *s.* 3½, with 6 *per cent. per annum* compound intereft for 15 years added, will amount to 1000 *l.*

On this ftate it appears, that the longer the term, the lefs the value, with regard to the fund alone. From whence it follows, that by increafing the term, this value may be reduced to a degree beneath eftimation. But whatever the value thus proved be, I call it *intrinfick*.

The FUND eftablifhed, I proceed to the USES as they next require our attention in regard to the value of the paper-money.

If value, in refpect to the ufes of things, fhall always be in direct proportion to thofe ufes, (which I prefume I have heretofore proved in general, and fhall hereafter fhew is true in relation to paper-money) and we defign to raife the power, it follows clearly, that

that to bring this to pass, we ought to give it all the uses of money, or coined gold and silver in other countries. From these uses alone it must derive all the worth it shall bear beyond what I called the *intrinsick* value. For the purpose *take the case stated* on the Fund only, that the possessor of 1000 *l.* paper shall receive 1000 *l.* proclamation money in exchange for it, at the end of 15 years. On this account the paper appeared to be worth but 417 *l.* 15 *s.* 3$\frac{1}{4}$. But suppose this 1000 *l.* paper may be immediately exchanged for 800 *l.* proclamation money, which is 382 *l.* 14 *s.* 8$\frac{1}{4}$ more than the intrinsick worth, how has it acquired this exceeding price or value? I think plainly from the uses. To prove the truth of this, suppose all the uses as money taken away; unquestionably then the worth of 1000 *l.* paper in proclamation money will be reduced to what I call the intrinsick value; because, depending upon the fund alone, it will be exactly in the state of a fund to be paid at a future day; for in neither case can the creditor use it in the mean time. But if the creditor can by any contrivance use the sum in that time, as he may the paper when it passes for money, that use must be something worth. And when experience shews, that under this use the value advances from 417 *l.* 15 *s.* 3$\frac{1}{4}$ to 800 *l.* I apprehend it is evident to a demonstration, that

that the difference is derived from the use. To deny it must be as irrational and absurd, as if, upon adding and extracting an ingredient to and from a composition, we perceived properties in the composition appear and disappear, and yet were to deny that such ingredient was the cause of those properties. This leads me to attempt the solution of a question I have known frequently made. If we in Pensylvania, upon a sufficient fund answerable in silver, at a future day, mint a quantity of paper equal to the uses of the people for money, and they willingly and universally accept of the paper in all payments, why should it not, at all times, have *value* equal *to the nominal value*, or to the sum chargeable on the fund at the day to come. This reason, urged by many, to support the paper to this degree, is drawn from the nature of money in general. Money, say they, is but a ticket or counter, which represents to the mind of the possessor a quantity or degree of power. No man, on the receipt of it, ever examines how, or from whence it acquired that power, but in order to discover its reality and duration. For instance, when an English crown is received, does the acceptor regard any properties in the metal, or the figures of it, but those which are to convince him that it is what it appears to be? a crown. It must be be confessed, he does not. If so, then why may not a piece of paper, under distinguishing characters and impressions, affixed by law and common consent, have the power of an English crown annexed to it? It is to pass in the same manner as a crown does, and in the end will as certainly be a crown as the real one.

Therefore they conclude, that the paper may, and ought at all times, to be esteemed equal to the quantity of silver the fund is to yield for it at the end of the term.

I confess I think this reasoning fair, and the conclusion just and satisfactory, if we do not use silver in our *commerce, foreign or domestick:* otherwise not. The fact is, we do use silver *in our foreign commerce.* I presume it will be easily admitted, as the paper represents the silver in the fund, and from thence obtains its credit, that it shall always be at least of equal use with, or be as readily received as paper. Then if silver in hand has one power, *one use more* than the paper, to wit, that of procuring foreign commodities, it is impossible we can esteem them equally. For that would be to controul the different virtues and influences of things over the mind of man, which necessarily depending upon the things themselves, no laws or
con-

consent can, by any means, vary or direct. Wherefore, in the case stated, it seems to me certain and undeniable, that the paper must have less worth than the silver.

Having said, that the uses of the paper should be as many as possible, it may be proper for me to speak of some of those uses, the equity and advantage of which have been very much controverted. But here let it be understood, that I proceed upon the case last stated, that the quantity of paper is to be equal to all the uses of money *within* the country. For that state, and a partial supply of paper credit, differing in principles, require different reasoning, and infer quite opposite consequences.

First, then, it seems just and reasonable to compel all persons contracting for silver money, after the law, that raises the paper money to be paid in the country is enacted, to receive the paper in lieu of it, and at the value struck from the fund, although that be inferior to the real value. This perhaps may not be strict equity *between the contracting parties*, but it is just *from the community*, who have power from the consent of every member, by laws, to prohibit the exercise of a particular natural right inconsistent with the welfare of the whole, and to inflict a penalty

nalty upon difobedience to the law. To ufe filver or gold with the paper, muft depreciate the latter. Therefore the law forbids it. This can't be unfair, becaufe every man has notice of what coin he is to be paid in, and *is not obliged to exchange more* for the paper, than he thinks agreeable to the *real worth*. And if any fhould endeavour fuch ufe, the lofs of the difference between gold or filver and paper, is a kind of penalty for violating the law, which muft be as juft as any other penalty impofed on an act, *not evil in itfelf, but prohibited* only.

Again, upon breach of contracts for payment of money in foreign countries, I think it both convenient and right, that fatisfaction fhould be made in the paper. The convenience of it will appear, if we fuppofe the debtor a member of the fociety amongft whom the paper paffes; for as fuch, being reftrained by law from trafficking for gold or filver, and thereby difabled from procuring them, he muft either pay paper in compenfation, or lie in a goal, if the feverity of his creditors requires it. In thefe circumftances, no man in his fenfes would dare to contract a foreign debt, or transfer foreign money in the ufual manner, by exchange; the bad confequences of which are too numerous and obvious to admit of, or

need

need particular mention, and evidently prove the convenience of allowing satisfaction to be made in paper.

The equity of this satisfaction will be indisputable, if the debtor pays a sum of paper really of equal value with the foreign money. It is the common case on breach of specifick contract. If it cannot be performed, the most exact justice requires no more than *an equivalent compensation.*

Some persons imagining the real worth of the paper equal to the nominal, have affirmed, that it ought to discharge these debts *at the nominal value*; others confessing a difference between these values, under some political views, have asserted the same. As I shall have occasion to speak on these opinions hereafter, upon a point similar to this I shall only add here, that if this mode of payment should take place, it would as effectually destroy foreign credit and negociations by exchange, as if gold or silver were to be insisted on here, to discharge a foreign debt. In one case, it would be the highest imprudence to be the debtor, in the other, it must be equally indiscreet to become a creditor.

Pur-

Pursuing the uses, I come to that of discharging by paper, the silver debts contracted antecedent to the law that raises the paper.

To shew the necessity of admitting this, I suppose it will be granted me, that there must at all times be a very great number of debtors who depend on their future labour and industry to pay their debts. This dependence is reasonable and just, founded on the natural right of all fairly to purchase silver, the then current money of the country. The debtor has the continuation of this right in view and expectation at the time of his contract; without it he cannot be supposed either prudent or honest to borrow. If then, for the convenience and advantage of the whole society, this right must be taken away by a subsequent law which he could not foresee, it cannot be agreeable either to reason or good conscience, to exact a payment in specie; for that would be requiring a performance when we had expressly taken away the means. Therefore I think it clear in respect to the debtor, that the paper should have this use. But how will this stand with the right of the creditor, who upon the contract as certainly expected to be paid silver, as the debtor did the opportunity of acquiring it to pay.

I pre-

I presume, if he receives as much paper as shall be equal in power or value to the silver, it will be just in itself, and perfectly satisfactory to him. But can any man offer so high a degree of violence to his own reason, and the understanding of others, as to affirm, if he is forced to accept less, that still he has justice dispensed him. If I borrow 100 *l.* in silver before the law, under agreement to repay it at the end of the ensuing year, and before the day of payment comes, the law takes place, commanding the lender to receive 100 *l.* paper for it, which shall be worth, or have power to procure 82 *l.* silver money only; with truth can this be called a rational or upright law? Certainly no. Nor shall it be any justification to me in conscience to detain 18 *l.* of my creditor's money.

The rules of natural justice flowing from our fixed and unchangeable relations to each other, and the invariable nature and order of things, inforced by the express commands of God, are of eternal and indispensible obligation. No laws, no combinations of human power, customs, usages, or practice, can controul or change them. We may, by the consent of a majority, tie up the compulsory hand on the civil magistrate, and thereby dissolve the power of coercive laws,

laws, but can no more abfolve from the moral duty, than we can reverfe decrees inrolled in heaven. If my debtor fhould be fo extremely weak, as to fuppofe this not criminal becaufe it is legal, (which I think next to impoffible to imagine of a rational creature, and I make bold to affirm, never was the cafe of a creditor of underftanding, fufficient to know the meafure of his demand) his opinion perhaps may ferve for an excufe, or extenuation of his crime, but never can prove the rectitude of the act, and ftill the guilt muft reft fomewhere. The law-makers, the authors of this miftake, are culpable, unlefs they are under the fame delufion, which is yet more difficult to apprehend. Some, who gave up the juftice of the law, defend their practice under it, by faying, they are creditors as well as debtors: and as they are obliged to receive, fo they fhould have liberty to pay. Alas! what feeble arguments fatisfy, when they are caft into the fcale of intereft, and gain is the confequence of conviction. If the actions of men towards us are to be the meafures of our dealing with others, then he that is cheated by any perfon, may juftly plunder the next he meets. And truly I can't fee why it fhould ftop here; for as we may be many times defrauded, and not know it, to be fecure, and keep the ballance on the right fide, side, we should pillage our neighbours as often as an opportunity offers. This may seem severe reasoning, but really I think it fair from the first position; that because one keeps back part of another's due, therefore he may honestly detain the right of a third innocent person.

Again, paying an equivalent cannot be injurious to the debtor. For suppose he pays 120 *l.* paper. If 100 pounds worth of coin'd silver, reduced to bullion, will then yield him so much, what does he more than perform his contract to pay 100 *l.* of coin'd silver? seeing a compleat recompence is perfectly consistent with the right of each contracting party. Any remaining objections must arise from its being hurtful or injurious to the society in general. This has been asserted, and endeavours have been used to support the truth of it, by this kind of reasoning.

First, if the law should oblige the debtor (for the purpose) to pay 120 *l.* paper in lieu of 100 *l.* silver, the legislature would thereby confess the inferior worth of the paper, which will be attended with this ill consequence, that the general current value of the paper shall be less than if the law had declared it equal to silver.

Secondly,

Secondly, That leſſening the current value will be a loſs to the ſociety in general. To the firſt, That obliging to pay a larger ſum of paper for a leſs of ſilver, acknowledges an inequality of value under the like denominations, is ſelf-evident. But from thence to infer, that the paper ſhall paſs in general, at leſs value than if they had been declared equal, with ſubmiſſion, I think miſtaken, and inconcluſive reaſoning.

To be clearly underſtood, permit me to examine this upon the fact. Suppoſe the law, in the ſtrongeſt terms, enacts that the paper ſhall be in value equal to ſilver money, according to their ſeveral denominations. Carry the paper from thence to uſe, by offering it in exchange or payment for ſome commodity, and then I aſk a ſhort queſtion, Who it is that really ſets a value on the paper, the legiſlature, or the perſon that has the commodity to ſell? If it be anſwered, the firſt, then I ſay, this cannot be, unleſs they alſo limit the price of the commodity. For if the ſeller can raiſe and porportion the price of it to what he thinks the real worth of the paper, the law-maker's declaration notwithſtanding, it is he that ſtrikes the value, and not they. For inſtance, put the caſe; a farmer, juſt upon emitting the paper, has a buſhel of wheat to ſell, which he rates at, and will not part with under, three silver shillings. The future current worth of the paper being unknown to him, let him by guess imagine these three shillings equal to four shillings paper. A purchaser then presses him, under the influence of the law, to accept of three paper shillings for this wheat; but he, without regard to the law, according to his own opinion, demands and receives four shillings for it. Will any man say, the legislature determined the value of the paper here? Apparently the seller did. For the legislature commanded, that the three paper shillings should be valued at three of silver, but the farmer has made his estimate at three fourths of that value only. Unquestionably the vender must always have this power, unless, as I said before, the law-makers can limit the price of all commodities, which is not practicable, consistent with the order of things, or the preservation of men's properties. But it may be alledged, although the receiver of the money is not bound to observe the legislative command, yet still it may have some weight. He may consider it to be the impartial opinion of the wisest part of the society, what the future current value of the paper shall be, and thereby add, in some degree, to its worth.

In

In anſwer I muſt obſerve, firſt, this gives up the point of power, and changes it to a matter of meer advice. Then, ſuppoſing that of any import, ſurely delivering it in a mandatory way, will be very little able to produce the deſired effect. Imperative advice (pardon the expreſſion) favours too much of ſelling the rabbit, to prevail or perſuade. In ſhort, the words command and adviſe, convey two ideas ſo widely different, and ſo oppoſite and repugnant to each other, that it is abſolutely impoſſible we ſhould take the firſt for the laſt. But granting it to be interpreted as a piece of cordial advice. Shall it be received implicitly, and paſs without any examination? I preſume not. When it comes to be examined, if the people ſhould be informed, that, upon a nice examination, the legiſlature had found a fourth, fifth, or ſixth difference between ſilver and paper, as ſuch calculations are generally out of the reach and comprehenſion of moſt people, it ſeems not improbable that the paper might paſs at firſt, agreeable to the given difference. *I ſay at firſt*; for I contend, if the calculation ſhould be erroneous, (which the uſe of the money in time will diſcover) this effect ſhall not be laſting. But if, on the contrary, they learn that the paper, without any calculation, by gueſs, was pronounced equal to ſilver, which every man's judgment, who knows the superior power of the last, must disapprove of, what influence can the legislative advice then have? Undoubtedly it will be universally rejected, and each person turned at large to make his estimate as well as he can, without the least regard to the legislative opinion.

Once more, take it, that the quantity of silver in 100 shillings proclamation money is now worth 120 paper shillings in Pensylvania, and suppose this requisite had hitherto been omitted in all laws relating to the paper: let the supreme authority to-day enact, that from henceforth all persons shall give as much for 100 shillings paper as they do now for that quantity of silver, would this make the least alteration in the current value of the paper? Might a man, with reason, expect to buy more bread or wine to-morrow with 100 paper shillings, than he can to-day? if the legislative power can bring this to pass, perhaps it may prove more than some people desire; for I conjecture it will shew, that we never had any occasion for paper. Whatever quantity of silver we had amongst us, when the paper was struck, might have been extended in value proportionable to our wants, and all the business of paper-money done at once. The absurdity of this lies open to the meanest capacity;
yet

yet I aver, that to raise the value of paper by authoritative words or commands, is equally irrational and unfeasible.

I know no just means whereby mankind can give value to things, but increasing or lessening the *uses* or *quantity*. The paper derives its *intrinsick worth from* THE FUND which is stable and fixed. The *uses* give it further value, but that shall always be in inverse proportion to the quantity. The quantity is absolutely under the direction of the legislature, but the uses not. As they are raised, so they must be limited, by our necessities, and the disposition and order of things. The utmost the legislature can do, or is needful to be done, is to make the paper answer *all those uses*. When they have ascertained the FUND, the *uses* and *quantity*, their power expires. And the current value, if the people receive it, flows from them by so unavoidable and a necessary consequence, that whatever the legislature or others will or do, (if it alters not the fund, uses, or quantity) can work no change in it in general. For a time, as long as people are ignorant, I confess it may; but when experience, that excellent mistress, has disclosed what worth they give, all imaginary value shall cease and vanish, and on the three requisites, as on a solid and firm foundation, it shall ultimately rest and settle.

I conclude what I have to say on this point with a short observation. That all the attempts of assemblies in America in this way even by penalties on disobedience, have proved fruitless and abortive. And it has been extremely remarkable, that although transgressing the law, by making a difference between silver and paper, has been every day's practice, not in secret, but openly, I have never heard, that any person has been so much as questioned publickly, or has lost any degree of reputation privately for doing it. So far do the dictates of just and right reason surpass and transcend the force and power of any human device or institution, that opposes or contradicts them.

I come now to consider the second position; that lessening the current value will be disadvantageous to the society in general.

This cannot be maintained without proving, that it will occasion a loss, or obstruct some gain.

A society can gain but two ways, from the earth, and from their neighbours. When I say

say from the earth, I do not mean from her simple productions only; for I include therein men's labour and manufactures upon them afterwards: and they can lose only by the contrary, neglecting the fruit and product of the earth, and suffering their neighbours to carry away their wealth.

I presume it will be very hard to shew, how a different valuation of the money can influence the industry of the land-holder or the artisan.

Upon the quantities of the fruits of the earth, and manufactures produced, entirely depend the wealth of the country. A farmer and tradesman, for a certain portion of their commodities one year, receive 8 shillings, and with them can purchase an ounce of silver. The money being raised in value next year, they can get but 7 shillings for the same quantities; but still that sum will buy an ounce of silver. Can this difference, in the value of the paper, cause the one to till the more or less ground, or the other to make a greater or less quantity of his manufacture? What is it to them how the money is rated, if they receive and part with it at the same value? Gold, comparing quantity to quantity, is more valuable than silver. If silver was to vanish out of the world,

world, and gold should be made the only medium of commerce, can any one imagine that mankind would grow more industrious to procure it, because more valuable than silver, when the quantity they shall get must be proportionably less? Do we in fact find these different effects from gold or silver at present? I think we may as reasonably expect, that varying the measure of the bushel or yard, will induce people to make more or less corn or cloth, as that changing the value of the money, which is another kind of measure for commodities, should excite or abate men's diligence to raise and make them.

All gain from our neighbours must be by getting their money or their goods. These are to be acquired only by conquest or commerce. The first I pass over as impertinent to this purpose. Then let us see whether advancing the value of the money can reflect any gain to us from them in the latter. Gain in trade may be considered as derived from the manner or the measure of it. The manner of trade in general is of short circuit, and consists of importing foreign money or commodities, and the exportation of our own. In these negociations we shall find the worth of the paper affords us no advantage over, or an opportunity to get from our neighbours.

Sup-

Suppose a foreigner imports 800 *l.* proclamation money, and finding That not the medium of our commerce, proposes to exchange it for paper. Let the value of the paper be such, that he can get but 800 *l.* of it for his silver. With the paper he purchases corn, which he transports. What have we got from this foreigner? 800 *l.* in silver. Should we have got less had he received 1000 *l.* for his silver, and with it bought the same quantity of wheat? Certainly no. Neither case makes us richer or poorer than the other; and the same consequence will be found to attend all foreign imports whatever.

When we export our commodities, the value of the paper is quite out of the question; for in their sales, or the returns, it is in no sort concerned. If we send the paper abroad, and sell it, unless it be kept in expectation of what the fund will yield for it at the end of the term (which I intend to speak to hereafter) we shall find it but an exchange of merchandizes between us and them. For the seller brings the goods he receives here, and the buyer, by means of the money, carries back our goods; the paper is but a measure, as it was in the case of imports and exports in return; and if it be rated alike abroad and at home, no
loss

loſs or gain can enſue to either country, or to the traders, from a high or low valuation of it.

He that is not ſatisfied by theſe reaſons, may perhaps be convinced by the experience of others. The coins of England being finer than thoſe of Holland, quantity to quantity, are of more value; but was it ever thought the Engliſh had therefore more power or traffick, to obtain the money and merchandize of other nations, than the Dutch?

Were it poſſible that the profit of trade could be affected by lowering the coin, that cunning and ſkilful generation would hardly have debaſed theirs by deſign, much leſs have continued for ſo long a time as they have done. * The paper-currency of New England, by a great exceſs in the quantity, is ſunk to a ſhameful degree. From hence we hear of much fraud and diſhoneſty amongſt them; but it was never yet objected that it injured them in trade. In truth, if it had, as they principally ſubſiſt by com-

---

* * Theſe facts muſt be referred to the time in which this treatiſe was written, twenty years ago.——Theſe evils have been remedied by the acts of parliament reſtraining the aſſemblies from making their money a legal tender.

merce, they muſt have been ruined and undone long ago.

* The currencies of North and South Carolina are in the ſame condition; but ſtill their trades go on as uſual, without the leaſt alteration. In reſpect to the meaſure of our commerce, it is evident that cannot be impaired by reducing the value of our money, unleſs we are thereby deprived of a ſufficient quantity to carry it on: for inſtance, if 60,000 *l.* proclamation money be neceſſary to carry on all our trade, and we ſtrike 60,000 *l.* paper, in hopes it ſhall have the value, upon experience it proves worth but 50,000 *l.* proclamation. Then, for want of the remaining 10,000 *l.* ſome of the wheels of trade muſt ſtand ſtill or move ſlower, which apparently will obſtruct a part of our gain. But the impediment vaniſhes, by raiſing an additional ſum of paper equal to the 10,000 *l.* deficiency. The power of doing this we have hitherto enjoyed and exerciſed without any reſtraint; and probably ſhall retain as long as we uſe it with diſcretion and prudence.

Seeing then, that by raiſing the value of our money, we are not likely to get any thing from our neighbours, let us now try whether by lowering it they can get any thing from us.

us. I presume I have proved, that in common commerce, receiving and returning the money for merchandizes, they cannot; consequently no method remains, but keeping the money to receive silver from the fund at the end of the term. By these practices they can gain from us only upon one supposition; that they purchase the money at less than what I call the intrinsick worth: for if at more they lose by it, and we gain from them. I have shewn, rating interest at 6 *per cent. per annum*, that 1000 *l.* payable at the end of 15 years, is worth 500 *l.* to take a round sum, in hand. If our neighbour can buy it for 400 *l.* he gets 100 *l.* from us. But on the contrary, if he gives 800 *l.* for it, he loses 300 *l.* For he lends us 800 for 15 years, at 2 *l.* 8 *s. per cent. per annum*, when it is really worth 6 *l.* and the difference, which on computation will be found in the whole to amount to 300 *l.* or nearly, we gain from him. But neither of these cases can possibly happen while men have the least capacity to discern and preserve their own interest. Indeed I have never heard one sound reason, either moral or political, for this manifest deviation from justice and equity. So far is it from good policy, that if I am not mistaken, it must work an effect contrary to the design; and

instead

instead of supporting the credit of the paper, undermine and diminish it.

The public authority is guarantee for the payment of all just debts. Every body must agree, that the value of paper money is nothing but so much public credit. Now, is it possible for the public authority to break its own engagements, in respect of the payment of the debts, without in some degree blasting that credit which is to be the support of the money? Public and private faith are, in this respect, exactly alike; and it is as easy to see how violating one public obligation shall impair the value of the paper-money, as how a known breach of private contract in a goldsmith should lessen the worth of his bills or notes.

A second inconvenience attending it, is loss of foreign credit, which must be a great misfortune to a trading country. This is occasioned in the same manner, by which I just now shewed the value of the money might be affected; and let it not be thought amiss that I mention a third inconvenience, namely, prostituting and debasing the dignity and excellence of the divine and moral laws in the eyes of the people, and encouraging them, by ill practices and examples, to depart from true honesty and virtue. For
if

if a man can once believe, he may juftly, by human authority, tranfgrefs thofe laws, he lofes much of the due and neceffary refpect that ought to be paid them, and fhall afterwards be able to refift their checks and admonitions with greater eafe and facility: and he that owes to 20 people, and pays them with five fixths of their due, and fees his neighbour do the like, under colour of law to-day, will, I am afraid, with lefs regret and compunction, defraud his creditors without a law to-morrow.

But now, granting entire recompence ought to be made, it may be afked how the quantum of paper to be paid for antecedent filver debts fhall be afcertained.

The legiflature cannot fettle it with exact juftice, becaufe no fkill can difcover what the future current value fhall be; and if the people are left to do it themfelves, it will introduce many law-fuits and oppreffions, and ftill they may be as far from right as if the legiflature had done it. The greater inconveniences in the latter, rationally determine the power to the former. When they come to exercife it, if it is the firft experiment of the kind, I imagine they can do little more than guefs at the value. But as it is within demonftration, that the paper cannot be
equal

equal to silver, surely it ought not to be rated so. Impartiality requires the guess to be as near as may be, and then, although it may be mistaken upon the laws of change, it may be perfectly equal, because either party may lose or gain. It is a common case in life, and must be always so in untried things, and no man can justly complain of the event, because all errors are owing to our weakness, not our faults.

If any of our neighbours have issued paper-money, the value of theirs will afford us strong lights to discover the worth of our own, and allowing for different circumstances, we ought to rate ours as they have found theirs upon trial. But when experience has taught us the true worth of the money, all difficulty ends, and whatever debts or pre-contracts remain (as many from their growing nature must) should be satisfied according to that value.

I have now run through all the uses that occur to me worthy of observation; and therefore shall proceed to the quantity.

When it is designed, that paper shall be the only money of a country, the quantity, according to the nominal value, ought to be, as near as possible, adequate to the uses, or in other words, to all commerce, foreign and domestick. It is easier to see the truth of this rule in speculation, than to reduce it to practice; because the number and extent of the uses of money, in a populous and industrious country, are far beyond our knowledge and comprehension. From the circumstances of other places, the quantity of money current before issuing the paper, and the value of their exports, rational conjectures may be formed, but experience alone can teach us what sum will suffice. To strike the necessary quantity at once, would be most advantageous to the society, and equal with respect to individuals; but as that cannot be known, let it be approached as near as may be. And since we may expect to err, I presume it will be better to err on the side of deficiency than excess, seeing additions are easy, but substractions oftentimes very difficult after the emission.

FROM what I have said above, which the foregoing treatise doth fully confirm and elucidate, the following propositions, which I apprehended to be truths, do arise. That in Colonies, the essence of whose nature requires a progressive increase of settlements and trade, and yet who, from the balance

lance of trade with the mother country being against them, must suffer a constantly decreasing quantity of silver money, *a certain quantity of paper-money* is necessary. It is necessary to keep up the increasing operations of this trade, and these settlements; it is also necessary, in such circumstances, to the equal distribution and general application of these benefits to the whole Colony, which benefits would otherwise become a monopoly to the *monied merchant only*: it is prudent, and of good policy in the mother country to permit it, as it is the surest means of drawing the balance of the Colony trade and culture to its own profit.

These reasonings further shew, how, by securing the *fund*, extending the *uses*, and regulating the *quantity*, this measure of a paper-currency may be carried to the utmost extent of which it is capable. Nor do they stop here; for as they give the rule whereby to judge of the excess or defect of money in any place whatsoever, so do they, at all times, shew the necessity of encreasing it, or the contrary.

Although the reasonings, which from my own sentiments of the matter, I have applied to this subject, and those, with which I am able to oblige the world, by publishing the above

above very judicious and able tract, do perfectly coincide in these points: yet upon the point of the USES, in considering the remedies to be provided against the quantity of any fallacious depreciation of this paper-money, our reasonings seem to divide on quite different sides of the question. The author of the above tract asserts, that in Colonies, where paper-money is created, the people of that Colony *should be compelled by law to receive* it in payments: and he states two or three different cases in proof of his assertion: My opinion suggests, that this paper-money ought *by no means to be a legal tender:* and yet, different as these propositions may appear, they will be found to coincide in the application of the remedy; in the only proper and radical remedy, *the not permitting the paper-money to be a legal tender.* This gentleman experienced in the politicks of the Colonies, and knowing the danger, if not the impracticability, of any legislature in these Colonies adopting this maxim, takes up the reasonableness and necessity of this paper-money being forced into payments by law;— but then, in all the cases wherein he states the remedy in equity, against the injustice, which may arise from the artificial value of this paper-money thus declared, he firmly and justly declares, that the payment thus by law forced upon the creditor *in paper,*

ought

ought not to be according to the nominal legal value of that paper, but according to the real value, an equiva'ent to the debt.——This judgment totally deftroys the maxim of its being a legal tender. In the application therefore of the remedy, our opinions do not differ, but the truth of them becomes the more elucidated by this coincidence of two thus feemingly different propofitions.—I will therefore proceed in faying, that by the reafonings above it appears, that the only and proper remedy, againft the iniquities of a fallacious, depreciating paper-currency, is *that radical one, of not permitting this paper-money to be a legal tender*.—On the other hand, fo confirmed am I in my opinion of the neceffity and propriety *of a certain quantity* of paper-money in the Colonies, that were I not convinced, that the reftraining of it from being a legal tender, will not deftroy the exiftence of it, but, on the contrary, amend its currency; I would even facrifice my conviction to this point of utility: but whatever apparent value this paper-money may feem at firft view to lofe by reftraint of this one ufe, this very reftraint, (if the Colonies will have paper-money) muft become an occafion of fo meliorating and fecuring the *fund*, of fo exactly regulating *the quantity*, and of adding fome *other valuable ufe*, namely an intereft, or fome premium equiva- lent

lent to it; that the paper-money shall become thus intrinsically, and of its own nature, a better and surer currency than all the power and authority of Colony-government could make it. For not being forced into currency, by any external value derived from authority, it must, like bullion in coin, derive its currency from its intrinsick value and applicableness to the purposes of money;— so that thus becoming, from necessity, a more determinate measure, a more practical instrument of trade, and a more beneficial deposit, as bearing an interest even while in currency, it becomes to have *all the uses* of bullion in coin, and one more,— so as even to bear a premium,—which in fact is the case of the treasurer's notes in the province of the Massachusetts-Bay in New England, though they are not a legal tender.

As the inconvenience of permitting the assemblies of the Colonies to issue paper-money, under the sanction of its being a legal tender, had been complained of and confessed; an act of parliament was made, to restrain that part of the Colonies, against which the complaint chiefly lay. Since that time, a general restraint hath been lain upon all the Colonies, by a like act of parliament, extending to the whole. The majority of
the

the men of businefs and property in the Colonies, have ever heretofore wished to have the assemblies restrained by act of parliament, from the power of giving the sanction of a legal tender to their paper-money: They esteemed that restraint to be the only effectual means of preventing the many bad practices, which have arisen from this illusory false coin; to the detriment of real business and real property. On the other hand, seeing the absolute necessity of some paper currency, schemes of the like nature, as that of the following proposal, have been thought of. I have had opportunities, not with governors and crown-officers, but with the leading men of business in the Colonies, of examining and considering several of these schemes. The following proposal may be considered as the result of these discussions, containing and comprehending, according to my best judgment, all which was thought consistent with the liberties of the people, safe in respect of their interest, and effectual to the point required. So far am I from assuming any merit in the invention or framing of it, that I desire it may be considered, as founded on what hath been actually practised in Pensylvania, by the good sense and good policy of the assembly of that province, with success and with benefit to the public. That the particular proposal, as it is now formed,

formed, and applied to the prefent exigences of America and Great Britain, was drawn up fome years ago, in conjunction with a friend of mine, and of the Colonies. It was, by us, jointly propofed to government, under fucceffive adminiftrations, in the years 1764, 1765, 1766, during which time, the publication was fufpended. It is now given to the publick, not by way of appeal againft adminiftrations, but as a fcheme which, although not attended to by a Britifh miniftry at prefent, may yet fuggeft fomething that may be of ufe to better politicians than we pretend to be.

We are fully apprifed how much we have rifqued, both in the propofing, and in the now publifhing this fcheme.—If the Britifh ftatefmen fhould ftill think that they can turn it to no good ; and if the American patriots fhould think that a dangerous ufe might have been made of it by government : We fhall be thought by the one to have been impertinent, and by the others to be mifchievous meddlers. If our ftatefmen fhould have the happinefs to find out the right ufe of it, and, like the humbler, but not lefs wife politicians in the Colonies, to apply it to the mutual benefit of government, and of the people; then we fhall not be allowed to have the leaft fhare, much lefs any

any merit in the forming of it, or in the application of it: twenty different people will prove, that it has been their scheme. About this we are not anxious, any more than disappointed that our British statesmen could not find their way to the use of it. We now propose it to the sober sense and experience of the Colonies. Who will know how to profit by it, how to convert this species of credit, into a real efficient currency; how to benefit *and to take the lead of that power and political interest,* which their taking the management of this will necessarily throw into their hands. *We need not point out to them* how that will arise.——They have the means, whenever our bad policy, or their own prudence shall lead them to make use of such, of giving this currency a general value throughout America, by establishing an intercommunion and reciprocation of credit, under acts passed by each particular assembly, all having reference to this one point;—regulating the quantity which each province or Colony shall issue—by the state of its depreciation; and regulating the proceedings in their several courts of law, as to the specialty of all bargains and contracts made in this special note-money. They also will know, which hath hitherto puzzled our statesmen, how to give it a *real intrinsick value*, without
calling

calling in the aid of the government of Great Britain, to give it *an artificial one*, by making it a legal tender; and without paying to that government *forty thousand pounds per annum*, which sum, at least, the interest of this money would have produced as a revenue.

As the paper-money act made and passed in Pensylvania, in 1739, was the compleatest of the kind, containing all the improvements which experience had from time to time suggested, in the execution of preceding acts: An account of that act will best explain and recommend the measure contained in the following proposal.

The sum of the notes, by that act directed to be printed was 80,000 *l.* proclamation money: This money was to be emitted to the several borrowers, from a loan-office established for that purpose.

Five persons were nominated Trustees of the *loan-office*, under whose care and direction, the bills or notes were to be printed and emitted.

To suit the bills for a common currency, they were of small and various denominations, from 20 shillings downwards to one shilling.

Va-

Various precautions were taken, to prevent counterfeits, by peculiarities in the paper, character, manner of printing, signing, numbering, &c.

The trustees took an oath, and gave security for the due and faithful execution of their office.

They were to lend out the bills on real security of at least double the value, for a term of sixteen years, to be repaid in yearly quotas or installments, with interest: Thus one 16th part of the principal was yearly paid back into the office, which made the payment easy to the borrower: *The interest was applied to public services,* the principal, during the first ten years, let out again to fresh borrowers.

The new borrowers, from year to year, were to to have the money only for the remaining part of the term of 16 years, repaying, by fewer, and of course, proportionably larger installments, and during the last six years of the 16, the sums paid in, were not to be remitted, but the notes burnt and destroyed; so that at the end of the 16 years, the whole might be called in and burnt, and the accounts completely settled.

The trustees were taken from all the different counties of the province, their residence in different parts, giving them better opportunities of being acquainted with the value and circumstances of estates offered in mortgage.

They were to continue but four years in office; were to account annually to committees of assembly; and, at the expiration of that term, they were to deliver up all monies and securities in their hands, to their successors, before their bonds and securities could be discharged.

Lest a few wealthy persons should engross the money, which was intended for more general benefit, no one person, whatever security he might offer, could borrow more than 100 *l*.

Thus, numbers of poor new settlers were accommodated and assisted with money to carry on their settlements, to be repaid in easy portions yearly, as the yearly produce of their lands should enable them.

Great inconveniencies had arisen in other Colonies, from a depreciation of their paper money, occasioned by emitting it in too great quantities.

It

It was difficult to know beforehand, what quantity would be sufficient for a medium of exchange, proportioned to the trade of the country, and not to exceed the occasions.

To prevent the mischiefs attending an over quantity; the government of Pensylvania began with a small sum of 15,000 *l*. in 1723, proceeded to increase it gradually, in following years, and thus prudently *felt* for a proportion they could not previously *calculate*; and, as they never exceeded a moderate sum, the depreciation was never so great as to be attended with much inconvenience.

The advantages that arise from this act, were from a view thereof, in 1752, thus expressed, by a committee of assembly, in their report of August, 19th.

" Furnishing the country with a medium
" of trade, and of a kind that could not, to
" any purpose, be exported; as it facilitated
" mutual commerce, *lessened our taxes by*
" *the interest it produced*; and made it more
" easy for every one to obtain ready pay for
" his labour, produce or goods, (a medium
" so evidently wanted at the time paper-
" money was first issued) has doubtless,
" been

" been one great means of the subsequent
" increase of our trade and people, by in-
" ducing strangers to come and settle among
" us. But your committee conceive that
" the manner of issuing this medium, con-
" tributed no less to those happy effects,
" than the medium itself. It was by the
" law directed to be emitted on loans, in
" sums of 12 *l.* 10 *s.* and upwards, not ex-
" ceeding 100 *l.* to one person for a long
" term, on easy interest, and payable in
" yearly quotas, which put it in the power of
" many, to purchase lands and make planta-
" tions; (the loan-office enabling them to
" pay the purchase so easily) and thereby to
" acquire estates to themselves, and to sup-
" port, and bring up families, but who
" without that assistance, would probably
" have continued longer in a single state,
" and as labourers for others, or have quit-
" ted the Colony in search of better fortune.
" This easy means of acquiring landed
" estates to themselves, has, we suppose,
" been one principal encouragement to the
" great removal hither of people from *Ger-*
" *many*, where they were only (and could
" scarce ever expect to be other than) ten-
" ants. That it should be easy for the in-
" dustrious poor to obtain lands, and acquire
" property in a country, may, indeed, be
" charge-

" chargeable with one inconvenience, to
" wit, that it keeps up the price of labour,
" and it makes it more difficult for the *old*
" *settler* to procure working hands; the
" labourers very soon setting up for them-
" selves, (and accordingly we find, that
" though perhaps not less than 30,000 la-
" bourers have been imported into this pro-
" vince, within these twenty years, labour
" continues as dear as ever) yet this inconve-
" nience is perhaps more than ballanced by
" the rise and value of his lands, occasioned
" by increase of people: and to the public in
" general numbers of substantial inhabi-
" tants, have been always reckoned an ad-
" vantage. In fine, by rendering the means
" of purchasing land easy to the poor, the
" dominions of the crown are strengthened,
" and extended; the propietaries dispose of
" their wilderness territory, the British na-
" tion secures the benefit of its manufac-
" tures, and increases the demand for them;
" for so long as land can be easily procured
" for settlements, between the *Atlantic* and
" *Pacific* Oceans, *so long will labour continue*
" *to be dear in America*; and while labour
" continues dear, we can never rival the
" artificers, or interfere with the trade of
" our mother country."

But

But the act being expired, and the proprietors and the people differing about the terms of renewing it, the former, though they and their deputies had received annual presents out of the interest, amounting to near 40,000 *l.* yet, insisting on greater future advantages, which the assembly did not chuse to allow, *this excellent machine for settling a new country, now no longer subsists.* And as by the late act of parliament, no more paper-money can be issued in the Colonies, that shall be a *legal tender*, it may perhaps be necessary for government here to make some provision of a currency for the Colonies. If this should be necessary, the Pensylvania scheme, which has by long experience, been found so practicable, and so useful, may, with a few changes, to accommodate it more to general purposes, be safely and advantageously extended to all the Colonies, by an act of parliament as follows.

Let   millions, in bills of credit (or paper-money) be printed here, for the use of the Colonies.

Let a loan-office be erected in each Colony, to issue the bills, take the securities, and to receive the quota's yearly paid in.

Let

Let the bills be issued for ten years, payable a tenth part of the sum yearly with interest, at *5 per cent*.

Let the Bills be made by the act, a *legal tender* in all the Colonies, and the counterfeiting made death. I desire to mark the very material difference of a paper currency created by act of parliament, and one issued to the Colonies, as the necessities only of the Colonists have occasion for it, from a paper currency poured like a deluge over a country, by act of assembly only: In the one case, the mischief of its being a legal tender, has been severely felt, and therefore forbidden: In the other case, the making it a legal tender, is not only beneficial but necessary.

Let there be no limitation of the sums to be borrowed by one person, but that every one may borrow as much as he can give double security for, by a mortgage of real clear estate.

And to prevent an over quantity being extant at one time, let an interest of 4 *per cent*. be allowed, for all sums lodged in the office, during the time the owner suffers it to remain there. *By this means, it is supposed, the due proportion of money that shall be be current, will find itself;* and adapt itself from time to time, to the occasions of commerce.

The effects of this scheme would be, that although the silver and gold acquired by the Colonies, would be all sent to England: Yet they would have among them, in consequence of this measure, a legal tender.

They would also have a sufficiency of cash current for all purposes.

They would not have too much current at one time, as the allowance for interest for sums lodged in the office, would always bring in the surplus.

The settlement and improvement of new tracts of land would be greatly encouraged and promoted, population encreased, trade extended, &c.

The means of remittance to England would be always at hand, and the commerce thereby facilitated.

A great annual sum, continually increasing, will arise to the crown for interest, which,

which, after deducting charges, may be applied to American purposes, in ease of this kingdom; and become *a permanent and effective revenue.* A considerable profit will also arise to government, from the wearing out, and total loss of a great deal of small money.

It will operate as a general tax on the Colonies, *and yet not actually be one*; as he who *actually* pays the interest, *has an equivalent*, or more, in the use of the principal. But the tax, if it can be so called, will, in effect, spread itself more equally on all property, perhaps more so than any other tax that can be invented; since every one who has the money in his hands, does from the time he receives it, to the time he pays it away, *virtually* pay the interest of it, the first borrower having received the value of it (to use for his own profit) when he parted first with the original sum. Thus the rich who handle most money, would in reality pay most of the tax.

These bills having thus *full* credit, the government can issue, on occasion, any quantity for service, in case of an American war, without needing to send *real cash thither, by hurtful contracts.*

Plenty of money thus continued in the Colonies, will keep labour high, and thereby prevent the apprehended danger of interfering manufactures.

For the more easy ascertaining of titles, there should be a clause in the act, requiring that all transfers, conveyances and incumbrances whatsoever should be recorded,—this of itself would be a great advantage to the Colonies.

The manner of carrying this proposal into execution may be as follows.

An office to be established in London, to be managed by two Commissioners, appointed by the treasury; their salaries   *per annum*, with   *per annum*, for clerks and incidents of office, to be paid out of the revenue only, arising from the interest.

The business of this office to be

1. The printing of the paper-money.

2. The signing of it by the Commissioners.

3. The distribution of it to the offices in America.

4. The

4. The entering of what is sent, according to its number and denomination.

5. The communication and correspondence with the several loan-offices in the Colonies.

6. The drawing up the instructions for the same.

7. The receiving from these offices, accounts of the issuing the paper bills, these accounts to contain, 1. Account of the numbers and dates of bills issued. 2. State of the mortgages and securities. 3. Account of interest received. 4. Account of interest paid for deposited money. 5. Account of government drafts paid by the loan-office, and salaries paid to its several officers. 6. Account of bills exchanged, for those that are over-worn. 7. Account of receipts of principal money by instalments, &c.

And in general, the Commissioners from the monthly reports of the several offices in America, of every branch of their duty, are to form monthly abstracts and reports for the treasury, of the state of the money current, of the amount of the interest money in the loan-offices, at the government's disposal, of the state of each office, and the
far-

farther regulations from time to time necessary to be made, either by orders from the treasury, instructions from the Commissioners, or further legal powers, or directions by act of parliament, or by instructions necessary to be sent to the governors in America, recommending acts of assembly proper to be made in that country.

The Commissioners are also to draw up directions and instructions to the *Inspectors*, whose office will be hereafter described.

And they are to superintend all the other parts of the administration and execution of this scheme, as will be more particularly pointed out hereafter, in the descriptions of the several offices and officers in America, with their respective duties.

Loan-Office in each province.

To consist of *Trustees, Solicitor,* and *Clerk*. The province to be divided into districts. A large province into eight districts, a small province into fewer.

Each district to have a Trustee appointed *out of its own resident inhabitants,* one who is a freeholder that can give sufficient security to the crown within the province. So that

that the loan-office of the largeft province will confift of eight Truftees, and the fmaller in proportion to their diftricts, into which they are divided, fome not having more than two.

The Truftees to be appointed by act of affembly, and upon their appointment to qualify themfelves, by giving the fecurity required to the crown, and taking the ufual oaths (or affirmation) and oath (or affirmation) of office.

Each Truftee to have 100 *l. per annum.* out of the intereft arifing by the loans of the bills.

The principal acting Truftee to refide in the capital of the province where the office is to be kept, and to have 200 *l.* or lefs in fome provinces, for his conftant attendance, and the incidents of office, befides his fallary in common with the reft.

The Truftees to be appointed, only for the term of five years, at the expiration whereof, they are to account fully to the governor in council, affifted by one of the infpectors hereafter defcribed, and deliver up all books, deeds, depofited cafh, &c.

to their succeffors, upon which they are to receive their quietus.

All the Trustees are to meet once a month at the office, to sign the bills to be issued, to consider the applications for money, examine the goodness of the security offered, and fix the sum to be lent on each security, not less than a majority of the Trustees to order the loans, and not less than two to sign and date the bills to be issued. They are also to take charge of, and keep in some safe place, the security deeds mortgaged, and *they* are to chuse a person, skilled in the law of titles, to be their *Sollicitor*, who is to be paid by the fees arising in the office, viz. 20*s*. on every mortgage, for which he is to examine, and make extracts of the titles or securities offered, for the inspection of the *Chief Justice* of the province, if referred to him, and of the Trustees; to prepare the mortgage and counterpart, with the bond and warrant of attorney, and to record the mortgage. He is also to keep a book of applications, noting them down in the order of time in which they are made, the sum desired, and the security offered in mortgage. He is to get blank mortgages printed, of a prescribed form. There are to be triplicates of each mort-

mortgage, the firſt is to be executed by the mortgager, and lodged in the office, the ſecond, an exact copy delivered to the mortgager for his direction, as it contains the times and proportions of payments, both of inſtallments and intereſt, the third to be kept in a bound book and there made the record.

The clerk is alſo to be appointed by the Truſtees. He keeps a book of allowances, ſo called, becauſe therein is put down what ſums the Truſtees think proper to allow or lend to each applyer, according to their opinion, of the ſecurity offered. He alſo computes the quotas or inſtallments and intereſt, making together, the ſum to be paid each year, by the mortgager, and gives a copy thereof to the Solicitor, to be by him, after the approbation of the Truſtees given to it, inſerted in the mortgage. He keeps alſo a day book, in which is noted,

The emiſſions and receipts of each day, viz.

The ſums lent in mortgage, and to whom.

The ſums received from each mortgager, diſtinguiſhing principal and intereſt.

The

The sums deposited in the office, for which 4 *per cent.* is to be allowed by the office.

The returning of such sums, with interest paid.

The sums of new bills exchanged for old.

The drafts of government for interest money, as paid by the Trustees.

The Trustees Salaries, when paid, and the allowance for incidents.

N. B. The person bringing any money bills to be deposited in the office, for the purpose of receiving the 4 *per cent.* is to prepare two schedules of said bills, one to be signed by the acting Trustee, and delivered to him, the other to be signed by him and delivered into the office, to be kept by the Trustees. And no sum under 100*l.* is to be deposited on the terms of receiving interest, and *the interest must not commence till one month after the deposite made.*

The clerk is to keep a ledger, in which the day book accounts are to be posted up, under their respective heads.

The Trustees, from these books, &c. are to form monthly abstracts of the whole state of the currency, and the business of the office, and to send the same signed by a majority of the whole number, to the commissioner's office in England, in order that the commissioners may form states from time to time, as the treasury shall require, of the whole of the currency throughout the continent, as well as of the state of each office in the respective Colonies.

Provision for check and control of the execution of the office in America.

1. The direction and instructions of the commissioners residing in England.

2. Two *Inspectors* to be commissioned by the treasury, to act under their instructions, and the instructions of the commissioners, and to report to them. They are to visit all the offices in America at least once a year, and to inspect the accounts, cash, &c. as often as they shall see occasion, or shall be directed by their superiors, and to join with the governor and council of each province in the auditing of the accounts of the office. And, if upon any of these inspections, an inspector shall discover any mismanagement which requires immediate remedy, he is

not

not only to report to the commissioners in England, but to the governor of the province, and if it appears to the governor and council necessary, the governor to call together the assembly immediately, in order to the appointing new Trustees, and to order, by advice of council, the prosecution of the delinquent Trustees, to the forfeiture of their securities, and such other penalties as they may have incurred.

3. The governor and council (the inspector assisting) to audit the accounts of the loan-office within each province annually. The governor and council to be allowed for their trouble.

N. B. In those provinces where the governor is not appointed by the crown, perhaps some addition may be thought proper to be made to this board for auditing.

4. A committee of the assembly to inspect the state of the office, for their own satisfaction and information, that in case they discover any mismanagement or delinquency, they may apply to the governor, that proper steps may be taken to remedy the same.

When the accounts are to be inspected and settled, the Trustees will be charged with

with the loan money put into their hands, and discharge themselves by producing mortgages for the whole, or for part, and the remainder in bills.

They will be charged with the new bills put into their hands, to exchange such as by wearing are become unfit for farther currency, and discharge themselves by producing such worn bills for part, and the remainder in new bills unexchanged.

They will be charged by the account, of interest received, and discharge themselves by their salaries, by government draughts which they have paid, by interest they have paid on sums deposited, and by producing the remainder in bills in their hands.

They will be charged with the parts of the principal sums received yearly, as instalments, and discharge themselves by mortgages on which the same was remitted, and the remainder in bills.

They will be charged with the sums deposited in their hands, to bear interest, and discharge themselves by producing receipts for what they have returned, and for interest paid, and bills in their hands for the sums they have not returned.

Having

Having now gone through the consideration of every point of internal administration, let us next review those external relations by which the interest of the American settlements stand connected with the Indian country and its inhabitants. Our Colonies must necessarily have connections both of trade and politicks with these people, of a nature different from any other, as they are are planted in countries inhabited by a race of people, who differ in their circumstances and in their politicks from any other nation with whom there remains, either in history or on record, any example of alliance.

Perhaps it may not be unentertaining, I am sure it is necessary to the true knowledge of Indian affairs, to take up this subject somewhat higher than has been usual in the ordinary way of considering it.

The different manner in which this globe of earth is possessed, and occupied by the different species of the human race which inhabit it, must form the specific difference in their interests and politicks.

The human race, which is at present found on this earth, may be precisely divided into three families, generically, and in their essential properties, distinct and different each from

from the other. And, for aught I know, it is to this natural truth, that the heaven-directed pen of the author of the books of Moses may refer, when he gives precisely and only three sons to Noah. These three different species, or race, are—The white race—the red—the black. It is not barely the colour of these two first, which distinguishes them; the form of their skull, and their hair, where there has been no mixture, is specifically different from each other; and a true Indian will not judge by any other distinction: the black race has wool instead of hair, as also a form of skull different from each.

These books, after having given a philosophical account, cloathed in drama, of the origin of things, seem to confine their real narrative to the history of the white family, to that race of people who have been land-workers from the beginning, who, wherever they have spread themselves over the face of this globe, have carried with them the art of cultivating vines, and fruit trees—and the cultivation of bread corn; who, wherever they have extended themselves, have become settlers, and have constantly carried with them the sheep, goat, oxen and horse, domiciliated and specially applied to the uses and labour of a settlement.

Of the black family I say nothing in this place, as not concerned in the present consideration.

The red family, wherever found, are wanderers. The Tartars are in one part wandering herdsmen, and in other parts hunters and fishermen. The American inhabitants, Indians, as we call them, from the word Anjô, or Ynguo, signifying a man in their language, are the same race of people from one end of the continent to the other; and are the same race or family as the Tartars, precisely of the same colour, of the same form of skull, of the same species of hair,—not to mention the language and their names.

America, in its natural state, is one great forest of woods and lakes, stocked not with sheep, oxen, or horses; not with animals of labour, and such as may be domiciliated, but with wild beasts, game and fish; vegetating not with bread-corn, but with a species of pulse, which we call maize, of which there is great doubt whether it be indigenous or not.—All therefore that this country afforded for food or raiment must be hunted for. The inhabitants consequently would naturally be, as in fact they were, *not land-workers, but hunters; not settlers, but wanderers.*

derers. They would therefore, consequently, never have, as in fact they never had, any idea of property in land, of that property which arises from a man's mixing his labour with it. They would consequently never have, as in fact they never had, any one communion of rights and actions as extended to society; any one civil union; and consequently they would not ever have any government. They know no such thing as administrative or executive power, properly so called: they allow the authority of advice, a kind of legislative authority; but there is no civil coercion amongst them: they never had any one collective actuating power among the whole, nor any magistrate or magistrates to execute such power.

The race of white people migrating from Europe, still continue land-workers, and have made settlements in parts of America which they occupy, and have transported thither bread-corn, sheep, oxen, horses, and other usually domestic animals, that are domiciliate with these settlers.

They are a community—they are a society——they live under government, and have a fixed property in their lands, have a fixed permanent interest, which must subsist *under a continued series of security*. The locality

cality of the labour of these settlers, necessarily produces a reciprocation of wants and an intercommunion of supply, by exchange of mutual necessaries. This also leads to an intercourse of commerce with others, who are not immediately within their community—And hence arises a commercial interest to these settlers.

From the European desire of having the furs and peltry of the Indian hunters, and from the Indian desire of having the more useful and necessary tools and instruments of improved life, an artificial reciprocation of wants has arisen between the European settlers, and the original inhabitants of America, which hath gradually extended itself to many articles not at first called for—— And from this intercourse of commerce has arisen a necessary relation of politicks between them.

The only true spirit which ought to actuate these politicks, must arise from a due knowledge of the circumstances and interests of each, and from a constant invariable attention to that composite interest which is formed by their alliance.

The interest of a community of settlers must lye in *a permanent series of security* to
their

their cultured lands, as the making settlements is by the successive yearly application of repeated labour, and of its eventual future effect. Settlers and landworkers want but small tracts of land; but must have a fixed and permanent local property therein. A nation of hunters require a much greater extent of country, in the proportion that the wide extended produce of a hunt, bears to the local bounded produce of a farm or settlement; so that the Indian property of country consists of two sorts, their dwelling lands and their hunt.

The interest of a tribe of wanderers lyes in the protection and support of the aged, of the women and children—under the temporary locations of dwelling, which the severity of the winter season, the occasion of the procuring pulse in the season of vegetation, and the times of parturition, render necessary even to wanderers.

As fixed regulations and protection of trade, must be the essential spirit of the politicks and the law of nations to a commercial nation *, so an exact and strict observance

---

* Hunting being but the amusement, the diversion of a nation of settlers, the rights and laws of it may not appear as national points—but to a nation of hunters

ance of the laws of sporting, the protection of the game, and the most rigid sanction of the *hunt*, (better perhaps understood by our sportsmen than our politicians) become the *laws of nations* to an *hunting nation*.

From these principles let us carry our considerations into facts.

The European landworkers, when they came to settle in America, began trading with the Indians; * obtained leave of the In-

---

ters these become the national interests and the laws of nations.—A violation of these laws of nations; as subsisting between nations of hunters, was the cause of the war between the Five-nation confederacy, and the Oïlinois. The Ohio hunt, to the south-east of lake Erie, was common to these nations; the laws of the hunt required, that at each beaver-pond, the Indians should leave a certain number of males and females; the Oïlinois, on some occasion of pique, destroyed all. The Five-nations declared war against the Oïlinies. The Indian war ends not but in the total reduction of the one or the other. The Oïlinois were totally conquered. The conquered country, as well as the hunt, became the right of the Five-nations, and were, amongst the rest of their lands, put, by them, into the hands of the English in trust.

* Perhaps New-England may be an exception: The Indians began an unjust war against them; they conquered these Indians, and their claim is best, as well as justly, founded in conquest, which the Indians acknowledge.

dians to cultivate small tracts as settlements or dwellings. The Indians having no other idea of property, than what was conformable to their transient temporary dwelling-places, easily granted this. When they came to perceive the very different effect of settlements of landworkers creating a permanent property always extending itself, they became very uneasy; but yet, in the true spirit of justice and honour, abided by the effects of concessions which they had made, but which they would not have made, had they understood beforehand the force of them.

From this moment the politics of the Indians were fixed on, and confined to, two points. The guarding their dwelling lands and their hunts from the encroachments of the European settlers; and the perpetually labouring, to our utter shame, in vain, to establish some equitable and fixed regulations in the trade carried on between them and the Europeans.

The European encroachments, not only by the extent of their settlements, but by their presuming to build forts in the Indian dwelling lands, and in the territories of their hunts, without leave, or by collusion; and the impositions and frauds committed against the Indians in trading with them, has been the occasion of constant complaint from the Indians, and the invariable source of Indian hostilities: and yet even these might have been surmounted, were it not that we have constantly added an aggravation to this injustice, by claiming a DOMINION in consequence of a *landed possession*. Against this the free spirit of an Indian will revolt, to the last drop of his blood: This will be perpetual, unremitted cause of war to them against us. Against it, they have at all times, and upon all occasions protested, and they will never give it up. As long as we keep up this useless, faithless claim of dominion over them, so long shall we be embroiled in war with them. The European power may perhaps finally extirpate them, but can never conquer them. The perpetually increasing generations of Europeans in America, may supply numbers that must, in the end, wear out these poor Indian inhabitants from their own country; but we shall pay dear, both in blood and treasure, in the mean while, for our horrid injustice. Our frontiers, from the nature of advancing settlements, dispersed along the branchings of the upper parts of our rivers, and scattered in the disunited vallies, amidst the mountains, must be always unguarded, and defenceless against the incursions of Indians. And were we able, under an Indian war, to advance our settle-

settlements yet farther, they would be advanced up to the very dens of those savages. A settler wholly intent upon labouring on the soil, cannot stand to his arms, nor defend himself against, nor seek his enemy: Environed with woods and swamps, he knows nothing of the country beyond his farm: The Indian knows every spot for ambush or defence. The farmer, driven from his little cultured lot into the woods, is lost: the Indian in the woods, is every where at home; every bush, every thicket, is a camp to the Indian, from whence, at the very moment when he is sure of his blow, he can rush upon his prey. The farmer's cow, or his horse, cannot go into the woods, where alone they must subsist: his wife and children, if they shut themselves up in their poor wretched loghouse, will be burnt in it: and the husbandman in the field will be shot down while his hand holds the plough. An European settler can make but momentary efforts of war, in hopes to gain some point, that he may by it obtain a series of security, under which to work his lands in peace: The Indian's whole life is a warfare, and his operations never discontinued. In short, our frontier settlements must ever lie at the mercy of the savages: and a settler is the natural prey to an Indian, whose sole occupation is war and hunting. To countries circumstanced

stanced as our Colonies are, an Indian is the most dreadful of enemies. For, in a war with Indians, no force whatever can defend our frontiers from being a constant wretched scene of conflagrations, and of the most shocking murders. Whereas on the contrary, our temporary expeditions against these Indians, even if succesful, can do these wanderers little harm. Every article of their property is portable, which they always carry with them—And it is no great matter of distress to an Indian to be driven from his dwelling ground, who finds a home in the first place that he sits down upon. And of this formidable enemy, the numbers, by [*] the latest accounts, are 23105 fighting men.

If we entertain an idea of conquest, in support of this ambitious folly of dominion, we must form such a series of magazines and entrepôts for stores, ammunition and provisions; we must maintain in constant employ such a numerous train of waggons for the roads, such multitudes of boats and vessels for the waters; we must establish such a train of fortified posts; we must support such a numerous army; we must form and execute such an enlarged and comprehensive system of command, as shall give us military possession of the whole Indian coun-

[*] This refers to the year 1763.

try.

try. Let now any soldier or politician consider the enormous endless expence of all this conduct, and then answer to what profitable purpose such measure leads, which may in a much better and juster way be obtained.

If our government considers this well, and will listen to those who are best versed in Indian affairs, it will be convinced that honesty is the best policy; and that our dominion in America, will be best and surest founded in faith and justice, toward the remnant of these much injured natives of the country.

In this hope, and with this view, I will endeavour to state the Indian rights and our duty toward them; and to point out that line of conduct, which leads to it—And first of the Kenunctioni, or the Five-nation confederacy.

The Indian lands are of two kinds——Their dwelling land, where their castles are, and their hunting ground. The dwelling lands of the Kenunctioni, or the Five-nation confederacy, is called Kenunctioniga, and is at the top or highest part of the continent, from whence the waters run every way—By the waters of Canada into the
gulph

gulph of St. Laurence, by all the rivers of the English Colonies into the Atlantic ocean, by the waters of the Mississippi into the gulph of Mexico. They may, in a general manner, be thus described, by a line run from near Albany, north-westward, along the Mohawk river on the north side of it, north round Oneida lake, to the north east corner of lake Ontario, thence along the lakes to Canahôga on lake Oswego or Erie; thence sixty miles directly back into the country; thence to Shamêkin, on the Susquehanna river; thence along the Cushïètung mountains; thence again to the lower Mohawk castles. The Indians themselves describing, under confidence, to a friend of mine at Onondaga, this their situation, said, "That it has
" many advantages superior to any other
" part of America. The endless moun-
" tains separate them from the English, all
" the way from Albany to Georgia. If
" they should have any design against the
" English, they can suddenly come down
" the Mohawk's river, the Delaware, the
" Susquehanna, and Potomac, and that
" with the stream. They have the same
" advantage of invading the French, by
" the waters of the river St. Lawrence,
" Sorel, &c. If the French should pre-
" vail against this country, they can, with
" their old men, wives and children, come
" down

" down the streams to the English. If the
" English should prevail in attacking their
" country, they have the same conveyance
" down to the French; and if both should
" join against them, they can retire across
" the lakes."

Their hunting lands are—*First*, Couxsachraga, a triangle, lying on the south-east side of Canada, or St. Lawrence river, bounded eastward by Saragtoga, and the drowned lands; northward, by a line from Regiôchne point (on lake Champlain, or, as the Indians call it, Caniaderiguarûnte, the lake that is the gate of the country) through the Cloven rock, on the same lake, to Oswegatchie, or la Galette; south-westward by the dwelling lands of the Mohawks, Oneidas, and Tuscaroraos.

Secondly, Ohio, all that fine country (and therefore called Ohio) lying on the south and east sides of lake Erie, south-east of their dwelling lands.

Thirdly, Tieuckfouckrondtie; all that tract of country lying between the lakes Erie and Oïlinois.

Fourthly, 'Scaniaderiada, or the country beyond the lake; all that tract of country
lying

lying on the north of lake Erie, and northwest of lake Ontario, and between the lakes Ontario and Hurons.

The right of the Five-nation confederacy to their dwelling lands and the hunting ground of Couxsachrága, and even down to the bottom of lake Champlain, was never disputed. The lands to the northward of Regiôchne, and la Galette, have long since been ceded to the Canada Indians as an hunting ground.

In the year 1684, the Five nations finding themselves hard pressed by the French and their Indians, did, by a treaty at Albany, put the lands and castles of the Mohawks and Oneidas *under the protection of the English government:* and the English accordingly undertook *the trust* to guarantee them to these Indians. And as the external mark, by which this act and deed should be anounced, the Indians desired that the duke of York's arms might be affixed to their castles.

The right of the Five-nation confederacy to the hunting lands of Ohio, Tieûcksouchrondite and 'Scaniaderiada, by the conquest they had made in subduing the Shaöanaes, Delawares, (as we call them) Twictwes

twes and Oïlinois, may be fairly proved as they ſtood poſſeſſed thereof, at the pace of Reſwick, in 1697.

In the year 1701, they put all their hunting lands under the protection of the Engliſh, as appears by the records, and by the recital and confirmation thereof in the following deed.

In the year 1726, the Seneccas, Cayougaes and Ononda-agaes acceded to the ſame terms of alliance, in which the Mohaws and Oneidas were already——So that the whole of the dwelling and hunting lands of the Five-nation confederacy were put under the protection of the Engliſh, and held by them IN TRUST, for and to the USE of theſe Indians and their poſterity.

Copy of Agreement with the Sachems of the Five Nations.

TO all people to whom this preſent inſtrument of writing ſhall come, Whereas the Sachems of the Five Nations did, on the nineteenth day of July, One thouſand ſeven hundred and one, in a conference held at Albany, between John Nanfan, Eſq; late lieutenant-governor of new-York, give and render up all their land where the beaver-hunting

hunting is, which they won with the sword, then 80 years ago, to Coorakhoo [*], our great King, praying that he might be their protector and defender there, for which they desired that their secretary might then draw an instrument for them, to sign and seal, that it might be carried to the King, as by the minutes thereof, now in the custody of the secretary for Indian affairs at Albany, may fully, and at large appear.

WE, Kanakarighton and Shanintsaronwe, Sinneke Sachems; Ottsoghkoree Dekanisoree and Aenjeueratt, Cayouge Sachems; Raclyakadorodon and Sadageenaghtie, Onondaga Sachems, of our own accord, free and voluntary will, do hereby ratify, confirm, submit and grant; and by these presents do (for ourselves, our heirs and successors, and in behalf of the whole Nations of Sinnekes, Cayouges and Onondages) ratify, confirm, submit and grant unto our most Sovereign Lord George, by the Grace of God, King of Great Britain, France, and Ireland, Defender of the Faith, &c. his heirs and successors for ever, all the said land and beaver-hunting, *to be protected and defended by his said majesty*, his heirs and suc-

---

[*] It is by this name that they mean the King of England.

cessors, *to and for the* USE *of us, our heirs and successors, and the said three Nations*; and we do also of our own accord, free and voluntary will, give, render, submit and grant, and by these presents do, for ourselves, our heirs and successors, give, render, submit, and grant unto our said Sovereign Lord King George, his heirs and successors for ever, all that land lying and being sixty miles distance taken directly from the water, into the country, beginning from a Creek called Canahôge, on the lake Oswego, all along the said lake, and all along the narrow passage from the said lake to the falls of Oniâgara, called Canaquaraghe, and all along the river of Oniâgara, and all along the lake Cataraqui to the creek called Sodons, belonging to the Sinnekes, and from Sodons to the hill called Tegechunckserôde, belonging to the Cayouges, and from Tegechunckserôde to the creek called Cayhunghâge, belonging to the Onondages; all the said lands being of the breadth of sixty English miles as aforesaid, all the way from the aforesaid lakes or rivers, directly into the country, and thereby including all the castles of the aforesaid three Nations, with all the rivers, creeks and lakes, within the said limits, *to be protected and defended by his said majesty, his heirs and successors for ever, to and for our*

USE,

use, *our heirs and succeffors, and the faid three nations.*——

In teftimony whereof, we have hereunto fet our marks and affixed our feals, in the city of Albany, this fourteenth day of September, in the thirteenth year of his majefty's reign, *Annoque Domini* 1726.

The mark of Raclyakadorodon.   a Sachem of the onondages. (L. S.)

The mark of Kanakarighton   a Sachem of the Sinnekes. (L. S.)

The mark of Otfoghkoree,   a Sachem of the Cayouges. (L. S.)

The

(273)

The mark of Sadegeenaghtie, a Sachem of the Onondages. (L.S.)

The mark of Dekaniforee, a Sachem of the Cayouges. (L. S.)

The mark of Shanintfaronwee, a Sachem of the Sinnekes. (L. S.)

The mark of Aenjeweratt, a Sachem of the Cayouges. (L. S.)

Signed, sealed, and delivered,
 in the Presence of us

Philip Livingston,   Mynderst Schuyler,
Peter Vanbrugh,   Lawrence Clausen.

Secretary's Office, New-York. The preceding is a true copy of the Record in Lib. Patents, Numb. 9. p. 253, 254. Examined and compared therewith by
    Geo. Banyer, Deputy Secretary.

Instead of executing *this trust* faithfully and with honour, by extending to the Indians our civil protection against the frauds of the English, and our military protection against the attempts of the French, we have used this trust only as a pretence to *assume a dominion* over them—We have suffered the English settlers to profit of every bad occasion to defraud them of their lands—We have
never

never made any effectual regulations to prevent their being defrauded in their trade; and until our own interest appeared to be affected, we abandoned them to their own chance and force, opposed to the strength of a powerful enemy. Nay, when at last we thought necessary for the sake, not of national faith and honour, for the sake, not of these our faithful allies, but for the sake of our own safety and interest to interfere, in opposing the French encroachments, we took it up as disputing the empire of America with the French; not as protecting and guarding the Indian lands and interest to their use, agreeable to the sacred trust by which we were bound.—And thus these savages (as we to our own shame call them) repeatedly told us, " That both we and the " French sought to amuse them with *fine* " *tales* of our several upright intentions; " that both parties told them, that they " made war for the protection of the Indian " rights, but that *our actions* plainly discovered that the war was only a contest " who should become masters of the country, which was the property neither of " the one nor the other." Since we have driven the French government from America, we have confirmed this charge of the Indians against us, by assuming that dominion which in faith and justice we cannot say we have gained over the Indians, which, in fact, we have not gained, and which, be it remembered, will coſt more blood and treaſure before we do gain it, than it is for the honour and intereſt of Great-Britain to expend in ſo bad and uſeleſs a cauſe. While theſe poor tribes of hunters remain, it will be our own fault if they do not remain in perfect harmony and good alliance with us. As hunters, their intereſt can never interfere with ours, as ſettlers; but, on the contrary, will become the ſource of the natural and moſt profitable trade to us as traders. They are continually wearing away, and as they diminiſh or retire, they cede their lands to us in peace; which we, thus in time as faſt as we can really want them, may poſſeſs in right and juſtice, untainted with the impeachment of having been gained by murder and fraud. While therefore we do remain a great and juſt nation, as we pride ourſelves Great-Britain is, we ſhould abhor the black baſe thought of uſing the power which providence hath given us, to the ruin and deſtruction of theſe brave and free people; of theſe people who gave us our firſt ſettlement in this country, and have lived with us, except under ſome temporary interruptions, in a ſeries of faithful alliance.

If

If these considerations, taken up in the course of that general review of the Colonies, and of the administration of their affairs, which I now publish, were intended as an express treatise on Indian affairs, I should think it right to examine all the complaints and several claims of justice which the Five-nations have made, and have repeated for many years, which I would found first on extracts from the records of Indian affairs, and secondly, on the history of the landed patents, and thirdly, on the occasions taken to erect, without their leave, forts on the Indian lands, which measure the Indians always consider as an act of dominion. In this general view I shall only point out that shameful patent of Ka-y-adarosseros above Albany: that pretence of claim by the corporation of Albany for the Mohawk-flats, the very residence of the Mohawks, and some others on the carrying place, at the head of the Mohawk river——all which ought to be taken into immediate consideration, that justice may be done both to the Indian and European claimants; and that the matter may not remain perpetual cause of umbrage, and perhaps the source of war. Government ought also very seriously to revise the principles on which they are now endeavouring to take possession of the Indian country by forts and garisons;

garifons; built many within the Indian dwelling lands, and many within their hunting lands, and on the paſſes and communications of theſe. It is undoubtedly right to maintain the command of that country; but there is a way to do it with ſafety and juſtice. The meaſures we are taking by force will be found to have neither the one nor the other in them; nor do I ſee how common prudence can adopt the enormous charge to which ſuch meaſures muſt lead.

We have ſeen that Sir William Johnſon, although he took Niagara *from the French* by force of arms, never conſidered this as a conqueſt of theſe lands *from Indians*; but has, agreeably to his uſual prudence and his perfect knowledge of Indian affairs, obtained by formal treaty, a ceſſion of theſe lands from the Indians to the crown of Great-Britain. The wiſdom, as well as the ſucceſs of this example, ought to lead our politicks to the ſame conduct in every other caſe, where we have built or obtained forts within their lands, eſpecially as many of them were built under expreſs promiſe of their being diſmantled as ſoon as the war ſhould ceaſe: and as the Indians were expreſsly and ſolemnly promiſed to have a ſatisfaction given to them for the uſe of theſe lands.

The

The Shawänese and Delawares are more immediately connected with the province of Pensylvania; and although, as subdued, they are under obedience to the confederacy of the Five-nations; yet, under tutelage and protection of the confederacy, they possess their rights to their own country. Was this, as I have said, a particular treatise on Indian affairs, I might here point out *" the causes of the alienation of the Delawares and Shawänese Indians from the British interest, by extracts from the public treaties, and other authentic papers relating to the transactions between the government of Pensylvania and the said Indians for near forty years past,"* as set forth in a memoir which I have had by me for many years. I could also from a series * of letters for ten years, from Monsieur de Vaudreüil, while governor of Louisiana, to his court, point out these neglects and errors, as also the manner in which the French profited of those our errors, by which we lost the Cherokees, and other southern tribes.

After what has been explained, it will be sufficient here to say, that, 1st, Doing justice

* These letters in manuscript are authentic; but I am not at liberty to say how they came into my possession.

to our faith and honour, by treating the Indians according to the real spirit of our alliances with them; 2dly, That doing the Indians justice in their lands, and 3dly, giving up that idle, useless claim of dominion over them, are points absolutely and indispensibly necessary to be adopted into our politicks, unless we have seriously taken the resolution to force our way by war. Until these points are adopted, we never shall have peace———And it deserves thorough and mature deliberation how we engage to settle and possess America by war.

These measures of sound policy once fixed upon, the next step is to establish an Administration for the conducting Indian affairs— This part of the plan which I proposed is in part adopted, by dividing the management of Indian affairs into two Intendencies—one for the northern, the other for the southern nations, but, as every thing which I could say further on this head hath been some years past stated in the memorial annexed to these papers, I will here refer the reader to that memorial on these points. The measures recommended therein I have by an opportunity of comparing them with the events of eight ‡ years, found to be such as I do most sincerely wish may be carried into execution. And if a

‡ This refers to the year 1755.

private

private person might presume to obtrude advice, which has not formerly been neglected, when the affairs of the plantations were full as happily administered, as they have been of late. I would now venture to recommend the consideration of these measures to those whose duty it is to act upon these matters. When these matters shall be settled as they ought to be, then it may be time to take up the consideration of proper regulations for the Indian trade; and when that time comes, if a plan, which I have accidentally seen, be carried into execution, I would venture to say, that every thing which can or ought to be done in Indian affairs will be effected.

If with the same spirit, guided by the same principles *, a revision was made of the laws of trade, so far as they respect the Colonies, it would answer more wise ends of government, and more the interest of the governed, both here as well as in the Colonies, than any endeavour, even though successful, to carry the present laws into execution.

The principles on which the act of navigation is founded are just, and of sound po-

* This hath been in part done by the late American revenue act.

licy;

licy; but the application of them, by the modes prescribed, as the laws now stand, to the present state of the Colony trade, is neither founded in justice or prudence. Any spirit that would force this application, would injure the principles themselves, and prove injurious to that commercial interest, which those very acts of trade mean to secure to Great Britain: whereas, upon a due revision of those laws, it would appear that there are means of producing this same end consistent with the particular interest of the Colonies, and what would carry the general commercial interest of the mother country to the utmost extent that it is capable of.

The laws of trade respecting America were framed and enacted for the regulating *mere plantations*, tracts of foreign country, employed in raising certain specified and enumerated commodities, solely for the use of the trade and manufactures of the mother-country—the purchase of which, the mother-country appropriated to itself. These laws considered these plantations as a kind of farms, which the mother country had caused to be worked and cultured for its own use. But the spirit of commerce, operating on the nature and situation of these external dominions, beyond what the mother country or the Colonists themselves ever thought

thought of, planned, or even hoped for, has *wrought up these plantations to become objects of trade;* has enlarged and combined the intercourse of the barter and exchange of their various produce, into a very complex and extensive commercial interest: The operation of this spirit, has, in every source of interest and power, raised and established the *British government on a grand commercial basis,* has by the same power to the true purposes of the same interest, extended the British dominions through every part of the Atlantic Ocean, to the actually forming A GRAND MARINE EMPIRE, if the administration of our government, will do their part, by extending the British government to wheresoever the British dominions do extend. If, on the contrary, we are predetermined to carry into strict and literal execution, the navigation act, and other laws respecting the plantation trade—without reviewing and considering what the very different circumstances of the Colonies now are, from what they were when they were first settled, merely as plantations, and when these laws were first made,—we must determine to reduce our Colonies again to such mere plantations: We must either narrow the bottom of our commercial interest, to the model of our plantation laws, or we must enlarge the

spirit

spirit of our commercial laws, to that latitude to which our commercial intereſt does actually extend. Thus ſtands the fact. This is the truth. There is no other alternative. But if we would profit of them in thoſe great commercial benefits, to thoſe great political purpoſes, which they are capable to produce; which they lead to; which the whole ſtrain of our politics have, for many years, taught us to value ourſelves upon; and which have really been the ſource of all our wealth and power; we muſt examine thoroughly the ſtate of this commercial intereſt, we muſt make a ſincere, unprejudiced and candid review of theſe laws of trade,—and by true and more enlarged principles, model them on the ideas of regulating the conduct and the intereſt, of various and widely extended parts of a one great commercial dominion.

I will firſt deſcribe the circuit of the North American commerce, and then ſuggeſt ſome ſuch meaſures as may tend to produce a happy eſtabliſhment of our trading intereſt, on true commercial principles. As the matters contained in the following repreſentation, are fairly ſtated, according to the truth and fact, and the conſequences thence deduced, are ſuch as actual experience

ence shows to be in existence, I am sure I cannot give a more clear, distinct, or better state of the American commerce than it contains.

† This representation states, that it is the singular disadvantage of the Northern British Colonies, that, while they stand in need of vast quantities of the manufactures of Great Britain, the country is productive of very little which affords a direct remittance thither in payment; and that from necessity therefore, the inhabitants have been driven to seek a market for their produce, where it could be vended, and, by a course of traffick, to acquire either money or such merchandize as would answer the purpose of a remittance, and enable them to sustain their credit with the mother country; that the prodigious balance arising in her favour is a fact too well known to the merchants of Great Britain trading to those parts to need any elucidation; but, as the nature of the petitioners commerce when free from restraints, *which they think of fatal effect, and destructive to it*, ought to be understood, they beg leave to observe that their produce then sent to our own and the foreign islands, was chiefly bartered for sugar, rum, melasses, cotton, and indigo; that the sugar, cotton, and indigo, served as remittance to

† New-York petition.

Great

Great Britain; but the * rum and melasses constituted essential branches of the petitioners commerce, and enabled them to barter with our own Colonies for fish and rice; and by that means to pursue a valuable trade with *Spain, Portugal,* and *Italy,* where they chiefly obtained money or bills of exchange in return; and likewise qualified them for adventures to Africa, where they had the advantage of putting off great quantities of British manufactures, and of receiving in exchange gold, ivory, and slaves, which last, disposed of in the West India islands,

---

* This rum and melasses became, to the Carolinas and other southern Colonies, not only a matter of aid in their own consumption, but also an article in their Indian commerce; became to the inhabitants of New England and New Scotland, an aid in their internal consumption, but also a considerable aid to the consumption in their fishery. The avowed and chief articles of commerce between North America and the parts of Europe to the southward of Cape Finistre are, fish and rice. Rice is the produce of Carolina, and the fishery is the more peculiar business of New England and Nova Scotia. Each of these countries produces and manufactures, the one more rice, the other more fish than they consume in their own subsistance and in their own foreign trade, and so each exchanges that surplusage for the rum, or rather the melasses which the New Yorkers fetch from the West Indies. By which the New Yorkers, like the Dutch in Father-land, chiefly carriers, are enabled to make out adventures to the Streights and to Africa.

com-

commanded money or bills: Rum was indispensable in their Indian trade; and, with British manufactures, procured furs and skins, which served for considerable returns to Great Britain, and encreased the revenue thereof; that the trade to the bay of Honduras was also very material to their commerce, being managed with small cargoes of provisions, rum, and British manufactures, which, while they were at liberty to send foreign logwood to the different ports in Europe, furnished them with another valuable branch of remittance; that, from this view, it is evident that sugar, rum, melasses, and logwood, with cotton and indigo, are the essentials of their return-cargoes, and the chief sources from which, in a course of trade, that they have extended their usefulness to, and maintained their credit with Great Britain.

That considering the prodigious consumption of West India produce in Great Britain, Ireland, and the continental Colonies, the rapid increase of those Colonies, their inhabitants already exceeding † two millions, the vast accession of subjects by the late conquests, besides the innumerable tribes of In-

† Including the Blacks.

dians

dians in the extensive countries annexed to the British crown, the utter incapacity of our own islands to supply so great a demand, must be out of all question: on the other hand, the lumber produced from clearing this immense territory, * and provisions extracted from the fertile soil, which most of the inhabitants are employed in cultivating, must raise a supply for exportation, with which the consumption of our own islands can bear no sort of proportion; ‡ that it seems therefore consistent with sound policy to indulge those Colonies in a free and unrestrained exportation of all the lumber and produce they raise and can spare, and an

---

* This includes bread, corn, biscuit, flour, beef, pork, horses, and the smaller articles of live stock.

‡ If we, by artificial restraints, endeavour to cut off from between the foreign West India islands, and our North American Colonies, that intercourse and exchange of supplies which is now necessary to them, or to clogg it in a manner that renders it detrimental or impracticable to those islands,——may we not force them into what should seem their natural course of commerce, an intercourse with their own Colonies, in the southern latitudes; whence they may be supplied with all those articles of lumber and live stock and bread, corn, &c. which at present, by a lucky, rather than a natural or necessary course of trade, create almost a monopoly to the Northern American Colonies of the West India supply.—

ample importation of fugar, rum, and melaffes, to fupply the various branches of their trade, to which they appear fo neceffary; that, without the one, the clearing of new lands, which is extremely laborious and expenfive, will be difcouraged; and provifions, for want of vent, become of little profit to the farmer; without the other, the petitioners muft be plunged into a total incapacity of making good their payments for Britifh debts; their credit muft fink, and their imports from Great Britain gradually diminifh, till they are *contracted to the narrow compafs of remittances, barely in articles of their own produce*; and that, how little foever their intereft of commerce could be promoted, the Colonies, thus checked, muft, from inevitable neceffity, betake themfelves to manufactures of their own, which will be attended with confequences very detrimental to thofe of Great Britain. The petitioners, having thus reprefented the nature of their commerce, proceed to point out the feveral grievances, which it labours under, from the regulations prefcribed by the laws of trade; and which, if not remedied, they conceive muft have a direct tendency to prevent the cultivation, and ruin the trade, of the Colonies, and prove highly pernicious to both the landed and trading interest of Great Britain *.

That the heavy embarassments, which attend the article of sugar, is a capital subject of complaint; and, besides the absolute necessity of a great importation to sustain their trade, it is a well known truth, that it often happens, at the foreign islands with which they have intercourse, that a sufficient return-cargo, independent of sugar, cannot be procured, which alone must render trade precarious and discouraging; but the high duty of five shillings sterling a hundred is proved, by experience, to be excessive, and has induced the fair trader to decline that branch of business, while it presents an irresistable incentive to smuggling, to people less scrupulous; that it answers not the purposes of the government, or of the nation, since it cannot be duly collected, and, if it could, would have a necessary tendency to contract remittances for British debts, while,

---

* Whether the British merchant will attend to this or not—it is nevertheless true. The views of merchants seldom, in course of trade, go beyond themselves and the present profit,——but the statesman, whether we look to him in administration or in parliament, ought thoroughly to weigh the truth and consequence of this asserted fact, as it may affect the British commerce in general.

at the same time, it is most mischievous to the Colonies, by cutting off one of the grand springs of their traffic; and, that the pressure of this duty is not aggravated, the petitioners appeal to the officers of the customs of their port, that the petitioners therefore most humbly intreat, that a moderate duty be laid on foreign sugars, which, they are assured, would not only greatly conduce to the prosperity of those Colonies, and their utility to the mother country, but encrease the royal revenue far beyond what can be expected under the present restraints.

† That the compelling merchants to land and store foreign sugars in Great Britain, before they can be exported to other parts of Europe, is another most expensive and dilatory restriction, without being of any material advantage to the revenue of Great Britain; for it effectually puts it out of the petitioners power, to meet foreigners at market upon an equal footing, is a great and heavy burden in times of peace and security, but in war will expose the trader to such

---

† That the New Yorkers, only carriers, should regard this regulation with uneasiness, is natural, but surely it is a wise and prudent regulation, for the benefit of the British Isles, to create and give a preference to the British produce and manufacture of the subjects of those Islands.

peril and hazard, as muſt wholly extinguiſh this uſeful branch of remittance; that Britiſh plantation ſugar exported from North America, ſhould be declared French on being landed in England, the petitioners conceive may juſtly be claſſed among the number of hardſhips, inflicted by thoſe regulations, as in effect it deprives them of making a remittance in that article, by expoſing them to the payment of the foreign duty in Great Britain, which appears the more ſevere, as their fellow ſubjects of the iſlands are left at liberty to export thoſe ſugars for what they really are, and a diſtinction is thus created in their favour, which the petitioners cannot but regard with uneaſineſs.

That foreign rum, French excepted, is the next article which the petitioners moſt humbly propoſe for conſideration, as the importation thereof, on a moderate duty, would add conſiderably to the revenue, prevent ſmuggling, promote the petitioners navigation, encreaſe the vent of their own produce with Britiſh manufactures, and enable them to bring back the full value of their cargoes, more eſpecially from the Daniſh iſlands of St. Thomas and St. Croix, from whence they can now only receive half the value in ſugar and cotton, conſequently rum alone can be expected for the other half,

thoſe

thofe iflands affording nothing elfe for returns, and having no fpecie but of a bafe kind.

That the exportation of foreign logwood to foreign markets, has already been diftinguifhed as one of the principal means, by which thofe Colonies have been enabled to fuftain the weight of their debts for Britifh manufactures, and it is with the greateft concern, the petitioners obferve it to be ranked by the late act among the enumerated articles; and confequently made fubject to the delay, the hazard, and expence, of being landed in Great Britain; the low price of logwood, its bulk, and the duty with which it is now burthened, muft totally deftroy that valuable branch of the petitioners commerce, and throw it into the hands of foreigners, unfettered with thofe heavy embarraffments.

That their lumber and pot-afh even when fhipped for Ireland, where they are fo neceffary, the latter particularly for the progrefs of their linen manufacture, and provifions themfelves, though intended to relieve that kingdom from a famine, are fubject to the fame diftreffing impediments; nor is flax-feed, on the timely importation of which the very exiftence of the linen manufacture of Ireland immediately depends, exempted, although it is a fact capable of the most satisfactory proof, that, without the delay now created, it has been with difficulty tranſported from that Colony, to be there in proper ſeaſon for ſowing; that what renders ſo injurious an obſtruction the more affecting is the reflection, that, while it deprives the petitioners of the benefits ariſing from flax-ſeed, lumber, and pot-aſh, theſe articles may all be imported into Ireland directly from the Baltic, where they are purchaſed from foreigners, under the national diſadvantage of being paid for with money inſtead of manufactures; and the petitioners therefore humbly beg leave to expreſs their hopes, that an evil in ſo high a degree pernicious to them, to the ſtaple of Ireland, and to the trade and manufactures of Great Britain, and which in times of war muſt fall on all with a redoubled weight, will not fail of obtaining the attention of the houſe, and an immediate and effectual redreſs.

That they beg leave further to repreſent, that the wines from the iſlands, in exchange for wheat, flour, fiſh, and lumber, would conſiderably augment the important article of remittance, was the American duty withdrawn, on exportation to Great Britain: and that it is therefore humbly ſubmitted,
whether

whether such an expedient, calculated at once to attach them to husbandry by expanding the consumption of American produce, to encourage British manufactures by enabling the petitioners to make good their payments, and to encrease the royal revenue by an additional import of wines into Great Britain, will not be consistent with the united interests both of the mother country and her Colonies.

That the petitioners conceive the North American fishery to be an object of the highest national importance; that nothing is so essential for the support of navigation, since by employing annually so great a number of shipping, it constitutes a respectable nursery for seamen, and is so clearly advantageous for remittances, in payment for British manufactures; that the petitioners therefore humbly presume, that it will be cherished by the house with every possible mark of indulgence, and every impediment be removed, which tends to check its progress.

That the enlarging the jurisdiction of the admiralty, is another part of the statute of the fourth of his present majesty, very grievous to the trade and navigation of the Colonies, and oppressive to the subject, the property

perty of the trader being open to the invasion of every informer, and the means of justice so remote as to be scarcely attainable.

That the petitioners beg leave to express the warmest sentiments of gratitude, for the advantages intended by parliament, to America in general, in the opening free ports at the islands of Jamaica and Dominica; yet, at the same time, they cannot but lament, that it is their unhappiness to be in no condition to reap the benefits which, as it was imagined, would flow from so wise a policy; that the collecting great quantities of the produce of Martinico, Guadaloupe, &c. at the island of Dominica, will be the natural consequence of opening that port, and would prove of real importance to those Colonies, were they at liberty to bring them back, in return for their lumber and provisions; but, as they are now prohibited from taking any thing, except melasses, and, it is justly apprehended, there cannot be a sufficient quantity of that commodity to support any considerable trade, the petitioners think it evident, that no substantial advantage can be derived to them under such a restraint; that they are, at the same time, at a loss to discern the principle on which the prohibition is founded; for, since sugar may be imported direct from the foreign islands, it

seems

seems much more reasonable, to suffer it from a free port belonging to Great Britain; that the petitioners therefore humbly hope, that it will be thought equitable to adapt this trade to their circumstances, by granting them liberty to import into the Colonies all West India productions, in exchange for their commodities. That upon the whole, although, at the last session, the necessity of relieving the trade of those Colonies seems to have been universally admitted, and the tender regard of parliament for their happiness highly distinguished, nevertheless, experience has evinced, that the commercial regulations, then enacted, instead of remedying, have encreased the heavy burthen under which it already laboured.

* " In this survey one thing must be
" taken notice of as peculiar to this country,
" which is, that as in the nature of its
" government, so in the very improvement
" of its trade and riches, it ought to be
" considered not only in its own proper
" interest, but likewise in its relation to

* Letter of Sir William Temple to Lord Essex, in July 22, 1673, concerning the state of Ireland, wherein the reader will see the survey taken of the trade of that country, at that time so apposite to the state of the trade of the Colonies at this season, it will be impossible not to apply it.

" Eng-

"England, to which it is subordinate, and
"upon whose weal in the main, that of this
"kingdom depends, and therefore a regard
"must be had to those points wherein the
"trade of Ireland comes to interfere with
"any main branches of the trade of Eng-
"land, in which case the encouragement
"of such trade ought to be either declined
"or moderated, and so give way to the
"interest of trade in England. Upon the
"health and vigour whereof the strength,
"riches and glory of his majesty's crown
"seem chiefly to depend. But on the
"other side, *some such branches of trade
"ought not wholly to be suppressed,* but ra-
"ther so far admitted as may serve the
"general consumption of the kingdom, *lest
"by too great an importation of commodities,
"though out of England itself, the money of
"this kingdom happen to be drawn away in
"such a degree, as not to leave a stock suffi-
"cient for turning the trade at home.*"

If many of these regulations above proposed and submitted to consideration, cannot
be admitted, while the Colonies are, by the
laws of trade, considered as *mere plantations*:
And if the improved commerce of the Colonies cannot any longer subsist as a branch of
the commercial interest of Great Britain, if
they are not admitted, Great Britain is reduced

duced to the dangerous alternative of either giving up the fubordination of the trade of its plantations, or of giving up its commerce, as it hath been extended and improved by its Colonies becoming commercial ftates; from which, otherwife inevitable danger, nothing but the general plan of union, as repeatedly above recommended, can preferve it.

The general principle of the laws of trade regulating the Colony trade, is, that the Colonies fhall not, on one hand, be fupplied with any thing but from a Britifh market, nor export their produce any where but to a Britifh market. In the application of this principle, the prefent laws direct, except in fome fpecial particulars, that the Colonies fhall import all their fupplies *from Britain,* and carry all their produce *to Britain.*

If now, inftead of confining this market for the Colonies to Britain only, which is a partial and defective application of the general principle whereon the act of navigation is founded; this Colony trade was made, amidft other courfes of trade, an occafion of eftablifhing *Britifh markets even in other countries,* the true ufe would be derived to the general intereft from thefe advantageous circumftances, while in particular the Colonies and the mother country would be mutually

tually accommodated. In the firſt caſe, the general intereſt, perverted to partial purpoſes, becomes ſo far forth obſtructed; in the ſecond, it would be carried by the genuine ſpirit of it to its utmoſt extent.—If, under certain reſtrictions, ſecuring alſo thoſe duties which the produce of the Colonies, carried to market, ought to pay to the mother country, the Colonies were permitted to export their produce (ſuch as are the baſis or materials of any Britiſh manufacture excepted) directly to foreign countries, if ſo be they ſold it to any *Britiſh houſe* eſtabliſhed in ſuch place, and were alſo permitted, if they bought their ſupplies from a *Britiſh houſe* eſtabliſhed in thoſe parts, to ſupply themſelves with the natural fruits and produce of that country (all manufactures that any way interfere with the Britiſh manufactures excepted) paying there to ſome Britiſh officer, or upon their arrival in the Colonies, the ſame duties as they would have paid by purchaſing the ſame commodities in England, every end propoſed by the principal of the act of navigation would be anſwered; the exports of the Colonies would be encouraged; and *the Britiſh market* greatly extended.

The Colonies would not only trade to, and be ſupplied by, a *Britiſh market*, but would

would become an occasion of establishing the British market in foreign countries. The same reasons of commerce, which, in a narrower view, became the grounds for establishing factories at Petersburgh, Riga, Hamborough, Lisbon, Cadiz, &c. would on a more general and extensive basis become the foundation for establishing and building up *these British markets* in every region to which our trade extended itself; for while it necessarily enlarged the special interest of the Colonies, it would enlarge it only at British markets, and to the final profit of the British general commerce. The profits of such market finally centering in Great Britain. If this maxim be not true, that the profits of the factories settled in foreign ports finally center in Great Britain, the measure of establishing such is false in policy; if the maxim be true, the permitting our Colony exports to go directly to the ports where such factories are established, is not contrary to the principle on which the act of navigation arose, but becomes coincident with, and aiding to it, in extending the British navigation and British markets, and securing the final profits thereof to Britain only.

If this method of reasoning be found not contrary to the principle of the act of navigation; if this measure at the same time
that

that it encourages the trade of our Colonies, is found to do it in a way subservient to the general commerce of Great Britain, extending the British markets, and securing the final balance of profit to Britain only; if this spirit of administration, so far as government has a right to direct the course of trade, be adopted in this part of it, the great points which it has to secure, are first, that the Colony exports to, and the supplies purchased by them from those foreign ports, *be sold and bought at a British market only.*—— The government has a right to extend its laws to these Colony traders, and to the factories established in foreign ports.——It can therefore, partly by such laws as it finds proper to enact, for the regulation of this factory trade, and partly by obliging these Colony traders to give bond before their departure from the Colonies, secure and confine all these transactions of that commerce, which is permitted at any such port, to a British market only, the laws that established these being a favour extended to the Colonies, and promoting the interest of these factories, would, as all laws of trade should do, execute themselves; and by giving the requisite powers to a consul or naval officer resident there, would be easily administered by such officer.

The next point to be guarded, would be the fecuring thofe duties which this trade ought to pay to the government of Great-Britain: If the fame duties were paid, or fecurity for them taken in thefe foreign ports, as would be or fhould be paid by the Colony trade, if the traders were ftill obliged to come to Britain, every end would be anfwered to the government revenue, and thefe charges might be fufficiently fecured, by obliging all thefe traders to fail under bond. The arrangements to be taken in fuch cafe ought to be that of adding to the office of conful, fuch powers as in the Colonies, before the eftablifhment of fpecial revenue officers there, were given to the naval officer, or to eftablifh a naval officer. The conful or naval officer, in this branch of his adminiftration, fhould be fubordinate to the commiffioners of the cuftoms and the lords of the treafury. If the duties were collected by him, in the ports of his diftrict, he fhould account and give fecurity for the fame; If bonds only, as fecurity for the payment at fuch Britifh or plantation ports, were given, he fhould keep the regifter of the fame, and correfpond with the commiffioners of the cuftoms, and fuch officers as they direct, as to the fulfilling, cancelling, or profecuting to effect faid bonds. Thefe general arrangements, taken, together with fuch further fpecial special regulations, as the experience of the commissioners of the customs should suggest, the revenue of the Colony and factory trade, under this mode of administration, would be well secured, chearfully paid, and easily collected.

Under the administration of such measures, there does not appear any reason why all the produce of the British Colonies, which are not the basis of, or do not interfere with the British manufactures, might not be carried directly to a British market at a foreign port,—and why the carrying of rice to foreign ports might not be extended, under these laws, to all such foreign ports whereat a British factory is established.—Nor under this mode of commerce can any sufficient reason upon earth subsist, why the Colony traders should not be permitted to load at these ports, the fruits, wine, oil, pickles, the produce of that country, and also such raw unmanufactured produce, as would not interfere with the manufacture of Great Britain, instead of being obliged to come to Britain to buy or reload here, after the expence of an unnecessary voyage, those very commodities which they might have bought in a *British market*, at the port which they left. Why not any of these as well as salt, as well as wines from the Madeiras and western isles?

In

In the same manner, by the same law, why may not our Colony traders be permitted to carry sugar, ginger, tobacco, rice, &c. to such ports in the rivers Weser and Elbe, in the Sound and in Russia, whereat a British factory is, or may be established? It can never be right policy to suffer labour in vain in a community: it is just so much lost to the community: and yet this coming round by England is labour in vain: If the subordinacy of the Colony-trade, and the duties arising thereon, can be by any other means secured, it is so much labour lost. The two points of a *British market,* and the revenue of the duties being secured, why may not these traders be permitted to load at these ports directly for the Colonies, hemp, yarn, and such coarse linens, as do no way interfere with the British manufactories? These measures taken, which would prove to be the true means of encouraging the Colony-trade, the best method to put a stop to the contraband trade carried on in this branch of business, and the true grounds whereon to establish the general commercial interests of Great Britain, government could not be too strict in enforcing the execution of the laws of trade, nor too severe in punishing the breach of them.—Wherever they found these traders endeavouring to carry from these ports to the Colonies raw silk, silks, velvets,

foreign

foreign cloths, laces, iron, steel, arms, ammunition, sails or rigging, or any manufactures whatever, that interfere with the manufacture of Great Britain: whenever they found these traders endeavouring to carry from the Colonies to those ports, any dying-wood whatever, indigo, cotton, silk, bees or myrtle-wax, flax-seed, naval stores, furs, skins or peltry, hides, provision, grain, flour, bread or biscuit; whale-oil, blubber, bone, or any other fish-oil, or tallow, or candles, with an exception perhaps to myrtle and spermaceti candles, government could not be too strict and watchful to restrain them. Under proper regulations, the rum of the northern Colonies should be carried to Africa, and the sale of it to the French on the banks of Newfoundland encouraged, if such vent could be procured, as we should thereby reap at least some share even of the profit of the French fishery.

In the above revision of, and the proposed regulations for the Colony trade, as connected with that of Europe, it will be seen that all mention of East India goods is purposely omitted. I think a special measure might be contrived of supplying the Colonies with East-India goods, in a way that would effectually put to a stop to that contraband trade, by which it is complained they are at present

sent supplied, in a way by which one of the greatest marts in the world, with every attendant advantage to the British general commerce, and the special interest of the East-India trade, might be established.

If measures were at this juncture taken, between the government and the East-India company, so that an East-India ship might annually stop at some island in the West-Indies, the traders, not only of the West-Indies, but of North America, would supply themselves with every advantage at such mart, not only for their own proper consumption, but also for a trade of the greatest extent; and this mart, in return, would be to the East-India company, the collector of all the surplus silver of America, and perhaps even of some of the gold and ivory of Africa also. The extensive advantages of this measure cannot but be seen; nor would this any way interfere with that supply with which the East-India trade, by way of the Manilla's, furnishes the Spanish West-Indies, so far as our East-India company may be supposed to be concerned, but would, in other respects, open a better channel of trade between the East and West-Indies, which our company must command. The difficulties in the execution lie in securing to government the revenue that should arise from

from the duties duly paid by this trade, and in securing the company against the perversion of this trade to the profit of their officers and servants.———

In the same manner, some revision of the state of the trade of the Colonies of the several maritime powers amongst each other will be necessary.———The laws and ordonnances of these do in general prohibit all trade of foreign Colonies with their own;— and yet, without some such trade as supplies the Spanish provinces with British goods and provisions, as supplies the British Colonies with Spanish silver, as supplies the French islands with British lumber, fish, provisions, horses, and live stock, as supplies the British Colonies with French mellasses, the trade and culture of these Colonies would be greatly obstructed and impaired; and yet notwithstanding this fact, our laws of trade, by an impracticable duty, extend to the prohibiting the importation of French mellasses into our Colonies.—If the government, under this law, could prevent effectually this importation, not only into the northern Colonies, *but into the British isles also*, the reward of that pains would be the destruction of a beneficial branch of trade, perhaps of driving the British American distillery into the

the French, Dutch, or Danish isles, or of forcing the French, contrary to their own false policy, into a profitable manufacture of that produce which they now sell as refuse materials. I need not point out here the very essential change that this would make in the Colony trade.——On the contrary, it is the duty of government to permit, nay even to encourage, under proper regulations, these branches of trade; in the first place, in order to extract out of the foreign Colonies, to the benefit of the British commerce, as much as possible the profits of these Colonies, and which is more material, in order to create a necessary dependence in the trade and culture of those Colonies for their supplies on the British commerce.—When it is remembered that the law, which lays a duty equal to a prohibition, on the importation of French mellasses in the British Colonies, was obtained at the solicitation of the British isles, it will be seen, that the obtaining this law is not so much meant to prohibit totally the introduction of French mellasses into the British trade, as to determine a struggle between the West-India and North American traders, who should have the profits of it. And thus, from the predominant interest of these partial views, has government been led to embarrass the general courses of its trade.——But as the West India

India traders see that this law has not, never had, and never will have the effect proposed, they will be better reconciled to its ceasing; and as government must now, after the experiment, see the false policy of it, * there is no doubt but that it will cease, so far as to reduce the duty to a moderate and practicable charge, such as will be paid, and such as will raise to the crown a very considerable revenue thus paid.

I speak not this by guess; but, from a comparison of the quantity of sugars and mellasses brought to account in the customhouse books of the *King's revenue,* with the quantity of the same article, in the same ports, brought to account in the impostbooks of the *Colony revenue,* for six years together, could, with some precision, mark the extent of it. I own I did always apprehend that two-pence *per* gallon on foreign mellasses imported into any British plantation, and so in proportion of sugars, was the best rate at which to fix this duty; that being thus *moderate,* it might be easier and with less alarm and opposition collected, and might therefore the sooner introduce the practice of fair trade, and the sooner become

* This measure hath, since the writing of the above, taken place by 6 Geo. 3. c. 52.

an *effective revenue:* But when I see a groundless clamour raised, which represents the rate fixed by the late revenue-act as destructive of the American distillery, as ruinous to the American fishery, as a prohibition of the returns made from the foreign islands for the North American fish; I must own that I have never seen any fact stated, or calculation fairly made on which such assertions found themselves.

The French isles, since the surrender of Canada and Louisiana, must depend entirely for their supplies of lumber, staves, heads, provisions, live stock, horses, &c. on the British Colonies, immediately exported from thence to those isles, unless by some means supplied from markets created at New Orleans and the island of St. Peter, as from another Isle of Man; it will therefore be the duty of government to keep a watchful eye to the formation and extent of these markets;—so at least, if they be permitted, as to have the command of them, and so as to prevent their being, to the French traders, the means of supplying the Spanish markets also, as well as their own.

Since the writing of what the paragraph above contains, very proper regulations have been by the late American revenue-act provided;

vided; and if proportionate care be taken in the execution of it, this danger is for the present guarded against.

Some revision also will be necessary in the laws about naval stores, especially that respecting the masts. The present law, under an idea of preserving the White Pine or mast trees, directs, That no White Pines shall be cut or felled within the limits of any township, if not actually private property.—This part of the law arises from a mistaken apprehension of a township, there being no lands within such but what are private property.—2*dly*, That no pines out of a township, of the dimensions of 24 inches and upwards, diameter, at the heighth of 20 inches from the ground, shall be felled.—This part of the law is *felo de se*.—Those who find their profits in cutting down these trees for logs or making shingles, &c. or who know the embarrassments which would arise to their property, if they should ever apply for a grant of these lands, by letting such Pine-trees, the property of the crown, grow there, never (if they have not other means to evade this law) will permit these Pines to come to *this dimension* which makes them royal property. The false policy of this law, and the defects in the establishment of an office of surveyor-general of his

Majesty's

Majesty's woods, will soon, if not obviated, be felt in the scarcity and price of masts, which will be the effect of it. The necessity of their going a great distance from the rivers for the masts has already taken effect, and the case of there being none within any practicable distance will soon follow. The navy-office finding that their mast-ships do come regularly hitherto to England, cannot entertain any fear of such want, and it will be the interest of others to suppress and contradict this fact; yet it is a fact, and will be soon known in its effects. On the contrary, if it is considered how disproportionate a value the price of the Pine-tree growing bears to the price of the mast when brought in the middle of winter, over the snow, with 70 or 80 yoke of oxen to the water-side; if, instead of aiming to make these trees, thus growing, *royal exclusive property*, the crown was not only to permit a free masting in lands not granted, and to make the mast-trees of all dimensions, *private property* on lands actually granted, but also (as it is done in other cases of naval stores) to give a bounty besides the price, to the person who should bring down any such masts to the water-side, it would have an immediate effect in supplying the crown with masts at a cheaper rate, and in the preservation

of

of thefe trees, thus become a branch of trade.

I would wifh here alfo to recommend the giving fome advantages and encouragement to the importation of American timber into Great Britain.

I have not gone into the thorough examination of thefe fubjects above-mentioned, nor have I pointed out, in all their confequences, the effects that this or that ftate of them would have. I have only pointed them out as worthy the attention of government; and, I am fure, whenever government takes them under confideration, they will be better underftood than any explanation of mine can make them

Were fome fuch arrangements taken for a revifion and further eftablifhment of the laws of trade, upon the principle of extending the Britifh general commerce, by encouraging the trade of the Colonies, in fubordination to, and in coincidence therewith, the trade of the Colonies would be adminiftered by that true fpirit from whence it rofe, and by which it acts; and the true application of the benefits which arife to a mother country from its Colonies would be made. Under this fpirit of adminiftration, the government, as I said above, could not be too watchful to carry its laws of trade into effectual execution.—But under the present state of those laws, and that trade, there is great danger that any severity of execution, which should prove effectual in the cases of the importation into the Colonies of foreign European and East-India goods, might force the Americans to trade for their imports, upon terms, on which the trade could not support itself, and therefore become in the event a means to bring on the necessity of these Americans manufacturing for themselves. Nothing does at present, with that active and acute people, prevent their going into manufactures, except the proportionate dearness of labour, as referred to the terms on which they can import; but encrease the price of their imports to a certain degree, let the extent of their settlements, either by policy from home or invasion of Indians abroad, be confined, and let their foreign trade and navigation be, in some measure suppressed;———their paper-currency limited within too narrow bounds, and the exclusion of that trade which hath usually supplied them with silver-money too severely insisted upon;——— this proportion of the price of labour will much sooner cease to be an object of objection to manufacturing there, than is commonly apprehended. The winters in that climate

climate are long and severe; during which season no labour can be done without doors. That application therefore of their servants labour, to manufactures for home consumption, which under any other circumstances would be too dear for the product created by it, becomes, under these circumstances, all clear gains. And if the Colonists cannot on one hand purchase foreign manufactures at any reasonable price, or have not money to purchase with, and there are, on the other, many hands idle which used to be employed in navigation, and all these, as well as the husbandmen, want employment; these circumstances will soon overbalance the difference of the rate of labour in Europe and in America. And if the Colonies, under any future state of administration, which they see unequal to the management of their affairs, *once come to feel their own strength in this way*, their independence on government, at least on the administration of government, will not be an event so remote as our leaders may think, which yet nothing but such false policy can bring on. For, on the contrary, put their governments and laws on a true and constitutional basis, regulate their money, their revenue, and their trade, and do not check their settlements, they must ever depend on the

the trade of the mother country for their supplies, they will never establish manufactures, their hands being elsewhere employed, and the merchants being always able to import such on * terms that must ruin the manufacturer. Unable to subsist without, or to unite against the mother country, they must always remain subordinate to it, in all the transactions of their commerce, in all the operation of their laws, in every act of their government:——The several Colonies, no longer considered as demesnes of the crown, mere appendages to the realm, will thus become united therein, members and parts of

---

* This is a fact too well known and understood to need any particular proof—but if need were, the writer of these papers could demonstrate this from the prices of wool, hemp, and flax, and the labour of carding, dressing, spinning, weaving, &c. in North America, compared with the prices of the same articles of produce and labour in Britain. It is therefore an idle vaunt in the Americans, when they talk of setting up manufactures *for trade* ; but it would be equally injudicious in government here to force any measure that may render the manufacturing for *home consumption* an object of prudence, or even of pique in the Americans. And yet after all, should any thing of this sort extend itself to a degree that interfered with the exports of Great Britain to the Colonies—the same duties of an excise which lie upon the manufactures of Great Britain, levied upon those of America, would soon restore the balance. This consideration, one might imagine, would induce those who are prudent in America, to advise the rest to moderation in their opposition.

the

the realm, as essential parts of a one organized whole, *the commercial dominion of Great Britain.* THE TAKING LEADING MEASURES TO THE FORMING OF WHICH, OUGHT, AT THIS JUNCTURE, TO BE THE GREAT OBJECT OF GOVERNMENT.

The END.

APPENDIX.

SECTION I.

ALTHOUGH the following papers, at the time in which they were written, had reference to the state of the service as opposed to the French measures and power in America: Although they are parts of another work intended to be published at some future time, yet they are here annexed to *the Administration of the Colonies*, as they treat of matters very worthy present consideration; and as in general they contain ideas of police, which respect the possession, preservation, and improvement of those acquisitions which our conquests have put into our hands,—and the forming them into some system of Empire that shall be the Empire of Great Britain.

The first paper, which had for its object the forming of the British possessions, together with those of our allies the Indians, into a system of barrier against the French, was written at a time when the subject was entirely new, scarce ever brought forward to consideration here in England, and when authentic accounts of the true state of the country as possessed by the English and French, were with great difficulty, if at all, to be be obtained; and I may venture to say, utterly unknown to our military.

The latter of these papers, was written after it became necessary to change the object of the war; and the only thing which I wish to say of the ideas that it contained, is, that they were literally justified by the events.

A MEMORIAL:

Stating the Nature of the Service in NORTH AMERICA, and proposing a General Plan of Operations, as founded thereon.

Drawn up by Order of, and presented to, his Royal Highness the Duke of Cumberland, 1756. By T. Pownall.

HIS Majesty has now united the service in North America into one power of action, and under one direction, by appointing a commander in chief over all North America, with powers to direct, and with force to carry on this service as a one whole. The next and necessary point therefore is, that there should be some *one general plan of operations* fixed, which may be carried on, not only by the general forces employed in the general and military part of this plan, but by every particular province and colony, within its own private councils, and own

private

private operations, coincident with the whole. When such plan is fixed, every sum of money that is raised for this service, will be applied to what shall be of real service and permanent use; and every the most minute operation that is undertaken, will become as part of such plan, Ἔργον εἰς ἀεὶ;——and every (the most otherwise insignificant) measure would become of more importance, and more service, than twenty the most expensive and bustling operations, that arise from momentary and partial starts of whim, vanity, or interest: There could not even a logg house be built, nor scarce a piquet stuck down in any part of the country, but what would be a necessary measure, and whose use (however trifling the thing in itself) would extend to the grand service of the whole: There would not be a pound, scarce a penny raised, but would have its share in this grand service. On the contrary, while private persons, or particular independent bodies of people, have consulted only the momentary partial starts of whim, vanity, party, or interest, under the influence of such motives, without any general scheme to the defence of the country, the *taking possession* of it, or the command of it, without any reference to any general idea, forts have been built up and down the country, that could never have been of use, have never been used, have never been supported, have been left to go to ruin, have been abandoned to the enemy; or, if they have been kept up at all, have been a private standing job to all concerned in them: While thus large sums of money have been squandered away to no use, or bad ones; while thus fruitless detached measures, that have

been

been of no use, but a perversion of, and incumbrance to the general service, and interfering amongst each other, have been pursued by vague, random fits and starts, the public service has not only been ruined, but the people have lost all opinion and confidence in military operations, have been discouraged and alienated from engaging in any active measures, and always suspicious, that whatever sums they give to such, are either thrown away, or put into the private pocket of some job. On the contrary, were there some one general plan of operations formed, upon the practicability and really intended execution of which they might confide, the assemblies might be persuaded, the people would be willing, and I verily believe, would be persuaded to give amply and chearfully: So that it is not only necessary to the gaining the end proposed, but also absolutely necessary to the gaining the means, that some such general plan should be fixed.

In order to which, the following paper proposes to consider,

1*st*, The site of the country:

2*dly*, The interests of the possessions and settlements:
As the basis of

3*dly*, The state of the service in America.

It becomes necessary to a right understanding of these proposed objects, to recur and run up to the first principles on which they were founded, not

not only because the subject is *new*, but because it has been misconceived, and misrepresented.

1*st*, Prior to any observations on the settlers and settlements, it will be necessary to take some notice of the peculiar state and site of the countries, in which they are settled: For it is the site and circumstances (I mean those that are unchangeable) of a country, which give the characteristic form to the state and nature of the people who inhabit it.

The consideration of the continent of America may be properly divided into two parts, from the two very different and distinct ideas that the face of the country presents, but more especially from the two distinct effects which must necessarily, and have actually arisen, from the two very different sorts of circumstances to be found in each tract of country.

All the continent of North America, as far as known to the Europeans, is to the westward of the endless mountains, a high level plane: All to the south-east of these mountains, slopes away south-easterly down to the Atlantic Ocean. By a level plane, I must not be understood, as if I thought there were no hills, or vallies, or mountains in it; but that the plane of a section, parallel to the main face of the country, would be nearly an horizontal plane, as the plane of a like section of this other part would be inclined to the horizon, with a large slope to the Atlantic Ocean. The line that divides these two tracts, that is the south east edge of these planes, or the highest

part

part of this slope, may in general be said to run from Onondaga, along the westernmost Allegehani ridge of the endless mountains, to Apalatche in the gulph of Mexico.

2*dly*, In considering first the main continent, this high plain, it may be observed, with very few exceptions in comparison to the whole, that the multitude of waters found in it is properly speaking but of two masses: The one composed of the waters of the lakes and their suite, which disembogue by the river St. Lawrence; the other that multitude of waters which all lead into the Mississippi, and from thence to the ocean; the former into the gulph of St. Lawrence, the latter into the gulph of Mexico.

There are in all the waters of Mississippi, at least as far as we know, but two falls; the one at a place called by the French St. Antoine, high up on the west or main branch of Mississippi; the other on the east branch called Ohio. Except these, and the temporary rapidity arising from the freshes of spring, and the rainy seasons; all the waters of the Mississippi run to the ocean, with a still, easy and gentle current.

As to all the waters of the five great lakes, and the many large rivers that empty themselves into them, the waters of the great Otawawa river, the waters of the lake Champlain, of Trois Rivieres, and the many others that run into the river St. Lawrence above Quebec, they may all be considered in one mass, as a *stagnation* or lake of a wilderness of waters, spreading over the

country

country by an infinite number and variety of branchings, bays, straits, &c. for although at particular places of their communications, and at the mouths of their streams, they seem to pour out such an immense ocean of waters, yet when they are all collected and assembled together, as at a general rendezvous where they all disembogue themselves into the river St. Lawrence, the whole embouchure of this multitude of waters is not larger than the * Seine at Paris; the waters of each respective mass not only the lesser streams, but the main general body of each going through this continent in every course and direction, have, by their approach to each other, by their interlocking with each other, by their communication to every quarter and in every direction, an alliance and unity, and form one mass, a one whole.

Let any one raise in his mind the idea of some low country incapable of being travelled, except on the roads, causeways, dykes, &c. that have been made through it, and that these roads have throughout the whole country a communication which connects and forms them into a one system of design, a one whole: Such person will readily conceive how easily and with what few numbers a General may take possession and hold the com-

---

* About 12 French leagues above Quebec, over against a place called la Loubiniere, the river St. Lawrence appears to be of a very considerable breadth; but when the tide, which runs up much higher than that place, has at its ebb entirely retired, that breadth which one would have judged to have been that of the St. Lawrence river, remains all dry, except a small channel in the middle, which does not appear to be much larger than the Seine at Paris, nor the waters of it that pass there to have a greater current.

mand of this country; and when once poffeffed how eafily he may defend it, by fortifying with redoubts and fuch works, the ftrong holds and paffes in it, and at what an almoft infurmountable difadvantage any one who aims to recover it muft act, even with twenty times the numbers. If thefe roads and lines have thus a communication forming a one whole, they are the foundation or bafis of a command throughout the whole country; and whoever becomes poffeffed of them has the command of that country.

Now let any one behold and confider the continent of America, as it really is, a wildernefs of woods and mountains, incapable of land carriage in its prefent natural unwrought form, and not even to be travelled on foot, unlefs by the good will of the inhabitants, as fuch travelling in thofe woods and mountains is perpetually and unavoidably liable to ambufcades, and to the having the communication from the one part to the other cut off. Let fuch perfon alfo know, that the waters for thefe reafons have ever been the only roads that the inhabitants ufe, and until art and force make others, are the only roads that any body of people can in general take. Compare this ftate of country with what is above defcribed, and the fame conclufion, *mutatis mutandis*, will be found to be derived from it.

Seeing this, as fact and experience fhews it to be, let fuch perfon then recollect what is faid above of the communication and alliance amongft the feveral waters of this continent—of the unity, one mafs, and one whole, which they form;—
he

he will see in a strong light how the watry element claims and holds dominion over this extent of land; that the great lakes which lie upon its bosom on one hand, and the great river Missisippi and the multitude of waters which run into it, form there a communication,—an alliance or dominion of the watry element, that commands throughout the whole; that these great lakes appear to be *the throne*, the *centre of a dominion*, whose influence, by an infinite number of rivers, creeks and streams, extends itself through all and every part of the continent, supported by the communication of, and alliance with, the waters of Missisippi.

If we give attention to the nature of this country, and the one united command and dominion which the waters hold throughout it, we shall not be surprized to find the French (though so few in number) in possession of a power which commands this country; nor on the other hand, when we come to consider the nature of this eastern part of America, on which the English are settled, if we give any degree of attention to the facts, shall we be surprised to find them, though so numerous, to have so little and languid a power of command even within the country where they are actually settled. I say a very strong reason for this fact arises out of the different nature of the country, prior to any consideration of the difference arising from the nature of their government, and their method of taking possession of this country.

Y 4

This

This country, by a communication of waters which are extended throughout, and by an alliance of all these into a one whole, is capable of being and is naturally a foundation of a one system of command: Accordingly, such a system would, and has actually taken root in it under the French. Their various *possessions* throughout this country have an order, a connection and communication, an unity, a system, forming fast into a one government, as will be seen by and by: Whereas the English settlements have naturally, neither order, connection, communication, unity, nor system. The waters of the tract on which the English are settled, are a number of rivers and bays, unconnected with, and independent of each other, either in interest or natural communication within land. The vague dissipated random settlements therefore, scattered up and down these, will have no more communication or connection amongst themselves, than there is amongst the various independent streams they are settled upon.— This country, instead of being united and strengthened by the alliance of the waters which run in it, is divided by these several various streams, detached from, and independent of each other, into many separate detached tracts, that do naturally and have actually become the foundation of as many separate and independent interests.

As far as the communion of the waters of any river, or the communion there may be between any two rivers extends, so far extended will arise a communication of system, of interest and command; the settlements therefore on this tract of country, would be naturally, as they are actually,

divided

divided into numbers of little weak, unconnected, independent governments—Were I to point out the natural division of these tracts and interests, it would point out a new division of the governments of the colonies, which is not the purport of this paper.——

The consideration of this country, so far as it is connected with, or has any effect upon the interests and politicks of the English settlements, presents itself to view divided in two ideas. 1*st*, The country between the sea and the mountains: 2*dly*, The mountains themselves. The first part is almost throughout the whole capable of culture, and is entirely settled: The second, a wilderness, in which is found here and there in small portions, in comparison of the whole, solitary detached spots of ground fit for settlements: the rest is nothing but cover for vermine and rapine, a den for wild beasts, and the more wild savages who wander in it.

Thus far of the site of the country, as it becomes the foundation of a natural difference between the English and French possessions in America. The next point that presents itself to consideration is, the manner in which the English and French have taken possession of, and settled in this country: And,

1*st*, Of the French.

The French in their first attempts to settle themselves in these parts, endeavoured to penetrate by force of arms, to fix their possessions by
military

military expeditions, till through the perpetual and conſtant abortion of theſe meaſures, and the certain diſappointment and ſure loſs that attended them, they through a kind of deſpair gave over all thoughts of ſuch attempts.

Whether the dear-bought experience that they learnt from hence, or whether deſpair leaving their colony to make its own way, or whether rather, the right good ſenſe of Mr. Frontenac and Mr. Calliers led them to it, is neither eaſy nor material to determine; but ſo it was, they fell afterwards into that only path, in which the real ſpirit and nature of the ſervice led.

The native inhabitants (the Indians) of this country are all hunters; all the laws of nations they know or acknowledge, are the laws of ſporting, and the chief idea which they have of landed poſſeſſions, is that of a *hunt*. The French ſettlers of Canada univerſally commenced hunters, and ſo inſinuated themſelves into a connection with theſe natives.

While the French kept themſelves thus allied with the Indians as hunters, and communicated with them in, and ſtrictly maintained all the laws and rights of ſporting, the Indians did eaſily and readily admit them to a local landed poſſeſſion; a grant which rightly acquired and applied, they are always ready to make, as none of the rights or intereſts of their nation are hurt by it: While on the contrary, they experience and receive great uſe, benefit, and profit, from the commerce which the Europeans therein eſtabliſh with them.

Whereas

Whereas on the contrary, the English with an insatiable thirst after landed possessions, have gotten deeds and other fraudulent pretences grounded on the abuse of treaties, and by these deeds claim possession even to the exclusion of the Indians, not only from many parts of their hunting grounds, (which with them is a right of great consequence) but even from their house and home, as by particular instances from one end of the continent to the other might be made appear. Upon these pretences they have driven the Indians off their lands.—The Indians unable to bear it any longer, told Sir William Johnson, *that they believed soon they should not be able to hunt a bear into a hole in a tree, but some Englishman would claim a right to the property of it as being his tree:*—And whatever the great proprietors, patentees, and land jobbers, may affirm or affect to prove, or however angry they may be with those who declare this truth; this is the *sole ground* of the loss and alienation of the Indians from the English interest, and this is the ground the French work upon.—On the contrary, the French possessions interfere not with the Indians rights, but aid and assist their interest, and become a means of their support.—This will more clearly and better appear, by a more minute and particular attention to the French measures in these matters.

1*st*, No Canadian is suffered to trade with the Indians, but by licence from the government, and under such regulations as that licence ordains. The main police of which is this. The government divides the Indian countries into so many hunts,

hunts, according as they are divided by the Indians themselves. To these several hunts there are licences respectively adapted, with regulations respecting the spirit of the nation whose hunt it is; respecting the commerce and interest of that nation; respecting the nature of that hunt.

The Canadian having such licence, ought not to trade and hunt within the limits of such hunt, but according to the above regulations; and he is hereby absolutely excluded under severe penalties to trade or hunt beyond these limits, on any account whatever.

It were needless to point out the many good and beneficial effects arising from this police, which gave thus a right attention to the interest of the Indians, which observed the true spirit of the alliance in putting the trade upon a fair foundation, and which maintained all the rights and laws of the hunt, that the Indians most indispensably exact.

But the consequence of the most important service which arises out of this police, is a regular, definite, precise, assured knowledge of the country.

A man whose interest and commerce are circumscribed within a certain department, will pry into, and scrutinize every hole and corner of that district: When such a hunt is by these means as full of these coureurs des boix, as the commerce of it will bear, whoever applies for a licence must betake himself to some new tract or hunt,

hunt, by which again begins an opening to new discoveries and fresh acquisitions.

When the French have by these means established a hunt, a commerce, alliance and influence amongst the Indians of that tract, and have by these means acquired a knowledge of all the waters, passes, portages, and posts, that may hold the command of that country, in short, *a military knowledge* of the ground, then, and not before, *they ask and obtain leave* of the Indians to strengthen their trading house, to make it a fort, to put a garrison in it.

In this manner, by becoming hunters and creating alliances with the Indians as brother-sportsmen, by founding that alliance upon, and maintaining it (according to the true spirit of the Indian law of nations) in a right communication and exercise of the true interest of the hunt, they have insinuated themselves into an influence over the Indians, have been admitted into a landed possession, and by locating and fixing those possessions in alliance with, and by the friendly guidance of the waters, whose influence extends throughout the whole, they are become possessed of a real interest in, and real command over the country. They have thus throughout the country sixty or seventy forts, and almost as many settlements, which take the lead in the command of the country, *not even one of which forts, without the above true spirit of policy, could they support, with all the expence and force of Canada:* Not all the power of France could; 'tis the Indian interest alone, that does maintain these posts.

Having

Having thus got poſſeſſion in any certain tract, and having one principal fort, they get leave to build other trading houſes and entrepôts, at length to ſtrengthen ſuch, and in fine to take poſſeſſion of more and more advanced poſts, and to fortify and garriſon them, as little ſubordinate forts under the command of the principal one.

Though theſe principal forts have ſubordinate forts dependent on them, they are yet independent of each other, and only under the command of the governor general; there is a routine of duty ſettled for theſe, and the officers and commanders are removed to better and better commands: What the particulars of this are, and of the diſtribution of the troops, I have not yet learned as to Canada; but in general the preſent eſtabliſhment for this ſervice is three thouſand men, of which there are generally two thouſand three or four hundred effective.

I have not been able to get an exact liſt of the forts in Canada, but the following is ſufficient to ſketch out the manner in which they conduct this ſervice.

It will be neceſſary firſt to deſcribe the line which now divides Canada and Louiſiana in the Illinois country. It begins from the Oubaſch at the mouth of Vermillon river, thence to the poſt called Le Rocher on the river Pæorias, and from thence to the peninſula formed at the confluence of Rocky river and the Miſſiſippi.

Forts

Forts in CANADA.

ST. FREDERICK, { St. John.
              { Carillon or Ticonderôga.

FRONTENAC, { L' Presentation.
           { Les Coudres.
           { Quintez.

NIAGARA, { Torento.
         { One other.

MISSILIMAKINAC, and its Dependencies.

DU QUESNE, { Presq' Isle.
           { Riviere au Bœuf.
           { One other.

LE DETROIT, Two { 'Twas proposed to the Court in the year 1752, to erect this into a Lieutenancy du Roy.

THE POST MIAMIS and SIOUX.

NIPIGON, { Two or three.
         { One on the River Michi-
         {   pocoton.
         { One other on the Long
         {   River.

ST. JOSEPH, and one other
LE PETIT PARIS.
ALIBI.
SAGUENAY.
ST. JOHNS, in Nova-Scotia.

In all about sixty.

Most of these forts have fine settlements round them, and they do entirely support themselves;

it

it being ufual for both officers and men to defer receiving their pay till the garrifon is relieved, which is generally in fix years; and fcarce any thing is fent to thefe garrifons, but dry goods and ammunition.

There is a fine fettlement at Detroit, of near two hundred families; a better ftill at St. Jofeph, of above two hundred; a fine one at St. Antoine, many fine ones about Petit Paris. But the French government does not encourage thefe, and has, by a pofitive ordonance, abfolutely forbid any one to make a fettlement without fpecial licence; which meafure they found neceffary to take, in order to reftrain the Canadians from totally abandoning Canada.

The eftablifhments, pofts, and fettlements of Louifiana, are as follow:

Thirty feven companies of fifty men each, and two Swiffe companies of feventy five men each.

1. The garrifon of New Orleans:

French - 900 }
Swiffe - - 75 } - - - - - - - 975

Out of which are garrifoned the outpofts of Báliffe, and other fmall pofts.

Detour Anglo's: The garrifon of this confifts of four companies, which have their tour of duty with the Mobile, Illinois, &c.

Mobile,

Brought over 975
Mobile, eight French companies, and one Swiffe - - - - - 475

"It is neceffary to fix this number here, on account of the proximity of Panfa- cola, on one part, and of the Englifh on the other; as alfo to influence the In- dians, as there are at our meetings and treaties, held here annually with the In- dians, fometimes 2, fometimes 3,000 Indians prefent *."

Tombechbé, } One company each, a de-
Alibamous, } tachment from the garrifon of Mobile.

Four companies of this garrifon relieved every year.

The Illinois, fix companies - - 300

The pofts were, in 1752, { Cafkafias.
Fort de Chartres.
Village de St. Philip.
Praire de Rocher.
Cohôkias.
Village de St. Jeune Veuve.

The Akanfas, a lefs principal poft, one company - - - - - 50
The Natches, one company - - - 50
———
1850

* Mr. Vaudreuil to the court.

The

Brought over 1850

The Nachitoches, one company - - 50
for the present on account of their not being able to prevent desertions to the Adages, a Spanish post within 7 leagues of it. They propose, when they shall be able to settle a cartel with the Spanish governor, and his Majesty approves of it, to fix two companies there, it being a frontier post.
The Point Coupe, one company - - 50
The German Settlement, one company - 50

Total 2,000

The settlements of Louisiana in general, produce Indigo equal to the Guatimalo, which admit three cuttings or crops annually; rice in great abundance, and cotton, but they find great difficulty in cleansing it from the seeds that accompany its growth here; tobacco, pitch, tar; they have a trade to their own islands with flour, peas, beans, salted or corned wild beef, and pork, hams of hogs and bears, tallow, grease, oil, hides, lumber, planks; they have also myrtle wax, which they export to France; they do also, in small quantities, manufacture the buffalo wool. From the abundance and natural growth of mulberry trees, they have their thoughts turned to silk; they have iron, lead, copper, and coals in abundance; besides the skins and coarse furs, arising from the Indian trade and hunt; they had, so long ago as in the year 1744, several vessels at their port, which came from Florida and Havanna, and the bay of Campeachy, to trade for boards, lumber, pitch, dry

dry goods, and live stock, to the value of 150,000 pieces of eight. They had a settled treaty of commerce with the Royal Company of Havanna, by the terms of which, the French were to deliver them at Louisiana, pitch at two piastres a barrel, tar at three piastres a barrel, boards at two reals each. Their settlements towards the mouth of Missisippi, are almost deserted and ruined, the settlers not being able to support the expence of banking against the inundations of the sea and land floods. Mr. Vaudreuil says, in a letter to the court, September 28, 1752, he thinks it would be much better, to defer for some years attempting settlements here, till the ground be more raised and elevated by the accretion of soil, as it has been three feet in fifteen years last past.

I mention nothing here of the posts of New Orleans, Detour Anglois, and Balife, nor of Mobile; because, being marine posts, the consideration of them does not come within the scope of this paper. I will observe, that they require our particular attention: They are become the ports to which all the men and stores, with which the country of the Ohio is furnished, are sent annually and constantly; as from New Orleans to this country, the way is much shorter than through Canada, the distance being at the most, where they are obliged at low water to follow all the windings of the river, not more than 340 French leagues; but at the usual times that they send their convoys, not more than 300, and to which they can go up with decked sloops, nine or ten months in the year. The trade comes down from the Illinois, about the latter end of

(22)

December, and goes up towards the latter end of January, or the beginning of February.

I shall describe the post of Tombechbé, from Mr. Vaudreuil's letters.

<small>April 20, 1751.</small> This post restrains the Alibamóus, Talapouches, Abekas, and Cowêtas, preserves the communication between the waters of Mobile, Alibamous river and the Missisippi; 'tis necessary for us in order to keep up amongst the Chactaws, the spirit of warring against the Chickasaws; tis also necessary as an entrepôt in our expeditions against the Chickasaws and English. From hence we can go within seven or eight leagues of the villages of the Chickasaws with periaugces, by the river Tombechbé, over which, seven or eight leagues of land carriage, we can easily go by land, and carry cohorns and light field pieces: from hence also it is, that we must send out our parties against the Carolinians; yet this fort being a heavy expence, and with great difficulty supplied, and being so situated as to be of no use to hinder the English from going to the Chactaws, when that nation is inclined to receive them, as they may conduct their convoys a little above, or a little below the fort, without our being able to oppose them. This being the case, were the Chactaws entirely secured in our interest, were the Chickasaws destroyed, and had the English lost and given up all hopes of strengthening themselves in that quarter, as we hope to effect, I then think it would be no longer necessary to keep up this post; yet till this be effected, it must be kept up, and more especially as by sup-

<small>January 6. 1746.</small>
<small>October 28, 1746.</small>
<small>March 6, 1749.</small>
<small>September 21, 1751.</small>
<small>January 12, 1751.</small>

pressing

pressing it now, the Chactaws would think themselves abandoned. This post, as well as Alibamous, should always be victualled for a year, lest by any revolution in Indian affairs, the road to it should be obstructed.

May 30, 1751.

As to the posts in the Illinois country, I am not able to describe them particularly; but what appears to be of more consequence, I collect from Mr. Vaudreuil's letters, (from 1743, to 1752) the general idea upon which the fortifying and securing that country is founded.

The first fort of their plan, in fortifying the Illinois country, was on the peninsula, in lat. 41. 30. This was a check upon, and barrier against the several nations of Sioux (not then in confederacy with them.) The next post in this plan was on the river Dorias, (so called after the junction of the Illinois river and Theakiki) which would be of more especial use, if situated on the north of the lake on that river, whence the roads divide, that lead to Massilimakinac and St. Joseph; This he describes as the key to the Illinois country from Canada.

July 18, 1743. August 30, 1744.

The next is the garrisoning and fortifying the country, from the mouth of Missouris to Kaskasias, where there are five posts. Mr. Vaudreuil thinks that Kaskasias is the principal, as it is the pass and inlet of the convoys of Louisiana, as also of those of Canada, and of the traders and hunters of the post Detroit, and that of the greatest part of the savage nations.

May 15, 1751.

There

(24)

There is also at this post, a river where the sloops which come from New Orleans, may be safely laid up in winter.

<small>Mr. M'Carty to Mr. Vaudruile, January 20, 1752.</small> But Mr. M'Carty, who was on the spot, thinks the environs of Chartres a far better situation to place this post in, provided there were more inhabitants. He visited fort Chartres, found it very good, only wanting a few repairs, and thinks it ought to be kept up.

The next post (I take them in order of place, not of time) which comes into this plan, is on the Ohio, over against the mouth of the Cherokee <small>November 4, 1745.</small> river: This, he says, would be the key of the colony of Louisiana, would be a sufficient <small>August 30, 1744.</small> barrier against the English, and restrain their in- <small>May 15, 1751.</small> croachments, and would obstruct their designs in alienating the Indians of the Ohio; it would restrain the incursions of the Cherokees, on the river Ouabash, and river Mississippi; it would also check the Chichasaws, and would by these means secure the navigation of the Mississippi, and the <small>November 4, 1745.</small> communication with our posts. He here expresses the greatest uneasiness, (as the French court did not care to engage in the measure at that time) lest the English should build a fort here, in which case, says he, we must give up all communication with the Illinois; for the English would become masters of all the navigation of that country.

<small>April 8, 1752.</small> Mr. Jonquiere proposes another fort at the mouth of Rocky river, (this is in the government

ment of Canada) which, he says, would secure the tranquillity of the south of Canada. This, says Mr. Vaudreuil, together with the post of the Illinois, would restrain and become a barrier against the English, and cover all our Indian allies to the west, from our enemies, the English, the Cherokees, Catawbas, and others.

By these posts above, and the posts of the Miamis, this whole country is secured and fortified. This country, says Charlevoix, (in 1721) will become the granary of Louisiana, and in 1746 we find it actually becoming so; for in that year it sent down to New Orleans fifty ton of flour; in 1747, we find it well furnished with provisions, and having fine crops; and in a letter of Mr. Vaudreuil's 1748, we have an account of its produce and exports—flour, corn, bacon, hams, both of bears and hogs, corned pork and wild beef, myrtle wax, cotton, tallow, leather, tobacco, lead, copper, some small quantity of buffalo wool, venison, poultry, bearsgrease, oil, skins, and some coarse furs; and we find a regular communication settled with New Orleans, by convoys which come down annually the latter end of December, and return at latest by the middle of February.

Thus the French do not only *settle* the country, but also *take possession of it*; and by the form, site, and police of such possessions, (led on and established by the guidance of, and in alliance with the waters,) a natural foundation of a sore command, have they acquired, and become possessed of *the command of this country.*

By thefe means, I repeat it, have they created an alliance, an intereft with all the Indians on the continent; by thefe means have they acquired an influence, a command throughout the country: They know too well the fpirit of Indian politicks, to affect a fuperiority, a government, over the Indians; yet they have in reality and truth of more folid effect, an influence, *an afcendency* *, in all the councils of all the Indians on the continent, and lead and direct their meafures, not even our own allies, the Five nations, excepted; unlefs in that remains of our intereft, which, partly the good effects of our trading houfe at Ofwego, and partly General Johnfon, has preferved to the Englifh, by the great efteem and high opinion the Indians have of his fpirit, truth, and honour.

* I mention nothing here of the influence of the Jefuit miffionaries, becaufe nothing is meant lefs than religion by them.

(27)

EAST.

In the French Interest.
Esquimaux.
St. John's.
Micmacs.
Penobscots.
Noridgwalks.
Abenakais.
St. Francis Indians.
Cachnewage.
Scaatecoke.
Oswegatchie.

Senekes. } Supposed to be in
Onondagas. } the British Inte-
Cayuges.   } rest, but greatly
Oneides.   } debauched by the
Tuskaroras.} French.

Mohawks.   } Wholly in the Bri-
Mehikanders.} tish Interest.

Delawares. } Lost to the English,
Shawenese. } except a few on
           } Susquehanah.

Catawbas.   } Supposed in the En-
Cherokees. } glish Interest, but
Chickasaws. } much debauched
            } by the French.

WEST.
French
Sioux.
Nadonesseries.

Illinois.
Tawigtwaes.
Miamis.
Piankeshanaes.
Wawyactaes.
Picques.
Kaskuskies.
Cawetas.   } The four Na-
Abekas.   } tions of the
Talaponches.} Creeks, as
Alibamôus. } above.

NORTH.
Wholly French.
Assinipoeles.
Adirondacks.
Algonkins.
Outawawaes.
Chononderdes } Skaniadere-
or Hurons.   } roenues.
Messisagues.
Outagamies.
Miscontiris.
Sakis.
Christinaux.
Almipogins.
Nipisenes.

SOUTH.
Osagaes.
Akansies.
Chactaws.   } Wholly French.
Panimaes.
Adages.

The English American provinces are as fine *settlements* as any in the world; but can scarce be called *possessions*, because they are so settled, as to have no possession of the country: They are settled as farmers, millers, fishermen, upon bays and rivers, that have no communication or connection of interest, consequently, the settlers belonging to these rivers, bays, &c. have no natural connection.

But

But further, the settlers upon any one river or set of waters, which waters having a connection, might become the natural seat of a one interest, are yet so settled, that they have no connection nor union amongst each other, scarce of comunion, much less of defence.

Their settlements are vague without design, scattered, independent; they are so settled, that from their situation, 'tis not easy for them to unite in a system of mutual defence, nor does their interest lead them to such system, and even if both did, yet through the want of a *police* to form them into a community of alliance, unity, and activity amongst themselves, they are helpless and defenceless; and thus may the English be considered as having, for many hundred miles, a long *indefensible line of frontiers*, prior to the consideration of the nature of the enemy they may be engaged with.

3*dly*, The state of the service as arising from the above facts.

It appears from the first cast of the eye, that the English, without some *preparative measures*, will not be able to carry into execution any military expeditions against the French in the upper part of America; because from any post where they can form an army, and lay in all its stores, ammunition and provision, they must undertake for many hundred miles, a long, dangerous, and tiresome march, by roads the most harrassing, and of almost insuperable difficulty, through a wilderness of woods and mountains, without magazines

zines of forage, &c. or any other affiftance; through a coun.ry liable to ambufcades, and all the ftrokes of war; through a country whereof the French are poffeffed of the command, or if through any part where their perfonal command does not actually exift, yet where Indians, (the moft dangerous enemies in fuch a wildernefs) where the Indians, I fay, are mafters, and poffeffed of every hold and pafs.

To put this matter in a ftill ftronger light, let any one confider, whence arifes the danger of marching through a fortified country; whence the danger of a general's leaving behind him any enemy's fort or garrifon, not taken.—It is that the enemy, who has poffeffion of thefe, has the command of the whole country, except the fole confined fpot, where the ftronger army is prefent, can forbid and reftrain the inhabitants from furnifhing you with fuch affiftance as the country is otherwife capable of affording; can, by fa lies from thefe pofts, cut off and intercept all your parties and convoys, all your intelligence; can cut off all communication with your magazines, and your own pofts; can perpetually harrafs and obftruct your march, and return within cover, before any fuperior party, fent out from the main body, can reach them; you are alfo always liable to furprize, even within your camp.

A march from any poft where the Englifh can *at prefent* form any army, and collect its ftores, ammunition, provifions, carriages, &c. through the country, as at this day above circumftanced,

is

is, literally and precisely in its effect, the same thing as the march here described.

While the Indians, whose chief art of war is that of forming ambuscades, who have acquired, from practice and art, a peculiar method of secretly traversing the woods and lying concealed in them;—while the Indians, whose military skill of fighting either single or in parties amidst these woods, renders the situation to them equivalent to fighting under cover;—while the Indians thus trained, and incredibly expert in the art, can at any time sally out from the holds, fastnesses, lurking places, and ambushes, in which the country abounds, (and all which they know) nay, even from the cover of the woods, and drive in all your small out parties, prevent such foraging as the country will afford, intercept and obstruct your convoys, cut off your communication of intelligence, provisions and succours, and retire again within cover, out of danger of any pursuit, and continue thus constantly to harrass, and, perhaps, surprize your army: while they can do this, and (believe it) all this they can do and will do, your army is to all intents and purposes, (as to the war with the Indians) marching through a country of forts and fortresses. Let any one here, compare this state of the case with the cause and reasons of the failure of the several military expeditions on this continent, and its truth will be still more evinced.

As then no general would think of making a campaign in any country, to reach which, he must march through an enemy's fortified country,
without

without some *previous measures* to maintain his march and secure his retreat through such: so here (I repeat it) there are some *previous measures necessary*.

The *first* of these measures is, the settling the police of our alliance with the [Kenunctioni] or Five-nation confederacy, upon a permanent, solid, and effectual basis, so as to restore and re-establish our interest with them.

The *second* is, taking possession of, and fortifying a system of advanced posts, entrepôs, *viz.* magazines whereat to collect stores and provisions, camps from whence (within a reasonable distance and by a practicable way) to make our sortis.

Thirdly, The securing the dominion of lake Ontario for the present, and laying a foundation for the like dominion on lakes Erie, Huron, and Michigan.

Let now any one consider the above stating of the form of the country that the English inhabit, and in which the operations of our arms must lie: Let him raise in his mind seriously, the precise idea of the native inhabitants who possess this country, and of the kind of operations by which we are, and shall be attacked, and by which we may be able to defend ourselves: Let any one, I say, by a serious attention to the above facts, form to himself that idea, which an actual and practical knowledge of the country would give him: Let him then be told a melancholy

lancholy truth, that almost all those Indians, whose friendship and alliance were once our best and securest barrier, are now by the French debauched and alienated from us, nay even turned against us, and become the servile instruments of the French robberies, massacres, and treacherous incroachments: Let then his eye be turned upon the state of our back inhabitants, settled in a vague, unconnected, defenceless manner, up to the mountains, to the very mouth of the dens of these savages.——Any one attentively considering the above facts, will see the English colonies in not only a weak defenceless state, but exposed to, and almost at the mercy of a very powerful enemy: Considering this, and the above facts, he would see how superficial, wild, and false an idea of the service that is, which would create a barrier by a line of forts; a barrier that might as well pretend to cut off the bears, wolves, and foxes from coming within it, as the Indians; a barrier that would have no more effect than so many scarecrows, unless you could actually build another Chinese wall, and so another, still advancing your wall-fence, as you advanced your settlements; a barrier that would take more troops to man it, than the country inclosed within it would take people to cultivate it; a line of 13 or 14 hundred miles, that is at last no line at all; he would, I say, see this measure not only impracticable, but ineffectual: Nay, were it practicable, and could it take effect, yet the insupportable expence of it, would render it impossible to be engaged in. Any one reasoning on the ideas as above stated, and knowing them to be what they really are, *facts*, would turn his

thoughts

thoughts on those objects which experience, fact, and reason point out to be one part of our barrier: Namely, a real and stable alliance with the Indians, formed on such articles as should give us the same kind of possession and command in the Indian country, the same influence in Indian affairs, as the French have. And,

First, As to that part of our barrier, and the service which is connected with, and depends on our alliance and interest with the Kenunctioni, the confederacy of the Five nations, I can only repeat what I have said formerly on this subject.

* " The original natural form under which the Indian country lay being that of a forest, stocked not with sheep, or oxen, or horses, not with beasts of labour and domestic animals, but only with wild beasts and game, all that the country afforded for food or raiment must be hunted for: The Indians, therefore, would constantly be, as they were in fact, not land-workers, but hunters; not settlers, but wanderers; they would therefore, consequently never have, as in fact they never had, any idea of property in land; they would consequently never have, as in fact they never had, any one common fixed interest, any one communion of rights and actions, one civil union, and consequently not any government;

* This proposal, amongst others, was contained in a paper, delivered by the author of this memoir, to the commissioners of all the Colonies, assembled at Albany in 1754. and transmitted to government with their minutes.

they

they know no such thing as an administrative or executive power, properly so called. They allow the authority of advice, a kind of legislative authority, but there is no civil coercion; they never had any one collective, actuating power of the whole, nor any magistrate or magistrates to execute such power.

But the country now appearing under a very different form, and they, the Indians, being under very different circumstances, arising from trade, treaties and war, begin to feel rather than see, to find by experience rather than reason, the necessity of a civil union of power and action; and that these circumstances have in fact, for many years been formed, and have at length formed to them such a collective power: These people are precisely in that point of circumstances, where a community, that was before only a community of society, is becoming that of government.

In all their actions, therefore, of late years, whether of treaty or war, they have recurred to *some agent* to actuate this power: They are not only become capable of such a general leading, but their circumstances require it. The circumstances with which they are connected, had formed them into a state, but from the circumstances of the society under which they live, they can never have amongst themselves a *stateholder*; their circumstances require and look out for some such; some such they must have, and if we do not find such for them, the French will, and are, actually attempting it. Further, as they know not, nor
acknow-

acknowledge any leading power, but that of authority, there can be no nominal, visible appointment of such leader; they will never appoint such within themselves, nor will they ever submit to any one appointed from without. This was the mistake of the governor of Canada, which had like to have lost him all the Cachnuagas two years ago.

* Therefore such person or persons only, as can acquire, or actually are, in possession of this leading power, this authority with them, can be *this agent, this leader, this* STATEHOLDER."

For this manager, this stateholder, the government hath appointed Sir William Johnson; a person not only the proper one, but precisely the very and only person that the above circumstances and nature of things pointed out; the person whose knowledge of Indians, whose influence, by the opinion the Indians have of him, whose very uncommon zeal for the interest of his country, whose integrity and bravery, will, by such measures as the Indians can really and indeed trust in, if properly supported, restore this branch of our affairs to its salutary effect.

He has, in his papers, communicated by me, mentioned every thing necessary, as to the management of this Indian administration: I cannot but add, as a collateral measure, that would

---

* This paper was drawn up, in the year 1754. not only to suggest the necessity of the office, but to recommend Colonel, since Sir William Johnson, to be the officer. It succeeded accordingly.

strengthen and finally confirm such our interest amongst the Indians, the making little settlements at Oswego, Niarondaquat, and Niagara *, and at our other forts, by leave of the Indians.

Secondly, We should then, according to good faith and truth, leave the Indians in full and free possession of their dwelling country and hunting grounds, which the English have, in the most solemn manner, confirmed to them by treaty, and of which, by the same treaty, we have undertaken the protection: We should guaranty and protect such to them, to their use, and also all their hunting-grounds.—This part of the general scheme also, is in some degree carried into execution, by the instructions given by general Braddock to general Johnson, for his direction in his late treaty with the Indians; which instructions were, at the desire of general Braddock and governor Shirley, drawn up by your memorialist, having been first proposed by him. This measure will be absolutely necessary to preserve these Indians to our alliance, as may be seen in almost every treaty held with them since the first surrender of those lands; it is also necessary to support ourselves against the western French Indians: This proposed measure will be so far from being an impediment or hurt to our interest, that the greatest advantages may be made of it, both in the means towards executing the general plan, and in the final execution of it. The uses that

* If we had done this, or would now do it, we need never suffer ourselves to think of abandoning our several distant posts, on account of the very enormous expence of maintaining them.

may be made of this measure towards the executing of this plan, are, That while we are undertaking the protection of the Indian country and hunting grounds, we are actually becoming possessed of the command of the country. Of which, in the whole, when we are possessed of the command and protection (by means of a very few forts necessary to be erected, which I do not here mention) upon which, in part, according to the proposed colonies and settlements, when we are settled, the Indians will be preserved and protected to their satisfaction, and yet cannot move to war, nor even to hunt, nor subsist, but as they maintain their alliance with the English; and yet in conjunction with us, their whole force by these means being become infinitely greater, may be directed at any time into the heart of the enemy's country.

Thirdly, As to the administration of * Indian affairs to the southward, the first step necessary to

* These Indians are the Catawbaes, Cherokees, Chickasaws, and Creeks. The Creeks are in part debauched and alienated from us by the French, and attend the French treaties constantly at the Mobile, especially the Alibamôus, Cowëtaes, Talapôuches, and Abekaes, and are in great measure held under subjection by the French forts at Alibamôus, and tombeckbá.

The Chickasaws are greatly weakened, and almost ruined by the intrigues of the French within them, and by the wars with the Chaćtaws, and other French Indians, being unsupported by us.

The Cherokees and Catawbaes; but ill supported by us, are constantly harrassed and warred upon by the Five Nations, at the instance of the French influence among that people.

be taken is, that there be an abfolute ftop put to all provincial adminiftration; that there be no more agents, commiffaries, or interpreters, appointed by, and acting under the private orders of a particular province or proprietories, from whence arifes interferings and confufion, and oppofition in our Indian affairs, always to the obftructing, often to the utter ruin, of the Britifh general intereft.

Inftead of thefe, there fhould be one only principal commiffary (who underftands the language and intereft, and is acquainted with the people of that nation) appointed feverally to each nation: This perfon fhould have under him feveral ftore-keepers and fmiths.

All thefe principal commiffaries fhould be fubordinate to a one general agent or fuperintendent *, who fhould be under the orders of the commander in chief only,—acting by his orders and inftructions, form'd on a *one general idea* of the Englifh and Indian intereft, of our alliance, and of the meafures to be conftantly and uniformly purfued.

As the being fupplied with European goods, is to the Indians the firft effential intereft of their politicks, is the fole and actual object of their alliance with us, and the only real and permanent motive of their attachment to us; and as, according to the cuftom of thefe people, all pub-

* *N. B.* There has been one fince appointed, Mr. Stewart, a very active, intelligent, and able man.

lic transactions are executed by exchange of presents, all public friendship preserved and animated by public hospitality and liberality, the first and fundamental object of the English measures should be to provide for these, in a regular and sufficient manner. The being able to do this, is our peculiar advantage and superiority over the French in these affairs; their measures are perpetually impeded and distressed, through their being unable to do this; it is the only difficulty that they have not surmounted, and cannot surmount; it is this that makes our alliance, if we did conduct it as we ought, the true and natural interest, the true and natural politicks of the Indians.

There ought therefore to be concluded with these southern nations, a general alliance of friendship and mutual defence and assistance, founded on the British general interest, not any provincial private one, upon a one general, uniform plan: The 1*st* article of which should be, To do justice to all their claims, to redress all their wrongs.

2*dly*, To maintain with them all public hospitality and friendship, by public, annual, and occasional presents, by entertaining them, and by all other usual assistance, to establish a fair and just trade with them, and settle stores within their countries, or wherever is most convenient for them, with a constant supply of goods at a settled and cheaper rate than the French do supply them.

3*dly,* Mutually to affift each other againft all attempts of the French or their Indians, or any hoftile attempt whatfoever upon either; conftantly and faithfully to give all intelligence to each other, to mend their guns when they have occafion to go to war, to fupply them at fuch times with ammunition, and always to fend fome of our people along with them if they require it, except againft Indians in alliance with the Englifh; and whenever the Englifh call upon them, to go out with them to war, that the Englifh fupply fuch as want them, with arms, and *all* with provifions and ammunition, and defend and maintain their wives and children in the mean time.

This being done, a fund capable of anfwering the above engagements, and of conftantly and faithfully executing them, and alfo capable of fupporting an adminiftration of Indian affairs, that may work effectually to the preferving and maintaining the Britifh intereft in fuch meafures, fhould be fettled on a general and permanent foundation; which may be as follows:

That the feveral colonies who have hitherto conftantly raifed monies for Indian affairs, as a private provincial fervice, fhould for the future appropriate fuch monies to this general fund.

That fuch colonies as have never raifed any monies for thefe fervices, fhould, for the future, raife and appropriate to this fund, fuch fums under a quota, in proportion to the benefit received, or the harm avoided, by the barrier arifing from
this

this general alliance and administration of Indian affairs; and it becomes worthy of consideration, whether the islands in the West Indies, their interest being inseparably connected with that of the continent, should not bear a certain proportion of taxes towards the charge of the war.

Matters within ourselves being thus prepared and provided for:

The first step of our measure in this branch should be, establishing, by the advice of people of the best authorities, and most knowledge of the affairs of each nation respectively, at proper places, general magazines for this service, at the most convenient entrepôts between *marine and inland navigation* of carriage, whence lesser stores, respectively subordinate to these, might be best supplied within the Indian countries, or where is most convenient for the Indians: As for instance, one at Schenectady, or rather at Mount Johnson;——one either at William's ferry on the Potomac, or at Fort Cumberland on Will's creek;——one other somewhere on the Roanoak, or James river;——one other at fort Augusta, on the Savanah.

From these general magazines, the several national or tribe-stores should be constantly supplied: These stores should be also public truck-houses, and the store keeper be also a public truck master: These to be fixed in each particular nation, in such places, and in such number as hath been usual, or will be best for the good of the service, at each of which there should also be a smith.

a smith. The commissary appointed to the affairs of each nation, to command and superintend all the store keepers, truck masters, smiths, and all the stores, and to be constantly circuiting through these, living always at some one of them, and attending respectively at any of them, wheresoever he is commanded by the general agent, or the good of the service requires: Also at all times (unless in matters of a more public general import, when the general agent is to attend) to negotiate and transact all matters of business which such nation may have to do with any other, or with any colony, and to interpret between the Indians of the nation he is appointed commissary to; and in general, within the powers of his instructions, to do all those matters and things as have usually been done by provincial agents or interpreters; that the store keepers and smiths do keep constant journals, and make report to the commissary; that the commissaries keep a regular journal of these reports, and of their own transactions, and report to the general agent, and he likewise to keep a journal and record, and report to the commander in chief.

The order then of the public presents, the public hospitality and liberality being settled, according to the nature of those Indians and our alliance with them:

The method and laws of the trade with them being also settled:

The next step to be observed, I take entirely from the French; and it is a measure, according to to my idea, abſolutely neceſſary. Obſerving the want of ſubordination among the Indians, the French make a number of ſachems, to whom they give medals and appoint them to preſide as chiefs, leaders, counſellors, ſpeakers, &c. ſome over eight, ſome over ten villages, and ſo on as their influence extends; being eaſily, by preſents and money, poſſeſſed of theſe medal-chiefs, they thus eaſily acquire a more uniform and ſtable management of their Indians, than the Indians even know of amongſt themſelves.

Let it be a ſtanding inſtruction, faithfully in all and every matter, to execute and fulfil, according to the true ſpirit and intent, the above treaty and alliance, both as to the true intereſt of the Indians, and as to the forming their alliance into a firm barrier againſt the French, and enemy Indians.

The ſeveral people employed in Indian affairs to have conſtantly in view, the ſcheme *of uniting the ſeveral nations into a confederacy* like that of the Five Nations. In order to this, that there be found out and fixed upon ſome one place in the back country, whereat the general agent ſhould hold all his general treaties and parlies with theſe Indians, as the French do at the Mobil; which place, upon the ſuccefs of this ſcheme, to be the council place,—as Onondaga is to the Five Nations. Let any one conſider how a little republick, formed by the Welinis on the river Ouäbaſch, by ſome free and independent Indians, did greatly embaraſs, and had well nigh ruined the French affairs there.

This

This third branch (according to my idea of our barrier) being thus or in some such way provided for and administered;

The fourth, is, that of *a system of magazines and fortified camps* as entrepôts, whereat either to collect for defence, or from whence, within a reasonable distance and by a practicable way, to make our sortis. This branch is in part provided for; for by removing and advancing these stores, and at length, when a proper place is found to fix them on, that would defend and command the country, getting leave to fortify them, and so erect them into forts, the Indians are defended, are at the same time held within proper terms, and we have within a friend's country, advanced posts or entrepôts,——that would answer all the purposes of defensive or offensive operations against the enemy; and all that could be in this place said on that head, I have very minutely entered into in that part, where I explain the nature and state of the country and its inhabitants. I will only add their opinion of one post, which we once had, and of another that they feared we were about to make.

Mr. Vaudreuil, governor of Canada, in his letter to the court, May 10, 1744, mentioning the leave which the English had got to build a fortified trading house at Ockfusques, amongst the Creeks, says, "If the measure of which this might be a foundation, should be properly carried into execution, it would oblige the French to retire from their fort of Alibamôus down to the Mobile."

And again in another letter, September 17, 1744, he mentions this store-house having opened a traffick with the Chactaws,—yet this the English abandoned; and the French have now a fort on each main branch of the river Mobile; one at Tombechbé, and fort Toulouse at Alibamôus.

In another letter of November, 1748, he says, it would be very easy for the English, by means of the river Ohio, to form an entrepôt at Prudehomme to serve them as a retreat, having the nations of the Shawoänaes, Cherokees, and Chickasaws, on their back to support them. From this entrepôt, it would not be difficult for them to penetrate to the Ackansas, Panis, Osages, Padouces, and Misouris, and all the other nations of that country, if the posts and settlements of the Illinois were broke up, as they would certainly be, did the English settle and fortify at Prudehomme; not only the inhabitants of the Illinois would be lost to us, but also the inhabitants near New Orleans, would be so greatly distressed for the want of the succours and provisions of this country, the granary to it, by loss of the benefit of the trade with that post, it would be difficult for them to subsist, it would be impossible to maintain the expence they must live at without it, and they must be obliged to abandon the colony: But should not matters be so bad as this, yet, were the post of
the

the Illinois taken away, the colony would not be able to extend itfelf at furtheſt, beyond the poſt of the Natches, without a very ſtrong garriſon at the poſt of the Ackanſas, and at beſt that poſt would be too low to cover the hunting country.

When ſuch forts are erected, the commanding officer at each fort ſhould be a kind of comptroller on the commiſſary or ſtore keepers for that diviſion, and ſhould be furniſhed with proviſions and neceſſary ſtores to make preſents to, and to entertain the Indians when they come to him, and to ſupply their neceſſities: He ſhould, for this reaſon, have a right to make an order on the magazine of his diviſion for this purpoſe.

Fifthly, In other parts of our frontier, that are not the immediate reſidence and country of Indians, ſome other ſpecies of barrier ſhould be thought of, of which nothing can be more effectual than a barrier colony; but even this cannot be carried, as is hereafter explained, into execution and effect, without this previous meaſure of a ſyſtem of entrepôts in the country between us and the enemy. *The nature of this* ſyſtem, muſt depend on the nature of the ground, which can only be determined by a particular view, and will then immediately be beſt known to military men; but all mankind muſt know that no body of men, whether as an army, or as an emigration of coloniſts, can march from one country to another, through an inhoſpitable wilderneſs, without
maga-

magazines, nor with any safety without posts, communicating amongst each other by practicable roads, to which to retire in case of accidents, repulse, or delay.

It is a fact which experience evinces the truth of, that we have always been able to outsettle the French, and have driven the Indians out of the country more by settling than fighting; and that wherever our settlements have been wisely and completely made, the French neither by themselves, nor their dogs of war, the Indians, have been able to remove us. It is upon this fact that I found the propriety of the measure of settling a barrier colony in those parts of our frontiers, *which are not the immediate residence or hunting grounds of our Indians.* This is a measure that will be effectual, and will not only in time pay its expence, but make as great returns as any of our present colonies do; will give a strength and unity to our dominions in North America, and give us *possession* of the country as well as *settlements* in it. But above all this, the state and circumstances of our settlements renders such a measure not only proper and eligible, but absolutely necessary. The English settlements, as they are at present circumstanced, are absolutely at a stand; they are settled up to the mountains, and in the mountains there is no where together, land sufficient for a settlement large enough to subsist by itself and to defend itself, and preserve a communication with the present settlements.

If

If the English would advance one step further, or cover themselves where they are, it must be at once, by one large step over the mountains, with a numerous and military colony. Where such should be settled, I do not now take upon me to say; at present I shall only point out the measure and the nature of it, by inserting two schemes, one of Mr. Franklin's; the other of your memorialist; and if I might indulge myself with scheming, I should imagine that two such were sufficient, and only requisite and proper; one at the back of Virginia, filling up the vacant space between the Five Nations and southern confederacy, and connecting, into a one system, our barrier: The other somewhere in the Cohass on Connecticut river, or wherever best adapted to cover the four New England colonies. These, with the little settlements mentioned above, in the Indian countries, compleats my idea of this branch.

The dominion then of the lakes being maintained by a *British navy* of armed vessels, suited to the nature of the service, according to a plan proposed by your memorialist, in June 1754, to the commissioners met at Albany; which part of the general frontier is, according to that proposal, by order from England, and at the expence of the crown, now carried into execution, compleats the whole of my idea of this frontier.

These matters being thus proposed, I do not at all enter into that point of their execution which is the duty of the military, as it is a matter in which the judgment of a civil man may not have its weight, nor into the manner of removing the French from their encroachments; yet I cannot but in general obferve, that as the prefent military object of his Majefty's fervice in this country, is either to erect forts, or to demolifh thofe erected by the French on his Majefty's lands; and as the way to all fuch lies through woods and wildernefses, there is a proper fphere of action peculiar to each, both for his Majefty's regular troops, and for the provincial troops of the country. The provincial forces of thefe countries, as irregulars or light troops, can, the beft of any forces in the world, efcort his Majefty's troops through thefe woods, to where their proper fcene of action lies; they can alfo in the fame manner hand up all their convoys, and would, I am perfuaded, fhould any occafion call for their fervice, act with bravery and fpirit: They are alfo fit for what may be properly called an expedition, fome excurfion a la brufque of ten or twenty days continuance: They fhould therefore be employed either as a covering army, or kept with the regular army, in companies of light infantry, for efcorts, fcouring and fcouting parties; while the regular troops, as a main body, marching by thefe means without being harraffed, fuftain them; while his Majefty's troops alone are fit for the various duties and fervices of a continued regular campaign, and for the fatigues and perfeverance, and fkill, neceffary in a fiege.

I muft

I must also observe, that this is not proposed as a scheme to be executed all at once; but, as a general plan of operations, to be preserved and attended to in the whole; to which every part of our measures, as they shall arise into action and come upon the field, are to be referred; to which, in all seasons and at all occasions, as from time to time such shall offer or serve, our measures must be directed; and to which every individual, and every part, must conspire and co-operate to form a whole.

T. POWNALL.

SECTION II.

THE ideas of the service contained in the paper above, lead by fair consequence to the following proposition, that after the English had been repeatedly disappointed in their attempts to penetrate the country, by the way of Crown-point and lake Champlain, and had lost Oswego and the command of the lake Ontario, considering the reason there was also to expect the defection of the Indians in consequence of it, there remained no other alternative, but either to make peace, *or to change the object of the war*, by making a direct attack, up the river St. Lawrence, upon Quebec itself, urged to a total destruction of Canada. The writer of these papers came over to England in the latter end of the year 1756, to propose and state these measures, nearly in the same form as was afterwards repeated by the paper that follows, particularly marking the necessity of two fleets, and two armies: One army destined for the attack; the other under orders to invest Canada, by taking post somewhere between Albany and Montreal, so as to cover the English colonies: One fleet to escort and convoy the army up the river St. Lawrence; and the other to cover and protect the sea-line of the colonies. The object was adopted. Why nothing was done in the year 1757, and why no more was done in the year 1758, than the taking of Louisbourg, will be explained on a future occasion; the ideas contained in the following paper lead to the rest.——

Idea of the Service in America, for the year 1759.

Boston, December 5th, 1758.

IF the point disputed between us and the French, be determinately and precisely understood, the manner of conducting it may be soon fixed: If we are still, as we were at the first breaking out of the war, disputing about a boundary line, and for the possession of such posts, communications and passes, as may be *a foundation* to our possessions *of a future dominion* in America, we are still engaged in a petty skirmishing war: from the state of which it was always plain, and experience now proves it, that we shall ever be inferior, and beaten by the French; for the French have long ago, by a continued system of measures, been taking possession of such posts as hath given them that foundation: They have already established that which we must fight to establish, inch by inch.

If we have changed the point, and brought it to its true issue, its natural crisis, whether we, as provinces of Great Britain, or Canada as the province of France, shall be superior in America; then the service to be done, is *a general invasion of of Canada, in conjunction with the European troops and fleet*; then is our natural strength employed; and we must consequently be as naturally superior.

This being fixed, the next point is, where the real attack must be made: the same reasons that show the necessity of such a general attack, show that it will *never effectually be carried on over land*; for, if it could, Canada might as effectually be destroyed, by the petty skirmishing war, for posts, passes, &c. as by a general invasion. But experience has now shown, what reason might have seen some time ago, that as the state of the service is circumstanced between us and the French, that cannot be; the possession which the enemy has of the posts of strength, the carrying places, passes, water communications, and roads, by forts, redoubts, and their Indians, would render the passage to Canada by land, the work of a campaign; even with success; but finally also, the success doubtful. The road to Quebec, up St. Lawrence river, we possess by *the superiority of our marine navigation*. There is neither danger nor difficulty, nor do I see how there can be any opposition, to hinder the fleet getting up to the island of Orleans; and a superior army in possession of that, may, by proper measures, command the rest of the way to Quebec. If our army can once set down before Quebec, it must take it: If Quebec be taken, the capitulation may at least strip Canada of all the regulars, after which the inhabitants might possibly be induced to surrender.

If this attack be determined, the fleet of transports will be escorted up the river by the frigates, bombs, and other small vessels of war: *But while our forces are all up the river, a very strong squadron seems necessary to cover the maritime parts of our own colonies.*

I am told, that many French vessels proceed early in spring, to the bay of Gaspee, before the river St. Lawrence is navigable, and lie there till the river breaks up, then slip up without danger, when for some time it would be almost impossible to cross the gulph; for as soon as the ice breaks up in the river, it is presently clear; but the ice embayed in the gulph, swims about for a long time, and renders the navigation of that gulph extreamly dangerous, long after the river may be navigated with safety. If this fact be true, it seems necessary, that two or three of the ships of war should proceed to Gaspee, before the river St. Lawrence breaks up, in order to prevent any succours being sent up the river in spring.

But although this attempt on Quebec, by way of St. Lawrence river, may be the only real, and will be the only effectual attack on Canada; yet one other, if not two false attacks will be necessary, one by way of lake Champlain; the other by way of lake Ontario. That by way of lake Champlain may, as far as Crown-point, be offensive, and should then change into a defensive measure, by taking strong post there, with a garrison which will effectually check the enemy at that gate of the country, and from whence continual scouting parties, to harrass the settlements, and beat up the quarters of the enemy, should be sent down the lake. As there are now so many regiments at Albany, Sckenectady, fort Edward, and the posts on the river, the taking fort Carillon, at Ticonderôga, and of consequence fort St. Frederick at Crown-point, might be effected with these, together with such provincials as shall be thought necessary, (if not in winter) yet, before the time for embarking for St. Lawrence river approaches: and this time appears the more proper, as it may possibly be before the French can sufficiently relieve it. The reason that makes me think that this should be attempted is, that the possession of this post is an effectual investing of Canada in that quarter: The reason why I think no more should be attempted is, that it *would prove unsuccessful*, and that all the labour and expence that is employed in the attempt, is lost as soon as it is given over.

As we have now so good an entrepôt towards lake Ontario, as the fort at the Oneida carrying place, it is now in our power to attempt acting on that lake; the want of this rendered all attempts there before, abortive and unsupportable. An appearance of an attack on Canada by that way, must greatly alarm the enemy at Montreal; and, though I do verily believe we shall never succeed to make an effectual irruption that way, *until Quebec be taken*, yet as whatever shall be done on that lake towards such an attempt, viz. taking post at some part on the lake, and building vessels, will have a collateral effect; even

sup-

supposing the first to prove abortive, that will prove a most essential point of service, namely, the gaining dominion of the navigation of the lake. So that should nothing else be done, yet what is done, and what is spent, will not be thrown away; but remain a chief corner-stone in the foundation of the British dominion in America:—Besides, if we remain, during the campaign, superior in the lake, the enemies communication with their southern posts is cut off, their connection with the Indians of the Five Nations interrupted; and we may, in the course of chances, possibly take Niagara. This amphibious kind of service seems adapted to the provincials, especially those of New York and Rhode Island, accustomed to privateering and batteauing: but these should be supported by good garrisons of regulars, in such posts as may be found necessary to be taken at the entrepôt on the Oneida carrying place, and at the port it shall be found necessary to possess on the lake.

As to the number of regular troops necessary for the attack on Quebec, I have not presumed to speak, for I am no judge; but a number of provincials will certainly be necessary, and these such as are used to the water, and marine navigation, for such will be of the most essential service in the passage of the army from the lower end of the Isle of Orleans to Quebec, where most of the difficulty and danger will lie. Now for this service, none can be so well adapted as the people of the province of Massachusetts Bay, as they are all, in the southern parts, whalers and fishermen. After the troops are landed near Quebec, numbers will

be

be wanted, such as are used to carrying heavy lumber and timber, &c. through the woods. Now for this service, none can be so well adapted as the inhabitants of New Hampshire, and the county of York, in the province of Massachusetts Bay, who are so perfectly accustomed to the masting service, that is, fetching the great masts down from the woods; besides, the people of Massachusetts in the counties of Hampshire, Worcester and York, are the best wood hunters in America; and would therefore, disposed in proper out-posts, be the best adapted to the keeping the camp before Quebec quiet from the enemies partizans and Indians, or perhaps in breaking up the enemies settlements in the country, while the regulars were taking their towns. For this purpose also, I should think, if about a hundred thorough wood hunters, properly officered, could be obtained in the county of York, a scout of such might make an attempt upon the settlements by way of Chaudier river. Such a scout, to the purposes of alarming and keeping the enemy in abeyance there, or perhaps breaking up the settlements, is practicable; and, I think, with early notice, such a scout may be obtained.

These are the services our people are fitted for; and therefore, as far as relate to the people of the province his Majesty has committed to my care, I can be positive, that if his Majesty's General would have a real and effectual service from them, they must be employed in such. Take those who live inland and carry them to sea, or those who have lived by the sea, and march them through the woods, they will be useless and sickly.

Employ each in their proper element; let those who are naturally connected with Hudson's river, and acquainted with inland navigation, be employed up in the back country, and lakes to the westward; and those who border on the sea, and are used to marine navigation, be employed in the service that goes by sea to the eastward; and then for every ten men on paper, there will be ten men's real service.

I have in this paper confined my idea to the invasion of Canada, and the attacks on that country, and so have said nothing of that very necessary service, the erecting a fort at Penobscot river, which on different occasions I have before repeatedly expressed.

I have confined my idea to Canada, and have therefore said nothing of fort Du Quesne; but if I had extended my idea to that part, I should have endeavoured to consider how far, or not, it might be practicable to break up the enemies settlements on the Ohio, and the Illinois country, founded on this opinion of Mr. Vaudreuil himself, in his letter to his court, when governor of Louisiana, November 1748.——" It would be very easy
" for the English, by means of the river Ohio,
" to form an entrepôt at Prudehomme, to serve
" them as a retreat, having the nations of the
" Shawöanese, Cherokees and Chickasaws on their
" back and to support them. From this entre-
" pôt it would not be difficult to penetrate to the
" Akansaes, Panis, Olagnes, Padouces, and
" Missouris, and all the Ohio nations of that
" country, if the posts and settlements of the
" Illi-

" Illinois were broken up, as they would cer-
" tainly be, did the English settle and fortify
" at Prudehomme; not only the inhabitants of
" the Illinois would be lost to us, but also the
" inhabitants near New Orleans would be so
" greatly distressed for want of the succours and
" provisions of this country, *the granary to it*,
" by the loss of the trade with that post, that it
" would be difficult for them to subsist, it would
" be impossible to maintain the expence they
" must live at without it, and they must be
" obliged to abandon the colony: But should
" not matters be so bad as this; yet, were the
" posts of the Illinois taken away, the colony
" would not be able to extend itself at furthest
" beyond the post of the Natches, without a
" very strong garrison at the post of Akansaes,
" and at best that post would be too low to *cover*
" *the hunting ground.*"

I should have extended my idea to an attempt by a West India squadron, with troops raised in the islands on Mobile, for nothing would more embarrass the enemy's Indian affairs in Louisiana, than the taking this place, the grand rendezvous at all their treaties. For they support a garrison here; amongst other reasons, for this also, (as Mr. Vaudreuil, in one of his letters to the court, says) " to influence the Indians, as there are
" at our meetings and treaties, held here annu-
" ally with the Indians, sometimes 2, sometimes
" 3,000 Indians present."

I should also have recommended the taking post at Ockfuiqué amongst the Creeks, because, says Mr. Vaudreuil, "If the measures of which this might be a foundation, should be properly carried into execution by the English, it would oblige the French to retire from their fort at Alibamôus down to the Mobile."

T. POWNALL.

To the Right Honourable
  Mr. Secretary Pitt.

The reader is here desired to refer to the events of the year 1759 in America.

Quebec was taken by general Townshend, the moment that the army was enabled to set down before it, by the greatly hazarded, and gloriously successful stroke of general Wolf.

The operations of the army under general Amherst, could not, by all the skill and determined perseverance of that excellent officer, be pushed further than Crown-point, and there became defensive by fortifying that point.

The operations up the Mohawks river, and on lake Ontario, were carried just to that effect which opened the way for the next campaign, 1760, when general Amherst went that way to take possession of Canada.

Amidst these objects, I mention the taking possession of the Penobscot country, and the building a fort there by the governor of the Massachusetts province, merely as it was proposed in the paper above,

above, and as the proposal and execution of it was approved by the King and his ministers at that time.

The whole fleet was taken up the river St. Lawrence, where, as general Wolf expresly declares, it was a part of the force least adapted to the object: The sea-line of the colonies was left uncovered and open. If the French had had sense enough to have sent two ships of the line, with a frigate or two, and one or two bomb-ketches, they might have burnt Halifax, Boston, New York, or Philadelphia, without interruption; or even if such measure had not been carried to that degree of success, they might have raised such an alarm as should have broken up some of our active, offensive operations, in order to come to the defence of this sea-line; and, perhaps, thus the whole of the operations of 1759, have been disconcerted and defeated. To enquire why this was done, would at this time become a mere criticism, for as, by good luck, no such accident happened, it is right that success should justify every measure,

To give reasons why nothing was attempted towards the quarters of Louisiana at that time, will be the solution of some future discussion.

SECTION III.

The following instructions, referr'd to in page 36, Appendix, drawn up by T. POWNALL, and recommended to General BRADDOCK, were, by that Officer, sent to Col. JOHNSON.

YOU are to produce to the Indians of the Six Nations, a deed which will be delivered to you by Col. Shirly, and in my name, to recite to them as follows.

Whereas it appears, by a treaty of the Five Nations, made at Albany on the nineteenth day of July 1701, with John Nanfan Esq; Lt. Governor of New York, That the said Five Nations did put all their Beaver Hunt, which they won with the sword, then eighty years ago, *under the protection of the King of England*, to be guarantied to them and their use. And it also appearing, by a deed executed in the year 1726, between the Three Nations Cayouges, Senecaes, and Onondagaes, and the then Governor of New York, that the said Three Nations did then surrender all the lands lying and being, sixty miles

miles diſtance, taken directly from the waters into the country, beginning from a creek called Canahoqué on the lake Oeſwego, extending along the ſaid lake to the falls of O'niagära, and along the lake Cataraquis to Sodons creek, and from Sodons creek, to the hill called Tegechunckſerôde, and from thence to the creek called Cayhunghâge, as is particularly deſcribed in ſaid deed, including all the caſtles of the aforeſaid Three Nations, with all the rivers, creeks, and lakes within the ſaid limits, to *be protected and defended* by the King of Great Britain his heirs and ſucceſſors for ever, to and for the uſe of them the ſaid Indians, their heirs and ſucceſſors for ever.

And it appearing that the French have, from time to time, by fraud and violence, built ſtrong forts within the limits of the ſaid lands, contrary to the covenant-chain of the ſaid deed and treaties: You are in my name, to aſſure the ſaid Nations, that I am come, by his Majeſty's order, to deſtroy all the ſaid forts, and to build ſuch others *as ſhall protect and ſecure* the ſaid lands to *them, their heirs and ſucceſſors* for ever, according to the intent and ſpirit of the ſaid treaty, and do therefore call upon them to take up the hatchet, and come and take poſſeſſion of their own lands.———

SECTION IV.

The following is referr'd to in page 47

Pro Johanne Caboto & filiis suis super t[erra]
incognitâ inveſtigandâ.

Rex omnibus, ad quos &c. Salutem.

A.D. 1496.
A. 11. H. 7.
NOTUM ſit et manifeſtum, quod d[edi]-
mus & conceſſimus, ac per præſe[ntes]
damus & concedimus, pro nobis & hæred[ibus]
noſtris, dilectis nobis Johanni Cabotto, civi [Ve]-
netiarum, ac Lodovico, Sebaſtiano, & San[cto]
filiis dicti Johannis, & eorum ac cujuſlibet eo[rum]
hæredibus & deputatis, plenam ac liberam au[cto]-
ritatem, facultatem & poteſtatem navigand[i ad]
omnes, partes, regiones, & ſinus maris o[rien]-
talis, occidentalis, & ſeptentrionalis, ſub [ban]-
ne[r]is, vexillis & inſigniis noſtris, cum qui[buſ]-
nabibus ſive navigiis, cujuſcumque porti[uræ]
& qualitatis exiſtant, & cum tot & tantis n[autis]
& nominibus, quot & quantis indictis nav[ibus]
ſecum ducere voluerint, *ſuis & eorum pr[opriis]
ſumptibus & expenſis*;

Ad inveniendum, difcooperiendum & inveſti‑
gandum quafcúmque infulas, patrias, regiones,
five provincias gentilium & infidelium, in qua‑
cumque parte mundi pofitas, quæ Chriſtianis
omnibus ante hæc tempora fuerunt incognitæ.

Conceſſimus etiam eifdem & eorum cuilibet,
eorumque & cujuſlibet eorum hæredibus & de‑
putatis, ac *licentiam dedimus affigendi prædictas
banneras noſtras & infignia in quacúmque villâ,
oppido, caſtro, infulâ fcu terrâ firmâ à fe noviter
inventis.*

Et quod prænominati Johannes & filii ejuf‑
dem, feu hæredes & eorum deputati quafcúmque
hujufmodi villas, caſtra, oppida & infulas à fe
inventas, quæ fubjugari, occupari, & poſſideri
poſſint, fubjugare, occupare & poſſidere valeant,
tanquam vafalli noſtri, & gubernatores, loca‑
tenentes & deputati eorumdem, dominium, titu‑
lum & jurifdictionem eorumdem villarum,
caſtrorum, oppidorum, infularum, ac terræ firmæ
fic inventarum, nobis acquirendo;

Ita tamen at ex omnibus fructubus, proficuis,
emolumentis, commodis, lucris & obventioni‑
bus, ex hujus modi navigatione provenientibus,
præfati Johannes & filii, ac hæredes & eorum
deputati teneantur & fint obligati nobis, pro
omni viagio fuo, totiens quotiens ad portum
noſtrum briſtolliæ applicuerint, ad quem omnino
applicare teneantur, & fint aſtricti, deductis
omnibus fumptibus & impenfis neceſſariis per
eofdem factis, *quintem partem totius capitalis*
lucri

lucri sui facti sive in mercibus sive in pecuniis persolvere;

Dantes nos & concedentes eisdem suisque hæredibus & deputatis, ut ab omni solutione custumarum omnium & singulorum bonorum ac mercium, quas secum reportârint ab illis locis sic noviter inventis, liberi sint & immunes.

Et insuper dedimus & concessimus eisdem ac suis hæredibus & deputatis, quod terræ omnes firmæ, insulæ, villæ, oppida, castra, & loca quæcúmque, a se inventa, quotquot ab eis inveniri contigerit, non possint ab aliis quibusvis nostris subditis frequentari seu visitari, absque licentia prædictorum Johannis & ejus filiorum suorumque deputatorum, sub pæna amissionis tam navium sive navigiorum, quam bonorum omnium quorumcumque ad ea loca sic inventa navigare præsumentium;

Volentes & stictissimè mandantes omnibus & singulis nostris subditis tam in terra quam in mare constitutis, ut præfato Johanni & ejus filiis ac deputatis bonam assistentiam faciant, & tam in armandis navibus seu navigiis, quam in provisione commeatûs & victualium pro sua pecunia emendorum, atque aliarum rerum sibi providendarum, suos omnes favores & auxilia impartiantur.

In cujus &c.

Teste rege westmonasterium quinto die Martii,

Per ipsum Regem.

SECTION V.

This Commission—erecting and establishing a board, for the purpose of governing the Plantations, is referr'd to in page 62.

De Commissione speciali domino archiepiscopo Cantuariensi et aliis.

REX &c. reverendissimo in Christo patri et perquam fideli consiliario nostro, Willielmo providentiâ divinâ Cantuariensi archiepiscopo, totius anglie primati et metropolitano. A.D. 1636.

Ac perdilecto & perquam fideli consiliario nostro Thome domino Coventrie magni sigilli nostri Angliæ custodi,

Ac etiam reverendissimo in Christo patri ac perdilecto & perquam fideli consiliario nostro Ricardo providentiâ divinâ Eborum Archiepiscopo, Anglie primati & metropolitano.

Necnon reverendo in Christo patri & perdilecto & perquam fideli consiliario nostro, Willielmo

lielmo episcopo London, summo thesaurario nostro Anglie;

Perdilectisque & perquam fidelibus consanguineis & consiliariis nostris,

Henrico comiti Manchester privati sigilli nostri custodi,

Thome Comiti Arundell & Surr', comiti marescallo Anglie,

Edwardo Comiti Dorchestrie, camerario perchariffime confortis nostre regine;

Ac perdilectis & fidelibus consiliariis nostris,

Francisco Domino Cottington, Cancellario & subthesaurario scaccarii nostri ac magistro Curie nostre Wardorum & Liberationum,

Thome Edmonds militi, thesaurario hospitii nostri,

Henrico Vane Militi Controrotulatori Hospitii Nostri,

Johanni Coke militi, secretariorum nostrorum primariorum uni, et

Francisco Windebanke militi, secretariorum nostrorum primariorum alteri, salutem.

Cum

Cùm subditorum nostrorum et nuper patri nostri domini Jacobi nuper regis anglie, memorie recolende, nonulli, regiâ licentiâ mediante, imperii nostri territoria, non tantum dilatandi studio, sed precipuè ex pio & religioso domini nostri Jesu Christi evangelium propagandi affectu & desiderio, copiosas gentis Anglicane Colonias, summa industria & magnis expensis in diversas mundi plagas incultas penitus & incolis vacuas, vel a barbaris nullam divini numinis notitiam habentibus occupatas, deduci fecerunt; nos eorum tranquillitati prospicere volentes gratiosè & quieti, vestrumque fide, prudentiâ justitia, et provida circumspectione plenius confidentes, constituimus vos predictos,

Archiepiscopum Cantuariensem, dominum custodem magni sigilli nostri Anglie,

Eboracensem archiepiscopum, dominum thesaurarium nostrum Anglie, dominum custodem privati sigilli nostri, comitem marescallum Anglie,

Edwardum Comitem Dorchestrie, Franciscum Dominum Cottington, Thomam Edmonds Militem, Henricum Vane Militem, Johannem Coke Militem, et Franciscum Windebank Militem, & quoslibet quinque vel plures vestrum commissionarios nostros & vobis & quibuslibet quinque vel pluribus vestrum damus & committimus potestatem ad regimen & tutamen dictarum coloniarum deductarum vel que gentis Anglicane inposterum fuerint in partibus hujusmodi deducte, leges, constitutiones et ordinationes, seu ad publicum coloniarum illarum statum, seu ad privatam singulorum utilitatem pertinentes, eorumque terras, bona, debita & successionem in eisdem partibus concernentes, ac qualiter invicem & erga principes exteros eorumque populum; nos etiam & subditos nostros tam in partibus exteris quibuscunque; quam in mari in partes illas vel retrò navigando, se gerant, vel que ad sustentationem cleri, regimen vel curam animarum populi in partibus illis degentis, exercentis, congruas portiones in decimis, oblationibus, aliisque proventibus designando spectant, juxta sanas discretiones vestras in politicis & civilibus, & habito consilio duorum vel trium episcoporum, quos ad vos convocandos duxeritis necessarios in ecclesiasticis, & clero portiones designandi, condendi, faciendi, & edendi, ac in legum, constitutionum & ordinationum illarum violatores, penas & mulctas, impositionem, incarcerationem & aliam quamlibet coertionem, etiam si oporteat & delicti qualitas exigerit per membri vel vite privationem infligendas providere; cum potestate etiam (nostro adhibito assensu) gubernatores & prefectos coloniarum illarum a locis suis amovere ex causis que vobis legitime vise fuerint aliosque eorum loco constituere, ac de eis rationem prefecture & regiminis suorum exigere, & quos culpabiles inveneritis vel a loci privatione, mulcte impositione de bonis eorum in partibus illis levando, vel abdicatione à provinciis illis quibus prefuerint, vel aliter secundum quantitatem delicti castigare, judicesque & magistratus politicos & civiles ad causas civiles, & cum potestate & sub formâ, quâ vobis quinque vel pluribus vestrum videbitur expedire, ac

judices,

judices, magistratus & dignitates ad causas ecclesiasticas, & sub potestate & formâ que vobis quinque vel pluribus vestrum episcopis suffraganeais (archiepiscopo Cantuariensi protempore existenti consulto,) videbitur expedire, constituere & ordinare; curiasque, pretoria, & tribunalia tam ecclesiastica quam civilia, judiciorum formas & procedendi modos in eisdem, & ab eis appellandi in causis & negotiis tam criminalibus quam civilibus, personalibus, realibus & mixtis pretoriis, seu de equo & bono, constituendi, & que crimina, delicta vel excessus, contractus vel injurias ad forum ecclesiasticum, et que ad Forum civile & pretorium spectare debeant, determinare;

Proviso tamen, quod leges, ordinationes, & constitutiones hujusmodi executioni non mandentur, quo usque assensus noster eisdem adhibeatur regius in scriptis sub signetto nostro signatis, ad minus & hujusmodi assensu adhibito, eisque publice promulgatis in provinciis in quibus sint exequende, leges, ordinationes, & constitutiones illas plenarie juris firmitatem adipisci, & ab omnibus quorum interesse poterit inviolabiliter observari, volumus & mandamus; liceat tamen vobis quinque vel pluribus vestrum, ut predictum est, leges, constitutiones & ordinationes sic edendas, licet promulgate fuerint, assensu nostro regio, mutare, revocare & abrogare; aliasque novas in forma predicta de tempore in tempus facere & edere, ut predictum est, novisque emergentibus malis vel periculis nova apponere remedia, prout decet, toties quoties expediens vobis videbitur et necessarium;

Sciatis

Sciatis ulterius, quod conftituimus vos & quoflibet quinque & plures veftrum, prefatos Willielmum archiepifcopum Cantuarienfem, Thomam dominum Coventrie——, magni figilli noftri Anglie cuftodem. Ricardum Eboracenfem archiepifcopum, dominum thefaurarium, Henricum comitem Manchefter, Thomam comitem Arundelle & Surrie, Edward comitem Dorcheftrie, Francifcum dominum Cottington, Thomam Edmonds militem, Henricum Vane militem, Johannem Cooke militem, et Francifcum Windebanke militem, commiffionarios noftros, ad audiendum & terminandum, juxta fanas difcretiones veftras, omnimodas querelas five contra colonias ipfas feu eorum prefectos vel gubernatores ad inftantiam partis gravate, vel ad delationem de injuriis hinc vel inde inter ipfas vel ipforum membra aliquod illatis movendas, partifque coram vobis evocare, ac partibus vel eorum procuratoribus hinc et inde auditis, plenum juftitie complementum exhibendum; dantes vobis & quibuflibet quinque vel pluribus veftrum, quod fi quas coloniarum predictarum vel aliquem prefectorum eorum ditiones alienas injufte poffidendo, vel ufurpando vel invicem feipfos gravando, feu nobis rebelles a fide noftra fubtrahendo, aut mandatis noftris non obtemperantes inveneritis, nobis prius in hac parte confultis, colonias hujufmodi & prefectos eorum ob caufas predictas, vel aliis juftis de caufis, vel in Angliam redire, aut ad alia loca defignanda divertere mandare, prout fecundum fanas difcretiones veftras equum, juftum vel neceffarium videbitur;

Damus

Damus insuper vobis & quibuslibet quinque vel pluribus vestrum, potestatem & mandatum speciale, ad omnia, chartas literas patentes & rescripta regia, de regionibus, provinciis, insulis vel terris in partibus exteris colonias deducentibus concessa, vobis duci facienda, iisque inspectis, si que eorum surreptivé vel indebité obtenta, vel per eadem, privilegia, libertates vel prerogativa nobis & corone nostre vel principibus exteris nociva & prejudicialia, indulta vel concessa fuisse, vobis quinque vel pluribus vestrum innotescat, ea secundum legem & consuetudinem regni nostri Anglie, revocari, jubere; ceteraque agendi, quæ ad regimen salutare & tutamen coloniarum predictarum & subditorum nostrorum in eisdem residentium fuerint necessaria; et ideo vobis mandamus, quod circa premissa, ad dies & loca que ad hoc provideritis, diligentes sitis intendentes prout decet, precipiendo etiam & firmiter injungendo, damus in mandatis omnibus & singulis prefectis provinciarum, in quas colonie predicte deducte sint vel fuerint, & singulis de coloniis ipsis & aliis quorum in hac parte interest, quod vobis in premissis sint intendentes, mandatisque vestris in eisdem obtemperantes & obedientes, quoties et prout ex parte vestra fuerint requisiti, sub periculo incumbenti.

In cujus rei &c.

Teste rege apud Westmonasterium decimo die Aprilis.

Per ipsum Regem.

FINIS.